MEDIUM ÆVUM MONOGRAPHS
NEW SERIES

MEDIUM ÆVUM MONOGRAPHS
NEW SERIES XX

STUDIES IN THE RECEPTION OF THE *HISTORIA SCHOLASTICA* OF PETER COMESTOR

The *Schwarzwälder Predigten*, the *Weltchronik* of Rudolf von Ems, the *Scolastica* of Jacob van Maerlant and the *Historiebijbel van 1360*

MARIA C. SHERWOOD-SMITH

The Society for the Study of
Medieval Languages and Literature
Oxford
2000

THE SOCIETY FOR THE STUDY OF
MEDIEVAL LANGUAGES AND LITERATURE

http://mediumaevum.modhist.ox.ac.uk

British Library Cataloguing in Publication Data

A catalogue record for this book
is available from the British Library

ISBN-13: 978-0-907570-13-4 (pb)
ISBN-13: 978-0-907570-83-7 (ebk)

First published 2000
Reprinted 2017

CONTENTS

LIST OF TABLES

ACKNOWLEDGEMENTS

This monograph is a revised version of a D.Phil. thesis. Pressures of space required the omission of various sections, which I hope to publish in another form.

The thesis was supervised by Nigel Palmer; he was as tireless in his general enthusiasm for the project as he was scrupulous when it came to details, and I am extremely grateful to him for all his help both then and in subsequent years. I would also like to thank Regina and Hajo Schiewer for their encouragement and for reading and commenting of draft versions of large parts of the thesis, and Annette Volfing for her advice on the revision. Many others have helped me with my research, but I would like to mention especially Professor W.P. Gerritsen, who first suggested Peter Comestor, and Tim Jackson, who suggested Nigel Palmer.

Finally, I would like to thank the Gerrans Memorial Fund of the University of Oxford for a grant as a subvention towards the cost of publishing this monograph and Dr David Pattison, Ms Val Tomlin and Ms Ruth Gwernan-Jones for their hard work and patience in preparing the rather unwieldy typescript for final publication.

1 INTRODUCTION

1.1 Peter Comestor and the *Historia scholastica*

The twelfth-century exegete Peter Comestor came from Champagne.[1] The name 'Comestor', commonly interpreted as a nickname alluding to his voracious appetite for books (and hence often replaced with the related word 'Manducator'), can be demonstrated to be a family name in that area in the twelfth century.[2] He was probably educated in the cathedral school of Troyes in the second quarter of the twelfth century, and became dean of St. Peter's in Troyes in or before 1145.[3] This connection with Troyes has been important in discussing possible influences on Comestor, and the sources he used. It has been suggested that the young Comestor, or at least his teachers, might have had contact with Peter Abelard through the latter's association with his nearby foundation, Paraclete.[4] Others highlight the vibrant Jewish intellectual community in Troyes centring on the grandsons of the seminal Jewish exegete Rashi, and suggest that Comestor was in personal contact with these Jewish scholars.[5] Though he seems to have remained dean of Troyes all his life, at some stage he moved to Paris, where he studied under John of Tours and Peter Lombard († 1160). Comestor himself also taught in Paris, and in about 1164 he became chancellor of Notre Dame. He held this post until his death on 22nd October 1178,

[1] For the principal handbook articles on Peter Comestor, see *DSAM*, XII (1986), cols 1614–1626, *DThC*, XII (1933), cols 1918–1920 and *LThK*, VIII (1963), cols 357–358, *LexMA*, VI (1993), cols 1967–1968.

[2] Saralyn R. Daly, 'Peter Comestor: Master of Histories', *Speculum* 32 (1959), pp. 62–73, here p. 63.

[3] Daly, 'Peter Comestor', p. 65.

[4] Daly, 'Peter Comestor', pp. 63–64.

[5] Daly, 'Peter Comestor', p. 63; Herman Hailperin, *Rashi and the Christian Scholars* (Pittsburgh, 1963), esp. p. 111; Louis E. Feldman, 'The Jewish Sources of Peter Comestor's Commentary on Genesis in his Historia scholastica', in: *Begegnungen zwischen Christentum und Judentum in Antike und Mittelalter. Festschrift für Heinz Schreckenberg*, ed. by Dietrich-Alex Koch and Hermann Lichtenberger (Göttingen, 1993), pp. 93–121, esp. pp. 94–98. For further discussion, see below, p. 8.

though he resigned from the chair of theology at the cathedral school in 1169.[6] Peter Comestor's best known work, the *Historia scholastica*, was written by 1173;[7] he also wrote a popular collection of sermons and a Gospel commentary.[8]

In a short prologue, Comestor dedicates the *Historia scholastica* to William, Archbishop of Sens, also known under the name of William of the White Hands as a generous patron of scholarly works, who held that office from 1169 to 1176.[9] Comestor explains that the work was written at the request of his colleagues.[10] It was intended as a text-book for courses in literal scriptural exegesis, aimed to provide basic background information for scholars, who would later progress to 'higher', more spiritual levels of understanding.

The *Historia scholastica* is a student's guide to the historical books of the Bible, and consists of summaries of the narrative, incorporating a great deal of direct quotation from the text itself, as well as commentary material from a wide range of sources.[11] Comestor narrates the biblical story and expounds

[6] Ignatius Brady, 'Peter Manducator and the Oral Teachings of Peter Lombard', *Antonianum* 41 (1966), pp. 454–490, here pp. 483–484. See also James H. Morey, 'Peter Comestor, Biblical paraphrase, and the Medieval Popular Bible', *Speculum* 68 (1993), pp. 6–35, esp. p. 10; n. 15 (p. 10) lists the main secondary literature on the life of Peter Comestor.

[7] *PL* 198 (Paris, 1855), cols 1049–1722. The dating of the work is based on the dedication, discussed below, and a reference to the *Historia scholastica* in the *Chronicon* of Robert of Auxerre for 1173 (his only entry for that year): 'Petrus Comestor celebris habetur in Francia, magistrorum Parisiensum primas, vir facundissimus et in scripturis divinis excellenter instructus; qui utriusque testamenti historias uno compingens volumine, opus edidit satis utile, satis gratum, ex diversis hystoriis compilatum' (MHG SS 26, p. 240; also quoted in Daly, 'Peter Comestor', p. 67 and Morey, 'Peter Comestor', p. 10, n. 16.

[8] Morey, 'Peter Comestor', p. 10; Johannes B. Schneyer, *Repertorium der lateinischen Sermones des Mittelalters für die Zeit von 1150–1350* (Münster, 1969–1989), IV, pp. 636–651; Friedrich Stegmüller, *Repertorium biblicum medii aevi* (Madrid, 1950–1980), IV, nn. 6575–6579.

[9] *PL* 198, cols 1053–1054. For further information about William, Archbishop of Sens (later of Reims), see Daly, 'Peter Comestor', pp. 67–68.

[10] Daly suggests that this assertion is 'largely motivated by a mannerly pretense at modesty', and points out that it has parallels in works by Abelard, Hugh of St. Victor, Peter Lombard and Richard of St. Victor ('Peter Comestor', p. 68).

[11] Bible and apocryphal books treated and columns in *PL* 198: Gn (1055–1142), Ex (1141–1194), Lv (1193–1216), Nm (1215–1248), Dt (1247–1260), Ios (1259–1272), Idc (1271–1292), Rt (1293–1296), I Sm (= 'I Rg', 1295–1324), II Sm (= 'II Rg', 1323–1348), III Rg (1347–1386), IV Rg (1385–1432), Tb (1431–1442), Ez (1441–1448), Dn (1447–1476), Idt (1475–1490), Est (1489–1506), I Mcc (1505–1522), II Mcc (1521–1538), Mt/Mc/Lc/Io – Gospel Harmony (1537–1646), [Act (1645–1722), added by Peter of Poitiers

difficult or important points with extra information gleaned from his own reading of Jewish and pagan authors in addition to the Church Fathers and more recent Christian exegetes.[12] The novelty of the *Historia scholastica*, and the reason for its popularity, lay in its concentration on the literal sense of the Bible and its fusion of various strands of narrative and commentary from diverse traditions into a continuous chronological account. The sources of the work are discussed in section 1.2.

The work was an immediate success. It was itself the subject of commentaries, including one by Stephen Langton, a former student of Comestor's who later became Archbishop of Canterbury. In 1215, at the Fourth Lateran Council, it was officially approved by Pope Innocent III; it formed the basis for lecture-courses, and was on the core curriculum at the universities of Paris and Oxford by the mid-thirteenth century.[13] The success of the *Historia scholastica* far outreached its original intention and sphere and extended to many other areas of religious and secular literary life, so that it became 'one of the most popular books of the middle ages'.[14] The 230 manuscripts listed by Stegmüller, which can only represent a small proportion of those actually surviving, bear witness to this popularity, as does the printed transmission of the work: it was first printed in 1473, exists in nine incunable editions, and was printed a further eleven times between 1500 and 1729.[15] The transmission of the work is discussed in sections 1.3 and 1.4.

1.2 The Sources of the *Historia scholastica*

There is no definitive work available to date on the sources employed by Peter Comestor in the compilation of his summary of biblical history, known as the *Historia scholastica*, despite the acknowledged popularity and importance of the work in the Middle Ages. Various theories have been advanced and

---

before 1183]. The abbreviations for books of the Bible follow *Biblia Sacra iuxta vulgatam versionem*, 2 vols, ed. Robert Weber OSB (Stuttgart, 1969).

12 For further discussion of Comestor's sources, see section 1.2 below; For a brief history of the development of biblical exegesis in the Middle Ages, see *LexMA*, II (1983), cols 47–65.

13 Morey, 'Peter Comestor', pp. 6–7.

14 Beryl Smalley, *The Study of the Bible in the Middle Ages*, 3rd edn (Oxford, 1983), p. 178.

15 Stegmüller, *Repertorium*, IV, nn. 6543–6572, pp. 280–300; for further discussion of the manuscript and printed tradition, see below, sections 1.3 and 1.4.

refuted with relation to various parts of the work, and generalizations based on these have formed the requisite sections of the more recent lexica, but the state of research is not entirely satisfactory, and much remains to be done.

However, to understand the use of the *Historia scholastica* by later writers, it is vital to know something of the substance of the work itself and the manner of its composition, the traditions from which it sprang, and the intellectual ingredients which went into it. Only by thus placing the work in context can one assess the individual input of the author and his role in shaping his material for later generations. The decisions of a vernacular author with regard to the biblical narrative can sometimes be understood on the basis of Comestor's earlier decisions; in this one can observe the role of the *Historia scholastica* as a mediator between the learned commentary tradition and the lay people who formed the readership or audience of the German and Dutch works studied.[16]

The *Antiquitates Judaicae* of Josephus are recognized by most to be the principal source (after the Vulgate) of the *Historia scholastica*.[17] Written in Greek in 93 or 94 A.D. by the Roman Jew Josephus Flavius, the work was more widely used by Christian authors.[18] It was first translated into Latin at the instigation of Cassiodorus in approximately 578, and it is in this form that it was available to Peter Comestor.[19] Schreckenberg gives a list of over eighty concordances with the *Antiquitates* in Comestor's treatment of the books of Genesis and Exodus alone, and suggests that even in this short section there are many more that he has overlooked.[20] 'Josephus steht für Petrus als authentische Geschichtsquelle gleichrangig neben der Bibel und

[16] Morey, 'Peter Comestor', p. 7; for further discussion, see Maria Sherwood-Smith, 'Die "Historia scholastica" als Quelle biblischer Stoffe im Mittelalter', in: *Die Vermittlunggeistlicher Inhalte im Mittelalter*, ed. by Timothy R. Jackson, Nigel F. Palmer and Almut Suerbaum (Tübingen, 1996), pp. 153–165.

[17] *TRE*, XVII (1988), pp. 258–264; see also Louis H. Feldman, *Josephus and Modern Scholarship: (1937–1986)* (Berlin, 1984) for bibliography and discussion of research to date.

[18] Heinz Schreckenberg, *Die Flavius-Josephus-Tradition in Antike und Mittelalter* (Leiden, 1972) and *Rezeptions geschichtliche und textkritische Untersuchungen zu Flavius Josephus* (Leiden, 1978).

[19] Franz Blatt, *The Latin Josephus. I. Introduction and Text. The Antiquities: Books I–V*, Acta Jutlandica XXX (Aarhus, 1958); introduction contains information about manuscript traditions, locations etc.

[20] Schreckenberg, *Tradition*, pp. 147–149.

den bedeutendsten Kirchenvätern und wird von ihm für seine Darstellung fast synoptisch herangezogen'.[21]

Manitius gives the disputations of Augustine and Jerome as another major source, and finds references to Roman secular literature as well as to Christian authors such as Isidor of Seville, Origen, Alcuin and Rabanus Maurus. He posits that Jerome is the direct source for the Hebrew material in the *Historia scholastica*.[22]

Smalley suggests that Peter Comestor's near-contemporary, Andrew of St. Victor, is frequently the source of such Hebrew material, which he gathered from discussions with Jewish exegetes.[23] In her article she demonstrates this in the case of the Comestor's commentary on the book of Numbers, and shows that 'very often the *Hebraei* and *alii* of the *Histories* mean Andrew'.[24]

Daly is concerned mainly with the biography of Peter Comestor, but gives Smalley's view of the Hebrew references and suggests that Peter Abelard might have been an influence. She discusses the similarity of sources between Abelard's *Expositio in Hexaemeron* and the Genesis section of the *Historia scholastica*: 'Abelard used Augustine *De Genesi ad Litteram*; Bede, *Hexaemeron* and his commentary on the Pentateuch; Josephus, *Antiquities of the Jews*; and probably Ambrose, *Exameron*. This list likewise comprises Comestor's major sources, though he may have taken some of his material second hand from the *Glossa ordinaria*'.[25]

Shereshevsky suggests that the Hebrew traditions in the *Historia scholastica* come from Comestor's own discussions with his Jewish neighbours in Troyes.[26] He gives a detailed analysis of the section on Genesis, showing which elements are similar to the Midrashic interpretations of Rashi, but seems unaware of the findings of Beryl Smalley. His case is rejected by Lachs, who argues that although there is 'material which ultimately derives from Hebrew sources, one cannot establish that the immediate source is the Jews'.[27] Lachs points out

21 Schreckenberg, *Tradition*, p. 147.

22 Max Manitius, *Geschichte der lateinischen Literatur des Mittelalters*, III (Munich, 1931), pp. 156–158.

23 Beryl Smalley, 'The School of Andrew of St. Victor', *RTAM* 11 (1939), pp. 145–167, and *Bible*, p. 150.

24 Smalley, *Bible*, p. 150.

25 Daly, 'Peter Comestor', p. 64.

26 Esra Shereshevsky, 'Hebrew Traditions in Peter Comestor's *Historia scholastica*', *Jewish Quarterly Review*, NS 59 (1968/69), pp. 268–289.

27 Samuel T. Lachs, 'The Source of the Hebrew Traditions in the *Historia scholastica*', *HThR* 66 (1973), pp. 385– 386, here p. 385.

that the word *Judaei* and not the *Historia scholastica*'s *Hebraei* is the more common term when referring to contemporary Jews and demonstrates that Jerome is the direct source of some of the disputed material.[28]

The most detailed work to date on Comestor's sources, though it makes no claim to be definitive, is Karp's 'The *Histories* of Peter Comestor: A Study of Literal Scriptural Exegesis'.[29] She investigates three traditions which provided Comestor with his source material – the Christian tradition, the works of Josephus Flavius, and the Hebrew tradition – showing how each of these contributed to the literal-historical interpretation of the *Historia scholastica*: 'The Christian tradition furnished the bones; the works of Josephus, the flesh and sinews; and the Hebrew tradition, the spirit'.[30]

The Christian tradition provided Comestor with the majority of his technical and explanatory material. Karp lists the many Christian authorities cited in the *Historia scholastica*, but shows that Jerome, Augustine and Bede from the patristic tradition, and the twelfth-century exegetes of the Victorine school, particularly Hugh and Andrew of St. Victor, are the main Christian sources consulted.[31] Josephus is credited with furnishing both the historical perspective of the *Historia scholastica* and a wealth of historical material; he provides psychological insights into the motivations of Old Testament characters and contributes to Comestor's positive presentation of the Jews.[32] The third section of Karp's chapter on the sources of the *Historia scholastica* re-opens the debate about Comestor's access to the Hebrew tradition. She shows that the majority of the technical and general historical information, which two categories together comprise approximately 58% of the Hebrew

[28] The rigidity of this distinction is called into question by the breadth of the semantic field covered by these terms, as discussed by Herman Hailperin in 'The Hebrew Heritage of Medieval Christian Biblical Scholarship', *Historia Judaica* 5 (1943), pp. 133–154. In Hailperin's opinion the field ranges from 'what Jerome or some other Church Father attributes to Jews' to 'what contemporary Jews are telling their Christian inquirers' (p. 145). Morey queries Lachs' definition on internal criteria: 'According to Lachs, [...] "Hebraei" describes "those of the biblical period or those who use their knowledge of Hebrew for biblical interpretation" (p. 386). But how the latter category excludes rabbinic scholars of Peter's acquaintance is unclear' ('Peter Comestor', p. 13, n. 31).

[29] Sandra R. Karp, 'The Sources of the *Historia scholastica*, in: 'The *Histories* of Peter Comestor: A Study of Literal Scriptural Exegesis' (unpublished doctoral thesis, Tulane University, 1978. UMI), pp. 129–224.

[30] Karp, '*Histories*', p. 131.

[31] Karp, '*Histories*', pp. 131–170.

[32] Karp, '*Histories*', pp. 183–197.

material, can be found in earlier authors (particularly Jerome, and Hugh and Andrew of St. Victor).[33] However, most of the Midrashic material cannot be located in Josephus or in Christian works before Comestor, and could have been derived by him in an oral form from direct contact with Jewish exegetes.[34]

Karp's systematic analysis of the sources drawn on by Comestor, the type of material taken from a given source and the manner in which this is incorporated in the *Historia scholastica*, is a considerable contribution to an understanding of the composition and nature of the work. She provides an overview and pointers towards possible avenues of enquiry, but, as she herself states, 'much work still remains to be done to complete our understanding of the sources of the *Historia scholastica*'.[35]

Further detail about the variety of Comestor's sources is added by Morey, who points out that several of the apocryphal motifs which occur in the *Historia scholastica* can be traced to texts with Irish affiliations.[36] He also discusses the question of Comestor's associations with Jewish scholarship, though without any new conclusions, and mentions his links with Andrew of St. Victor. Although he cites Karp (in footnote 15, p. 10, and footnote 30, p. 12), he does not appear to take full account of her analysis of the sources of Midrashic material in his brief discussion of the Hebrew legends in the *Historia scholastica*, and makes no reference to her substantial research in this area.[37]

The last word has by no means been said on the matter of Comestor's sources. The question of the Jewish sources is reopened by Feldman in his article of 1993, where he contributes to the ongoing discussion regarding

[33] Karp, '*Histories*', pp. 197–207; her suggestion that the then unpublished works of Andrew of St. Victor might be the direct source of more of this material is correct, although this does not account for all the untraced examples; a brief comparison located the following close parallels between the *Historia scholastica* (*PL* 198) and Andrew's *Expositio super Heptateuchum*, ed. by Charles Lohr, CCCM 53 (Turnhout, 1986): *PL* 198, col. 1157/CCCM 53, p. 116; *PL* 198, col. 1146, ll. 9–10/CCCM 53, p. 99, ll. 120–123; *PL* 198, col. 1146, l. 40/CCCM 53, p. 99, ll. 137–138; *PL* 198, col. 1147, ll. 30–44/CCCM 53, p. 102, ll. 231–245; *PL* 198, col. 1157, ll. 50–51/CCCM 53, p. 117, ll. 762–765.

[34] Of Comestor's 68 longer anecdotes from the Midrash, only 17 are found by Karp in traditional Christian sources or Josephus; Karp, '*Histories*', pp. 207–217, esp. p. 210. A compendium of traditions from the Midrashim is found in Louis Ginzburg, *The Legends of the Jews*, 8 vols (Philadelphia, 1909–1946), see esp. vol. VIII for a comprehensive index.

[35] Karp, '*Histories*', p. 131.

[36] Morey, 'Peter Comestor', pp. 11–14.

[37] Morey, 'Peter Comestor', pp. 13–14, esp. n. 35.

the provenance of Hebrew material in the Genesis section of the *Historia scholastica.* He examines the extent and nature of Comestor's debt to Josephus, Jerome, Hugh and Andrew of St. Victor and other Latin and Jewish traditions. Feldman suggests that the truth lies somewhere between the extremes in this debate marked by Shereshevsky and Lachs, though there is 'much more to be said for the latter position'. Feldman reiterates the conclusion that we have insufficient evidence to decide whether Comestor was acquainted with Rashi or his school: 'even though we have pinpointed a number of traditions that we are unable to trace in Jerome or the Victorines or other Latin writers or in Josephus, Comestor might have obtained such information from Jewish converts to Christianity'.[38]

1.2.1 Comestor's Sources for Exodus: Analysis of the First Six Chapters

The following brief analysis of Comestor's sources for the first six chapters of his account of Exodus forms the background for the subsequent studies of this section in the later works selected, giving a closer impression of the nature of the material that was passed on to the vernacular authors by the *Historia scholastica.* This section has been chosen because it demonstrates the range of sources consulted, the manner in which they are interwoven, and some of the difficulties that this collector's approach can present when one attempts to identify the provenance of the various strands.

The preface to the *Historia scholastica*'s commentary on Exodus explains the meaning of the word 'Exodus' and gives and explains the Hebrew equivalent. This information can be found at the beginning of Andrew of St. Victor's section on Exodus in his *Expositio super Heptateuchum*,[39] where the source is quoted as the Etymologies of Isidore of Seville.[40] Comestor

[38] Feldman, 'Jewish Sources', p. 121. See also C. Merhavyah, *The Church versus Talmudic and Midrashic Literature* (Jerusalem, 1970), pp. 167–193. Direct contact with Jewish exegetes has been demonstrated convincingly in the case of Andrew of St. Victor, Comestor's slightly older contemporary, leading Frans van Lieve to conclude that '... in the twelfth century, there was a body of exegetical material that was treated as common property in Jewish and Christian circles, and although there is seldom enough hard evidence to prove direct derivation, there must have been frequent and intensive exchange between the two circles', *Andreae de Sancto Victore Opera II. Expositio hystorica in librum Regum*, ed. Frans v. Lieve, CCCM 53a (Turnhout, 1996), pp. XXIX–XXXVII, here p. XXXVII.

[39] CCCM 53, p. 96.

[40] Isidore of Seville, *Etymologiarum sive originum libri XX*, ed. by W. M. Lindsey (Oxford, 1911), VI, 1,4; 2,4.

may have consulted either work, and in the light of Smalley's research on other chapters of the *Historia scholastica* it may seem likely that Andrew is the source here too, but it is also very possible that these facts were common knowledge to the medieval exegete. Comestor does not quote verbatim at this point, and gives no source-reference.

Comestor's second chapter, 'De servitute filiorum Israel', begins by quoting the Vulgate at the eighth verse of the first chapter of Exodus, with very minor changes such as the substitution of 'igitur' for 'interea' to give 'surrexit igitur rex novus in Aegypto'.[41] This is followed by the names of the two Pharaohs in question: Nephres, who was in power when Joseph was alive, and Ammonaphis, the eighth in the succession, who is the present ruler. This information can be found in the *Glossa ordinaria*, where it is attributed to the 'cronicis eusebij et hieronimi', Jerome's translation of Eusebius' chronicles.[42] In the older work, though, Ammonaphis – or Amenoptes, as he is here known – is the seventh Pharaoh and not the eighth as stated by Comestor and the Gloss.

The interweaving of material from the Vulgate and Josephus by Comestor can be observed in the following sentences if one juxtaposes the two sources and the section from the *Historia scholastica*:[43]

Historia scholastica	Vulgate	*Antiquitates*
Regno autem translato ad aliam domum, rex ille ab hoc quasi novus, ignoravit beneficia Joseph, quae contulerat Aegypto, et odiebat Israel maxime, ut ait Josephus, quia inviderunt eis Aegyptii propter virtutem ingenii, et laboris industriam, et	[8]surrexit interea rex novus super Aegyptum qui ignorabat Joseph [9]et ait ad populum suum ecce populus filiorum Israhel multus et fortior nobis [10]venite sapienter opprimamus eum ne forte multiplicetur et si ingruerit contra nos bellum	videntes enim Israhelitarum genus augeri et propter virtutem et laboris ingenium divitiarum adfluentia valde nobilitatos contra se eos augeri suspicabantur, oblitique bonorum propter longinquitatem temporis quae meruerant per Ioseph regnoque translato

[41] This sort of minor difference could of course be due to a variation in the exemplar of the Vulgate consulted by Comestor. In such cases I check the variants listed in *Biblia Sacra iuxta Latinam vulgatam versionem*, ed. Aidan Gasquet et al. (Rome, 1926–1978), and Carolus Vercellone, *Variae lectiones Vulgatae Latinae Bibliorum editionis* (Rome, 1860); for the persistence of readings from earlier Latin translations in Vulgate manuscripts, see Bonifatius Fischer, 'Zur Überlieferung altlateinischer Bibeltexte im Mittelalter', in: Bonifatius Fischer, *Lateinische Bibelhandschriften im frühen Mittelalter* (Freiburg, 1985), pp. 404–421. In this particular case, the search failed to reveal any parallels.

[42] *Biblia latina cum Glossa ordinaria*, Facsimile reprint of the Editio Princeps by Adolph Rusch of Strasbourg, 1480/81 (Turnhout, 1992), I, p. 112; *Sancti Hieronymi interpretatio chronicae Eusebii Pamphili*, *PL* 27, cols 150–162. The Eusebian-Hieronymian chronicles are the direct source for many of Comestor's *incidentia*.

[43] *PL* 198, col. 1141; Exodus 1:8–10; Blatt, *Latin Josephus*, p. 196.

affluentiam opum et sobolis nobilitatem. Et ait rex ad populum suum: 'populus Israel fere fortior est nobis; sapienter opprimamus eum ne multiplicatus, vel ipse contra nos insurgat, vel addatur hostibus nostris, et egrediatur liber. (col. 1141)

addatur inimicis nostris expugnatisque nobis egrediatur e terra

ad aliam domum, crudeliter opprimentes Israhelitas studebant varias illis inferre miserias.

Comestor processes the material from the two source works and combines the elements from them which he thinks most important. At this point Comestor follows the structure of the Bible account and supplements the information he finds there with details from Josephus.

The next sentence is a close paraphrase of Exodus 1:11, but the source for the subsequent discussion of the Vulgate phrase 'urbes tabernaculorum' is not clear. Similar information is found in Andrew of St. Victor's *Expositio*, where the source is Hugh of St. Victor's *Adnotatiunculae elucidatoriae in Exodum*.[44] It is possible that Hugh and Comestor drew on the same source, but it is more likely that Comestor reformulated and added to the material he found in either Hugh or Andrew's commentaries:[45]

Historia scholastica

Coxerunt ergo lateres ex quibus aedificaverunt regi civitates tabernaculorum, Phithon et Ramessen. Civitates quidem prius erant, sed non erant *tabernaculorum*, erantque in finibus Aegypti, et ideo muravit eas Pharao, ut ibi poneret armatos, quasi in tabernaculis semper excubantes, ne quis posset ingredi, vel egredi sine regis nutu: vel 'tabernaculorum', id est pauperum prius, et opere illorum illas ditavit; vel, ut alia littera habet, 'positionum', ubi scilicet fiscus reponeretur. (cols 1141–1142)

Adnotatiunculae

Aedificaverunt urbes tabernaculorum Pharaoni Phiton, et Ramasses. In Hebraeo ubi nos habemus tabernaculorum, est quidam sermo, qui transpositione puncti modo ad dextram modo ad sinistram, vel sonat in voce miscenoth, et significat positionum: et secundum hoc, quod prior vox subinnuit, urbes pauperum aedificatas intellegitur: urbes prius debiles, et pauperum mansiones operatione Hebraeorum fortiores effectas. Secundum hoc autem, quod miscenoth significat positionum, intellegitur ita fortes urbes compositas quod thesauri regis reponentur ibi in custodia pro firmitate loci, sive ante fuerint urbes, sive non.

Expositio

Aedeficauerunt urbes tabernaculorum etc. Secundum Hebraeos "vel pauperum" – ut scilicet, quae prius debiles et pauperes mansiones erant, operatione Hebraeorum factae sint fortiores – "vel positionum", id est, ita fortes, ut thesauri regis ibi reponerentur in custodia pro firmitate loci, siue ante fuerint ibi urbes siue non. Vel: *Vrbes tabernaculorum*, id est castrorum, ita scilicet firmae et munitae sunt, ut castra.

44 *PL* 175, cols 61–74.

45 *PL* 198, cols 1141–1142; *PL* 175, col 61; CCCM 53, p. 97, ll. 44–50.

Comestor mentions three tasks which are forced on the Israelites during their captivity. The first, the building of cities, is, as we have seen above, taken from the Bible, and seems to have been the subject of some debate among medieval exegetes. The second task listed by Comestor is the not so much hard, but rather humiliating job of cleaning the streets and disposing of refuse. A survey of the main Christian commentaries on Exodus which would have been available to Comestor fails to reveal any parallels.[46] The commentaries on Exodus generally concentrate on the spiritual sense, applying the 'symbols' of Exodus to the New Testament, to the Christian or monastic life or to the battle between Good and Evil in the world. Comestor's wish to concentrate on the literal sense draws him towards Jewish sources, and in this case it is the Midrash which supplies the idea of a servile task imposed on the Israelites.[47]

It is Comestor's main Jewish source, Josephus, who supplies the third of the labours of the Israelites, the deltafication of the river, and here Josephus is named:[48]

Historia scholastica	*Antiquitates*
Tertium etiam addidit opus, secundum Josephum, ut fluvium per multas derivationes dividerent, et circumdarent civitatis fossatis, ne eas inundare fluvius valeret, et jam quadringentos annos in his miseriis expenderunt, id est compleverunt. (col 1142)	fluvium namque per multas dirivationes eos dividere murosque civitatibus fabricare et fossata circumducere, ut eas inundare fluvius non valeret [...] quadringentorumque annorum tempus in his miseriis extiterunt [...]

Comestor begins his third chapter by paraphrasing the Vulgate (Ex 1:15,16), giving further details and explanations of various points. He gives two alternative reasons for the sparing of the Hebrew girl-babies. The first, 'quia fragilis sexus non poterat, et libidini Aegyptiorum deservirent', is based on the Midrash and has not been found in Josephus or in the Christian tradition before Comestor.[49] The second has parallels with Josephus, but here, unlike the previous example, he is not acknowledged as source:[50]

[46] *DSAM*, IV, cols 1976–1988, gives an outline of the commentary tradition on Exodus. The present survey focuses primarily those in Migne; see *PL*, Indices 2, XLIII: 'Index Generalis Commentariorum in Scripturas', 'In Exodum'.

[47] See Ginzberg, *Legends*, II, p. 248, quoted by Karp, '*Histories*', p. 213.

[48] *PL* 198, col 1142; Blatt, *Latin Josephus*, p. 196.

[49] Karp, '*Histories*', p. 210, n. 160; Ginzberg, *Legends*, II, p. 251.

[50] *PL* 198, col 1142; Blatt, *Latin Josephus*, p. 196.

Historia scholastica	*Antiquitates*
[...] quia quidam sacrorum scriba regi praedixerat eo tempore in Israel masculum nasciturum, qui regnum Aegypti humiliaret, et virtute universos transcenderet. (col. 1142)	quidam sacrorum scriba – cum sint exerti de futuris dicere veritatem – enuntiavit regi pariendum quendam illo tempore inter Israhelitas qui humiliaret quidem Aegypti principatum, augeret autem suo cremento Israhelitarum genus, virtuteque transcenderet universos, et gloriam in perpetuum memorabilem possideret.

Comparing these two passages with each other and with the two above, one notes that whereas the earlier passage quotes Josephus in full, here one has an abbreviating paraphrase, but which does retain close verbal parallels. This pattern of acknowledged quotation and unacknowledged paraphrase of the *Antiquitates* is followed throughout the section on Exodus. There are various possible reasons for this: either Comestor read and internalized the paraphrased information at an earlier date and was no longer aware of its provenance, which seems unlikely since he quotes from the same section a few sentences before, or he came upon the information in an indirect way. He may have used another work which in turn used Josephus, though the above objections still apply, or, alternatively, he distinguished consciously between the two types of use of source-material and did not judge it necessary to acknowledge the source when not quoting verbatim.

Comestor's treatment of the Bible is different: both quotation and paraphrase go unacknowledged in the text itself, and though in many manuscripts there are references to books of the Bible in the margins, these were probably not part of the original conception of the work, but were added with time. The phrase 'Timuerunt vero obstetrices Deum' (col. 1142), is quoted from the Vulgate, and concluded 'et servaverunt mares' for the standard Vulgate's '[...] sed conservabant mares', and the whole is absorbed into the main body of the text. This procedure too is followed consistently, as can be observed, for a further example, in the treatment of the Bible sections in Comestor's second chapter, quoted above.

Comestor quotes from the Vulgate the phrase 'Et quia timuerunt Deum, aedificavit illis domos' and concurs with Andrew of St. Victor in interpreting it figuratively to mean that God made them wealthy if they were poor, or fertile if they were barren. Whether Andrew was the immediate or original source is not clear, as the wording is very different:

Historia scholastica	*Expositio*
[...] id est locupletavit eas, cum essent pauperes, vel fecundavit eas, cum essent steriles. (col. 1142)	id est: In diuitiis vel prole multiplicauit.

The views of Augustine and Gregory the Great on the extent of the sin committed by the midwives in lying to protect the Hebrew children are given in the *Glossa ordinaria* and summarized here by Comestor, though he omits their allegorical and moral interpretations.

Comestor's fourth chapter on Exodus (*PL* 198, col. 1143) is mainly taken up with a digression about the gods of the Egyptians, the information for which is attributed to Pliny.[51] Comestor gives the massacre of the Hebrew children as the cause for the Egyptians non-recognition of God: 'Pro quo peccato creditur Deum Aegyptios tradidisse in hunc errorem, ut Apim pro Deo colerent', and proceeds to discuss the nature of Apis.

The fifth chapter (*PL* 198, cols 1143–1144) narrates the birth and childhood of Moses. The account follows the structure of the Vulgate (Exodus 2:1–10) for as long as this deals with Moses' childhood, but Comestor supplements the biblical information with details 'ut ait Josephus'. The *Glossa ordinaria* also draws frequently on Josephus for the historical side of its commentary on this section of Exodus. It is difficult to reconstruct Comestor's approach at this point: the extent of his summarization means that verbal similarities with either account are few, but he includes details from each which are not in the other. If one juxtaposes the three, the following picture emerges:[52]

Historia scholastica	*Glossa ordinaria*	*Antiquitates*
Quem dum quadam die Terimith obtulisset Pharaoni, ut et ipse eum adoptaret, admirans rex pueri venustatem, coronam, quam tunc forte gestabat, capiti illius imposuit. Erat autem in ea Ammonis imago fabrefacta. Puer autem coronam projecit in terram, et fregit. Sacerdos autem Heliopoleus a latere regis surgens, exclamavit: Hic est puer, quem nobis occidendum Deus monstravit, ut de caetero timore careamus, et voluit irruere in eum, sed auxilio regis liberatus est, [...] (col. 1144)	Refert iosephus quod filia pharaonis adultum moysen ad patrem suum adduxit. cui ille coronam suam imposuit: quam statim moyses proiicit. quoniam ibi sculptum similacrum vidit. Unde sacerdos qui ibi aderat voluit interficere eum dicens: quia egiptus esset subuertenda per ipsum. sicut ex oraculum daemonum acceperat. Sed pharaonis filia liberauit eum.	haec dicens posuit in manibus patris infantem: ille vero sumens eum et ad pectus applicans per amorem pro filiae gratia imposuit ei diadema. Moyses autem convolvens illud proiecit in terram quasi per infantiam conculcavitque suis pedibus. quod regi ferre videbatur augurium. contemplatus autem ille sacer scriba qui eius nativitatem praedixerat futuram ad humiliationem principatus Aegyptii impetum fecit ut eum occideret, et terribiliter clamans ait: 'hic est ille puer, o rex, quem nobis occidendum deus ostendit ut de cetero timore careamus

The detail about the image in the crown is not in Josephus' original account, but has been taken from the Gloss. The Gloss, in turn, does not quote the words of the Chief Scribe, which are taken directly from Josephus.

51 Pliny the Elder, *Naturalis historia*, VIII, 184–186.

52 *PL* 198, col. 1144; Blatt, *Latin Josephus*, pp. 200–201; *Glossa*, I, p. 115.

The situation is further complicated by the subsequent part of Comestor's account, which tells as a sequel to the story that Moses' innocence was put to the test and proved by the fact that he burnt his tongue by putting a hot brand into his mouth as a child might. This event is not narrated in either of the sources discussed above, but is based on Midrashim.[53] This is another story which Comestor may have derived from personal contact with contemporary Jewish exegetes.[54]

Chapter six of the *Historia scholastica* tells the apocryphal story of Moses' Ethiopian wife, and here the same pattern can be observed in Comestor's approach to his sources. The early part of the account contains similarities with both the original and *Glossa ordinaria*'s version of Josephus; the latter is summarized considerably, so that direct consultation of the original is undeniable.[55] A sequel tells how Moses disposed of his unwanted wife by giving her a ring containing an image which symbolized oblivion, so that in this way she forgot him and he could return freely to Egypt; this has no parallel in Josephus, and its source has not yet been traced.[56]

The search for Comestor's sources continues. It is only possible in a very few cases, where there is a direct quotation, or a straightforward paraphrase, to state with near certainty which work Comestor has consulted. In the vast majority of cases it is merely a question of suggesting possibilities or pointing out parallels, or the lack of them, with other exegetes. But the main point, on which most researchers agree, that Josephus' *Jewish Antiquities* are the principal source after the Vulgate, is borne out by the analysis of the first six chapters of the *Historia scholastica*'s account of Exodus.

1.3 The Manuscript Tradition of the *Historia scholastica*

The oldest surviving dated manuscript of the *Historia scholastica* is Paris, Bibliothèque Nationale, Ms. lat. 16943, which dates from about 1183, and the work is also preserved in over two-hundred-and-fifty manuscripts in

[53] See Ginzberg, *Legends*, II, p. 274, quoted by Karp, '*Histories*', p. 214; Jonathan Cohen, *The Origins and Evolution of the Moses Nativity Story* (Leiden, 1993), pp. 129–131.

[54] Karp, '*Histories*', p. 217.

[55] Blatt, *Latin Josephus*, pp. 202–203; *Glossa*, I, p. 115.

[56] Although it is not mentioned by Ginzberg, it is possible that it too derived from a Midrashic legend. Exodus is covered by Ginzberg, *Legends*, II; see also the index, vol. VIII.

libraries all over Europe and further afield.[57] As yet there exists no detailed or systematic survey of these manuscripts and their relation to each other, and no modern edition based on a manuscript tradition. In the absence of such an edition, the printed transmission of the work takes on added importance in tracing the antecedents of the most recent and widely-used version, that in Migne's *Patrologia Latina*.[58] For this reason, the printed transmission of the work will be discussed in detail in section 1.4.

In the present study, consultation of manuscripts is limited to spot-checks in those cases where Migne's text appears unreliable. For this purpose, I have assigned sigla to the manuscripts of the *Historia scholastica* in the Bodleian Library, giving preference to those consulted most frequently. The primary criterion for selection was the provenance of the manuscript, preference being given to continental manuscripts (A–C); other criteria included the age of the manuscript, its reliability (established in the course of these spot-checks), and the presence of marginal glosses and/or *additiones*.[59]

1.4 The Printed Transmission of the *Historia scholastica*

Any research into the *Historia scholastica* and its reception is undermined by scepticism about the representativeness of the most widely available version, that in Migne's *Patrologiae Latinae Cursus Completus*.[60] In the light of the very large manuscript tradition, and the lack of a study of the textual history of the work, all detailed observations are vitiated by uncertainty. Opinions about Migne's text vary: spot-checks against random manuscripts led both Margarete Andersson-Schmidt and Petra Berendrecht to the conclusion that

[57] Morey, 'Peter Comestor', p. 8. Stegmüller, *Repertorium*, IV, nn. 6543–6572 lists 230 manuscripts; that there are many more, is suggested by the case of Oxford: Stegmüller lists 9 manuscripts in the Bodleian library, but I have found records of 18 manuscripts and 5 fragments there, and a further 11 in college libraries.

[58] *PL* 198, cols 1049–1722; this is a reprint of the edition of E. Navarro (Madrid, 1699), see Morey, 'Peter Comestor', p. 7.

[59] For further discussion of the *additiones*, see section 1.4.

[60] For example, Frits van Oostrom, 'Slotbeschouwing: de *Rijmbijbel*, balans en perspectief' in: *Scolastica willic ontbinden. Over de Rijmbijbel van Jacob van Maerlant*, ed. Jaap van Moolenbroek and Maaike Mulder (Hilversum, 1991), p. 127: '...ook de *Historia scholastica* lijdt immers aan editoriale ondervoeding, waardoor bijvoorbeeld onze grondslag voor de vergelijking van Maerlant met zijn voorbeeldtekst filologisch uiterst twijfelachtig is'.

A	MS Laud Misc. 446	12th C.
B	MS Laud Misc. 74	13th C. France? annot. in German hand
C	MS Lyell 70	13th C. Italy/Sth France; extra additiones, glosses
D	MS Rawl. C 46	13th C.
E	MS Bodl. 164	13th C. English, list of chapters, Gen–Mcc
F	MS Laud Misc. 270	13th C. English?
G	MS Laud Misc. 151	13th C. English?
H	MS Bodl. 723	13th C. English
I	MS Bodl. 173	late 13th C. English
J	MS Bodl. 711	13th C.
K	MS Bodl. 208	late 13th C. English
L	MS Bodl. 397	late 13th C. English?
M	MS Bodl. 748	14th C. English
O	MS Rawl. C 889	14th C.
P	MS Rawl. 571	14th C., imperf.
Q	MS Rawl. C 283	12th C., N.T. only (Mcc – Gospels)
R	MS Laud Misc. 518	13th C., N.T. only (Mcc – Acts)
S	MS Rawl. A 363	13th C., N.T. only (Mcc – Acts)
Fragments:		
	MS Lat. misc. b.15 , fol. 3	(fragment, 12th C.)
	MS Lat. th. c.10, fols 23, 74	(fragments, 13th C.)
	MS Lat. th. c.10, fol. 33	(fragments, 13th–14th C.)
	MS Lat. th. c.23, fols 1, 6	(fragment, 13th C.) Mcc – Acts
	MS Rawl. D 893	(fragments)
Extracts/Adaptations/Abridgements/Commentaries:		
	MS Hatton 72	Adaptation, 13th C. English
	MS Laud Lat. 109	Abridgement, 15th C.
	MS Lyell 8	13th C. English, extracts (*PL* 198 cols 1108–1159)
	MS Lyell 35	15th C. 15 Last signs of day of Judgement
	MS Rawl. C 31	Glossa super P.C.'s *HS* usque ad Cap. X libri Exodi

Table 1: Manuscripts of the *Historia scholastica* in the Bodleian Library

Balliol College, MS 11	14th C.
Balliol College, MS 221	14th C.
Corpus Christi College, MS 159	14th C.
Merton College, MS 120	13th C., tables in 2nd hand
Merton College, MS 128	13th C., ref. to Aristotle in 2nd hand
New College, MS 101	13th C., excluding Acts, glosses in margins
New College, MS 102	14th C., excluding Acts
New College, MS 104	12th C., Tobias – Acts
St. John's College, MS 34	13th C., *HS* with glosses
University College, MS 112	13th C., incomplete
University College, MS 190	13th C. English, many marginal notes
Abridgements	
Magdalen College, MS 53	15th C.
University College, MS 42	15th C.

Table 2: Manuscripts of the *Historia scholastica* in Oxford College libraries

variation was minimal;[61] a similar procedure carried out by Koen Goudriaan gave him a rather different impression.[62] Vollmer too rejected Migne: 'die Ausgabe bei Migne erwies sich als durchaus unzureichend; es mußten die mir erreichbaren Frühdrücke, sowie stellenweise auch handschriftliche Überlieferung herangezogen werden'.[63] A full investigation into the

[61] Margarete Andersson-Schmitt, 'Zwei niederdeutsche Bibelfragmente und die Überlieferungsgeschichte der "sogenannten ersten" niederländischen Historienbibel', *Niederdeutsches Wort. Beiträge zur niederdeutschen Philologie*, 23 (1983), pp. 1–37 (p. 11, n. 21): 'Um einen Eindruck zu gewinnen, wie sich Mignes Text zu beliebigen ma. Texten verhält, habe ich Stichproben gemacht und Textstellen aus zwei mittelalterlichen Uppsala-Hss., C 129 und C 130, sowie aus zwei Inkunabeln aus dem Jahre 1485 (Hain *5533 und Copinger-Reichl 1709) miteinander und mit dem Text von Migne verglichen. Die Abweichungen waren erstaunlich gering'. Petra Berendrecht, 'Maerlants "Scholastica" (c.q. "Rijmbijbel") in relatie tot zijn directe bron. Een verkenning', *TNTL* 108 (1992), pp. 2–31 (p. 6): 'Bovendien is uit een steekproefsgewijze vergelijking met een aantal handschriften en incunabelen gebleken dat inhoudelijke afwijkingen ten opzichte van de door Migne bezorgde tekst in de overlevering van de *Historia scholastica* opvallend gering zijn'.

[62] Koen Goudriaan, 'Maerlants bronnen in de *Scolastica*: Comestor en de anderen', in: *Scolastica willic ontbinden*, p. 38, n. 14: 'De verschillen tussen de Migne-tekst en de beide genoemde handschriften [Bruges, Stadsbibl. 400 (Flemish, c. 1200) and Groningen, UB 5 (13th c.)] zijn soms aanzienlijk'.

[63] Hans Vollmer, *Eine deutsche Schulbibel des 15. Jahrhunderts. Historia scholastica des Petrus*

transmission of the work would be a very welcome project, but even a modern edition, taking into account every extant version of the text, could not rule out the possibility that a slightly different version has been lost. Though a better edition would facilitate research into the reception of the work, one still would not know exactly what the source manuscript used by a later author looked like. This problem is, of course, common to virtually all studies that proceed from the comparison of a medieval reworking or translation with a critical edition of the 'original' text.

The nature of the *Historia scholastica* might make it particularly susceptible to variation. It was conceived as a teaching-aid, developed by Comestor from his own lecture-courses and intended to form the basis of his colleagues' lectures on the literal sense of the Bible. The *additiones*, which are a distinctive feature of the text as found in Migne, reflect the genesis and primary function of the work: some reveal the voice of a lecturer further clarifying a difficult point ('Unde addam' in col. 1290) which echoes the tone of the main body of the text; others use such phrases as 'apposuit magister' (col. 1286) which situate them explicitly within an academic context. The term *additio* indicates their different status within the text, though some or all of them may stem from Comestor himself. It is not clear exactly when and by whom they were added, but they were an accepted feature of the work from early on in its transmission. However, though few manuscripts or early prints are completely free of *additiones*, comparison of manuscripts reveals that they are more liable to variation than the main body of the text, and can thus be seen as a more flexible element of the tradition.[64]

Another example of the way the *Historia scholastica* particularly lent itself to revision is the existence of many and various abbreviated versions produced in the 14th and 15th centuries.[65] Andersson-Schmitt posits the existence of

---

Comestor in deutschem Auszug mit lateinischem Paralleltext, Materialien 2 (Berlin, 1925/1927), I, p. XIV. He gives two examples in n. 2, p. XIV: 'Für die Unzulänglichkeit von Migne genügt als Probe wohl der Hinweis auf das sinnlose "nec romanticos" 288, 15 für "nigromanticos" (necromanticos) und das nicht minder rätselhafte "Scor regiae" 295, 3 statt "scenopegiae"'.

[64] L. Light, *The Bible in the twelth century: An Exhibition of Manuscripts in the Houghton Library* (Cambridge, 1988), p. 108, observes that 'a comparison of a limited number of manuscripts indicates that these *additiones* vary from copy to copy.' This observation is confirmed by spot-checks on manuscripts in the Bodleian Library (MSS ABCDEFGH).

[65] Vollmer, *Bibel und deutsche Kultur. Veröffentlichungen des deutschen Bibelarchivs in Hamburg*, Materialien 1, I, pp. 15–20; Morey, 'Comestor', p. 8, n. 6: 'Abridging the *Historia* was a popular fifteenth-century pastime'. Stegmüller lists three such abridged versions (6572, 1–3); the Bodleian Library contains two more: MSS Lyell 8 and 35.

selectively glossed Bibles to explain the striking conformity in the choice of Comestor material among vernacular authors for whom the *Historia scholastica* was a source.[66] Such a work would have to have been very widespread to span the distance and time that separate the works investigated, and it is surprising, if she is right, that no copies are known to survive.[67] This theory must remain speculation.[68]

In the light of these possibilities, the foundations for the study of the reception of such a work begin to look rather precarious. One can never be sure that the copy of the *Historia scholastica* used by a given medieval author is accurately represented by Migne, or that the omissions or additions which one attributes to him are not in fact merely a function of the version of the *Historia* at his disposal. However, as has been pointed out above, this problem is not unique. The very fact that there is recognizable uniformity among the manuscripts listed by Stegmüller, and that comparatively few copies of the individual shorter versions, the collections of excerpts, survive (and these from much later) emphasizes the very strong textual tradition of the original work. The persistence of the unabridged version of the text can be confirmed by comparing the various printed editions of the *Historia scholastica.*

The printed versions of the *Historia scholastica* are the culmination of a three-hundred-year process of handwritten transmission of the text. A comprehensive study of the relationship even of the printed transmission to Migne's text lies beyond the scope of this research. For present purposes a systematic study of all the available printed versions of a limited number of sections of the *Historia scholastica* will be undertaken to serve as an indication of the extent of variation that can occur within the main textual tradition. This is a first step towards the ultimate goal of establishing the overall contours of the tradition. It is important because it helps to evaluate the

[66] Margarete Andersson-Schmitt, 'Die Verwendung der "Historia scholastica" in einigen volkssprachigen Bibel werken des Mittelalters', *Årsbok Kungliga Humanistika Vetenskaps-Samenfundet i Uppsala/Annales Societatis Litterarum Humaniorum Regiae Uppsaliensis*, 1985 (1986), pp. 5–31 (p.19): 'Neben solchen Bibelwerken, die dem Text der Vulg. Stellen aus der Hist.schol. als laufende Glosse beigaben, müssen auch Bibeln verbreitet gewesen sein, die nur eine Auswahl aus dieser Glosse enthielten'.

[67] I know of no examples where material from the *Historia scholastica* was incorporated into a glossed Bible.

[68] The works investigated by Andersson-Schmitt are: the 'so-called first' Dutch (= Noordnederlandse) *Historiebijbel*, the *Weltchronik* of Rudolf von Ems, Merzdorf's edition of *Historienbibel I*, the *Historien der Alden E* and the Old Swedish Bible-paraphrase *Fem Moseböcker* ('Verwendung', pp. 5–7).

a	Strasbourg, not after 6 Feb. 1473: Printer of Henricus Ariminensis (Georg Reyser?) [Hain *5529; ISTC ip00460000]
b	Augsburg, 1473: Günther Zainer [Hain *5531; ISTC ip00458000]
c	Cologne, not after 14 Apr. 1477: Conrad Winters, de Homborch [Hain/Copinger *5530; ISTC ip00461000]
d	Strasbourg, 28 Aug. 1483: Johann (Reinhard) Grüninger and Henricus de Inguiler [Hain/Copinger 5532; ISTC ip00462000]
e	Chambéry, not after 1486: Printer of Breviarium Sedunense (Henricus Wirtzburg?) [Copinger 1709; ISTC ip00464000]
f	Strasbourg, 1485 ('post' 24 Feb.): Printer of the 1483 Jordanus de Quedlinburg (Georg Husner) [Hain *5533; ISTC ip00463000]
g?	Reutlingen, 1485 [Hain *5534]
h	Basel, 25 Nov. 1486: Johann Amerbach [Hain/Copinger *5535; ISTC ip00465000]
i?	Strasbourg, 1487 (after 24 Feb.) [Hain *5536]
j	Strasbourg, 15 July 1500: Georg Husner [Hain *5538; ISTC ip00466000]
k	New Testament only: Utrecht, 1473: Nicolaus Ketelaer and Gerardus de Leempt [Hain/Copinger 5540; ISTC ip00459000]
l	Strasbourg, 1503: Georg Husner [fol.] (ISTC ip00467000)
m	Paris, 17th Aug. 1513: Jehan Frellon/Jehan Petit (2 issues) [4o]
n?	n.n., n.p., 1515 [Univ. of Pennsylvania, Philadelphia]
o	Paris, 17th Nov. 1518: Franciscus Regnault [4o]
p	Hagenau, 1519: Heinrich Gran [fol.]
q	Lyon, 20th March 1526: J. Crespin [8o]
r	Lyon, 1534: Nicolaus Petit and Hector Penet [8o]
s	Lyon, 1542 [8o]
t	Lyon, 1543 [8o]
u	Benevento, 1699
v	Madrid, 1699: E. Navarro [4o]
w	Venice, 1729

Table 3: Printed Editions of the *Historia scholastica*

printed text that has formed the basis of all modern scholarship on Peter Comestor.

Migne's text is a reprint of the edition printed in Madrid by E. Navarro in 1699, which has not yet been available to me.[69] This would appear to

[69] Listed in: Antonio Palau y Dulcet, *Manual del librero hispanoamericano*, 2nd edn (Madrid/ Oxford, 1950).

contain minor revisions, but is substantially the same as the series of editions produced in France in the first half of the 16th century, and is apparently based on one of these. Only one major revision of the text was carried out in the whole printed tradition, and this revised version was published for the first time in Paris in 1513 in two issues, one sold by Jehan Frellon 'in vico Mathurinorum' and one by Jehan Petit 'in vico sancti Jacobi'. The principles of that revision are set out on the title-page:

> 'Historia scholastica magistri Petri Comestoris sacre scripture brevem nimis et obscuram elucidans nunc post exactam studiosamque diligentiam revisa ac in marginibus quotationibus capitulorum illustrata'

The colophon repeats the same information in slightly more detail, and claims, correctly, to be the first edition to note the exact provenance of the biblical quotations:

> Scholastica Historia magistri Petri Comestoris diligentissime revisa certisque sacre biblie capitulorum unde sumitur magno cum labore quotationibus nunc primum aptata. Ope atque impensa Honesti viri Johannis frellon Parisiensis librarij illic impressa' (f. 280^{v})[70]

These guide-lines are followed in all the subsequent sixteenth-century French editions. Apart from occasional textual emendations, the main innovation is in the systematic use of the margins, which contain various notes to guide the reader's interpretation: attention is drawn to certain sections with the word 'Nota' or a reference to the content-matter (e.g. 'Mors sisare', 'Gedeon nominatur ierobaal'); the source of each quotation from the Bible and of some other references is noted; and apocryphal or non-biblical material is marked with the phrase 'Incidens est et non de Biblia'.[71] The *additiones* continue to be found mainly in smaller columns inserted into the main column of text at the relevant point in the narrative, rather than at the end of the chapter as in Migne.

It remains to be seen whether the only sixteenth-century German edition, printed in Hagenau in 1519, is referring to an independent revision when it is introduced as 'diligenter revisa per industrium Henricum Gran'.[72] The

[70] These passages are identical in the issue made for Jehan Petit, with his name substituted in the colophon.

[71] In the manuscripts the margins are used, if at all, by the scribes as an 'overflow' for the main text columns (e.g. for the 'additiones' if they have not been included), or by later readers as a place to record their comments.

[72] It has not been possible to check this edition, which is not readily accessible; the copy

name of the revisor is not mentioned in any of the French editions. The introductions to the successive French sixteenth-century editions continue to intensify their claims of improved accuracy ('Mendis omnibus post primam editionem seclusis in lucem exit' or 'nunc melius quam antea fuerit'[73]), but the changes are minor, and the basic format remains the same.

At this later stage in the printed transmission relatively clear links are discernible between various editions. Not surprisingly, these reflect the geographical divisions, which are, in turn, divisions in time: there are no more Paris editions after the first Lyon edition. The relationship of the revised version to the incunabula and of the incunabula among themselves is more complicated. Although various similarities emerge at times between the incunabula, it has not been possible, on the basis of this survey, to identify a direct line of transmission. One example will show the complexity of the situation. Migne's version of the Gospel harmony contains an *additio* which gives alternative locations for the present whereabouts of the relic of Christ's foreskin: Charroux and Antwerp.[74] This reference to Antwerp is common to all the Paris and Lyon editions, but does not occur in the printed editions before the revision of 1513 discussed above. That this association with Antwerp is not just a sixteenth-century phenomenon but a much earlier addition to the tradition is demonstrated by its occurrence in Jacob van Maerlant's *Scolastica*, a thirteenth-century Dutch adaptation of the *Historia scholastica*.[75] Thus it is clear that the revised version is not based exclusively on a printed tradition, but draws also on manuscript material.

---

formerly in the library of Wadham College, Oxford is now missing, and there is no record of this edition in the catalogues of the main National and University libraries of Britain and Ireland. One copy is listed in the catalogue of the Bayerische Staatsbibliothek, Munich.

[73] Lyon, 1526 and Lyon, 1534 respectively.

[74] PL 198, col. 1541: 'Dicitur quod praeputium Domini delatum est ab angelo Carolo Magno in templo Domini, et translatum est ab eo Aquisgrani; Etiam post a Carolo Calvo positum in ecclesia Salvatoris apud Carosium. Alii dicunt Antuerpiam delatum, nam illic in summa veneratione habetur'. The first part of this story corresponds to the Legenda Aurea of Jacobus de Voragine, but in Jacobus' version the relic was then transferred to the Lateran in Rome. The Church of Our Lady in Antwerp claimed that it had acquired this relic from Jerusalem during the crusades in 1112, but it only became the focus of an individual cult in the late thirteenth century. See Floris Prims, *Geschiedenis van Antwerpen*, (Antwerp, 1927–1949), VI, pp. 118–124.

[75] *Sa*, ll. 21340–21351: 'Die besnidenesse van onsen here./ Was coninc carle dor sijn eere./ Van den inglen ghebrocht./ Dit lasic dar ict hebbe besocht./ Ende hi brocht dar na taken./ Nv seghemen in waren saken./ Dat soe tote andwarpen es./ Dar toghemense dies sijt ghewes'.

1473 marks the beginning of the printed transmission of the *Historia scholastica*, which was printed twice in that year: in Strasbourg, perhaps by Georg Reyser, and in Augsburg by Günther Zainer. These earliest editions are those which show most variation from the standard tradition, with frequent grammatical changes and mistakes. The work is printed between ten and twelve times before 1503, in six different locations.[76] Apart from such obvious pairs as the editions printed by Georg Husner in Strasbourg in 1500 and 1503, which scarcely differ at all, it is not clear how many of these editions derive from each other and how many draw directly on manuscript sources, but the differences between some of them are such that direct dependence is highly unlikely.

As most of the prints are based on different manuscripts, comparison of as many as possible of the printed editions is an indication of their reliability. Different approaches may yield different levels of similarity, and for this reason the problem is approached from various angles. The section of Exodus which forms the basis of textual analysis in the vernacular works studied is here quoted in full from Migne and all the significant variations in the earlier editions are noted. This section contains no *additiones*, and as these have been identified as the least fixed part of the tradition, their status in the printed versions of the books of Judges has been investigated. Finally the *incidentia* in the book of Judges have been considered as another possibly flexible component of the tradition. The investigation is thus based on three different sets of evidence, all from the Old Testament. I have included orthographic as well as substantial variants.

1.4.1 *Historia scholastica*, 'Historia Libri Exodi'

Cap. V. *De ortu, et educatione Moysi.*

'Egressus est post haec vir levita (*Exod.* II)', nomine Aram, vel Amram, qui accepit uxorem contribulem nomine Jocabeth, qui nolebat accedere ad uxorem post edictum, malens carere liberis quam in necem procreare. Cui Deus per somnium astitit, ut ait Josephus, dicens, ne timeret uxorem cognoscere, quia puer, quem timebant Aegyptii, nasciturus esset ex ea: etiam de sacerdotio

2 *Exod. II*] *A Exo. 2.* (supplied in margin) mopqrst, om. abcdefhjl. *Aram, vel Amram*] *amram vel amranus* b, *amramis vel amram* e. 3 *nomine*] om. be. *Jocabeth*] *iacobeth* acdfhjlmo, *iacobecth* qrstw. 4 *et malens* e. 5 *somnium*] *somnum* e. 6 *quem*] *quam* m.

[76] Hain lists two editions – Reutlingen, 1485 and Strassburg, 1487 – which remain untraced and do not occur in the ISTC.

Aaron ei significavit. Tandem 'concepit mulier, et peperit filium' sub silentio, eo quod non multum ei dolores partus instriterint. 'Et videns puerum elegantem, abscondit eum tribus mensibus. Cumque celare non posset, sumpsit fiscellam scirpeam' in modum fisci, id est sacci rotundi, vimine complexam, 'et linivit eam bitumine ac pice, et ponens intus infantulum in carecto ripae eum exposuit', ne impetu fluminis raperetur, et stante procul sorore parvuli Maria, exspectante rei exitum, ex matris praecepto. 'Ecce autem descendit Terimith filia Pharaonis, ut lavaretur in flumine, quae videns alveolum, et afferre sibi jubens, vidit parvulum vagientem, et miserta est ejus dicens: De infantibus Hebraeorum est hic'. Sic enim Deus eum venustaverat ut etiam ab hostibus dignus alimento haberetur. Et cum Aegyptiae plures ei admovissent ubera ad lactandum, faciem advertebat. Et ait Maria: Vis, inquit, Hebræam adducam, forte ubera gentis suae sequetur. Et praecepto ergo Terimith abiens, matrem parvuli, tanquam alienam, adduxit, et accessit ad ejus ubera puer. Suscepit ergo Terimith alendum puerum, et ablactatum reddidit filiae Pharaonis, quae adoptavit eum in filium, et dictus est Moyses. Aegyptii enim *Moys*, aquam, *is* salvatum dicunt. Quem dum quadam die Terimith obtulisset Pharaoni, ut et ipse eum adoptaret, admirans rex pueri venustatem, coronam, quam tunc forte gestabat, capiti illius imposuit. Erat autem in ea Ammonis imago fabrefacta. Puer autem coronam projecit in terram, et fregit. Sacerdos autem Heliopoleos a latere regis surgens, exclamavit: Hic est puer, quem nobis occidendum Deus monstravit, ut de caetero timore careamus, et voluit irruere in eum, sed auxilio regis liberatus est, et persuasione cujusdam sapientis qui per ignorantiam hoc factum esse a puero asseruit. In cujus rei argumentum cum prunas allatas puero obtulisset, puer eas ori suo opposuit, et linguae suae summitatem igne corrupit. Unde et Hebraei impeditioris linguae eum fuisse autumant. Tantae vero pulchritudinis fuit, ut ait Josephus, ut nullus adeo severus esset, qui ejus aspectui non haereret, multique, dum cernerent eum per plateas ferri, occupationes in quibus studebant, desererent.

7 *ei significavit*] *significavit ei* e. 8 *institerint*] *institurent* a, *intulerit* b, *insisterent* c, *insteterint* dhj. 9 *celare*] *celere* o. 10 *scirpeam*] *cirpeam* ac. *rotundi*] *rotundam* be. 12 *raperetur*] *reciperetur* b. *et*] om. acdeh. *et exspectante* acdelmqw. 13 *Terimith*] *tramuth* a, *termuth* be, *terimuth* c, *terinuth* d. 15 *est*] om. acd. *eum*] om. e. 18 *inquit*] om. acd. *Vis, inquit, Hebraeam adducam*] *Vis inquam ei adducam hebream* e. *suae*] om. b. 19 *Terimith*] *termuth* abde, *terimuth* c. 20 *ejus ubera*] *ubera eius* e, *eius verba* st. *Terimith*] *a termuth* ad, *a terimuth* c, *ad termuth* e, *a terimith* jlmoqr, *mater* w. 22 *Moys*] *mos* ade. 23 *et*] e. 24 *tunc*] om. e. 25 *Ammonis*] *hamonis* bdfhjlmoqrstw. 26 *Heliopoleos*] *eliopoleos* abcdfhjl moqrstw. *a latere*] *altare* e. 27 *nobis occidendum Deus monstravit*] *nobis deus occidendum monstravit* e. 30 *argumentum*] *augmentum* e. 31 *opposuit*] *apposuit* bcejloqr. *linguae*] *ligue* b. 32 *impeditioris*] *impeditiores* b. 33 *qui... haereret*] *quin ... adheret* bw, *horreret* h. *non* om. t. 34 *studebant*] *studebat* b.

Cap. VI *De uxore Moysi Aethiopissa*

Factum est autem cum adultus fuisset Moyses, Aethiopes vastaverunt Aegyptum, usque ad Memphim et mare, quo circa conversi ad divinationes Aegyptii, acceperunt responsum, ut auxiliatore uterentur Hebraeo; et vix obtinuerunt a Terimith, ut exercitui, quem paraverant, Moysen praeficeret ducem, prius praestitis sacramentis, ne ei nocerent. Erat autem Moyses vir bellicosus, et peritissimus, qui fluminis iter tanquam longius praetermittens, per terram duxit exercitum itinere breviori, ut improvisos Aethiopes praeveniret. Sed per loca plena serpentibus iter faciens, tulit in arcis papireis super plaustra ibices ciconias, id est Aegyptiacas, naturaliter infestas serpentibus, quae rostro per posteriora immisso alvum purgant, castraque metaturus praeferebat eas, ut serpentes fugarent, et devorarent, et ita tutus per noctem transibat exercitus. Tandem praeventos Aethiopes expugnans inclusit eos fugientes, in civitatem Sabba regiam, quam post Cambyses a nomine sororis suae Meroem denominavit. Quam cum, quia inexpugnabilis erat, diutius obsedisset, oculos suos injecit in eum Tarbis filia regis Aethiopum, et ex condicto tradidit ei civitatem, si duceret eam uxorem, et ita factum est. Inde est quod Maria et Aaron jurgati sunt adversus Moysen pro uxore ejus Aethiopissa (Num. 12). Dum autem redire voluisset, non acquievit uxor. Proinde Moyses tanquam vir peritus astrorum duas imagines sculpsit in gemmis hujus efficaciae, ut altera memoriam, altera oblivionem conferret. Cumque paribus annulis eas inseruisset, alterum, scilicet oblivionis annulum, uxori praebuit; alterum ipse tulit, ut sic pari amore, sic paribus annulis insignirentur. Coepit ergo mulier amoris viri oblivisci, et tandem libere in Aegyptum regressus est.

Cap. VII. *De fuga Moysi, et affinitate Jethro.*

In diebus illis egressus Moyses ad fratres suos in terram Gessen, vidit afflictionem eorum, et praefectum operis Aegyptium percutientem quemdam de Hebraeis, et secrete percussum Aegyptium abscondit in sabulo. Et egressus altera die vidit duos Hebraeos rixantes. Qui dum argueret eum, qui fecerat injuriam, respondit: 'Quis te constituit judicem super nos? Num me occidere vis, sicut occidisti heri Aegyptium?' Miratus est Moyses, quomodo palam factum erat

36 *fuisset*] *esset* be. 39 *auxiliatore uterentur Hebraeo*] *uterentur egypcij hebreo* c. 40 *Terimith*] *terimuth* c, *termuth* d *termuthe* e. *exercitui*] *exercertui* a. 44 *papireis*] *papirijs* ace. 45 *id est*] *scilicet* bcdehmo. *infestas*] *infectas* b. *rostro*] *rastro* c. 46 *metaturus*] *metatus* c. *ut*] *ub* c, *ubi* d. 47 *noctem*] *noctes* e. 49 *Meroem*] *merorem* h. 50 *obsedisset*] *obsideret* b. 53 *Moysen numeri duodecimo pro* b. *(Num. 12)*] om. abcefhmqrstw. 54 *Moyses*] om. cde. 55 *duas*] om. a. 57 *sic*] *sicut* abcdefjlmoqrstw. 61 *Gessen*] *iessen* abcdefhjlorstw, *iessem* q. 62 *quemdam*] *quandam* a, *quendam* lmqst. 63 *secrete*] *secreto* abcefjlmoqr. 64 *fecerat*] *fecisset* b. *injuriam (Stultus qui verba prudentie non recipit. xviii perum) respondit* b. 65 *judicem*] om. e. *me occidere vis*] *me vis occidere* e. 66 *palam*] *palem* o.

verbum hoc, et timuit, praesertim cum audisset Pharao verbum hoc, et quaereret eum occidere. Qui fugiens per desertum venit in terram Madian, et ciborum inopiam, ut ait Josephus, virtute tolerantiae superabat, et venit ad civitatem Madian circa mare Rubrum, sic nominatam a quodam filio Abrahae de Cethura, seditque juxta puteum. Erant autem sacerdoti Madian, id est primati, qui antiquitus sacerdotes dicebantur, septem filiae, et dicebatur Raguel, agnominatus Jethro, cognominatus Cinaeus, quae venerant ut haurierent aquam gregibus suis. Officium enim gregum alendorum tunc erat mulierum, maxime in regione Trogloditarum. Supervenientes autem pastores repulerant eas, quos prohibuit Moyses ab injuria virginum, et adaquavit greges earum. Quae maturius solito redeuntes rogaverunt patrem, ne beneficium peregrini retributione privaretur. 'Vocatusque Moyses, juravit ut habitaret cum eo. Et accepit uxorem filiam ejus Sephoram, quae peperit ei Gerson, quod sonat *advena*, eo quod in exsilio genuerat eum, peperitque alterum, quem dixit Eliezer, id est *Dei mei adjutorium*, deditque ei socer omnem curam gregum suorum, in quibus omnis antiquis barbaris erat possessio.

Cap. VIII *De Dei visione in rubo.*

Tandem mortuus est rex Aegypti, et clamaverunt filii Israel ad Dominum, et recordatus est foederis quod pepigerat patribus eorum (*Exod.* II et III). Moyses autem pascebat greges ovium in deserto. [...]

70 *nominatam*] *nominatum* c. *Cethura scilicet xxv .ge. seditque* b. *autem ibi sacerdoti* e. 72 *sacerdotes dicebantur*] *sacerdos dicebatur* ce. *et*] *qui* ad. 74 *tunc etiam erat* abcehjlmoqr. 75 *Trogloditarum*] *trogoditarum* abcdef, *drogoditarum* hjlmoqrw, *drogoditatum* st. 85 *(Exod. II et III)*] *G Exo. 2. A Exo. 3.* (supplied in margin) moqrst, om. abcefhjl. 86 *pascebat (Angelus ad pastores ait: annuncio vobis gaudium magnum luce .ii) greges* b.

The above comparison of Exodus chapters 5–7 in the various printed versions of the *Historia scholastica* gives some idea of the extent of variation from Migne's text and between the different editions. Some editions have more in common than others: b and e, for example, are frequently paired. However, even here there are only three instances where they are the only editions to correspond in a variant, and these are far outnumbered by the instances in which they differ from each other. The word-order frequently differs from Migne in e; b, the Zainer edition, is grammatically inconsistent, and contains several minor additions, as well as source-references, which do not occur elsewhere before the revision of the text.

Generally, though, significant variation is minimal, and Migne appears to give a version of the text that is representative, at least of the printed editions.

As can be deduced from the specific mention in the introduction to the revised edition of 1513, quotations from the Bible tend to be unattributed in the earlier printed editions, as in the manuscripts. The names have been standardized, but there has been little change in the basic text. There are some obvious mistakes in Migne's version, such as the omission of 'a' in 'suscepit ergo [a] Terimith', which seems to be derived from the Lyon edition of 1542, or the change from 'sicut' to 'sic', which goes against the entire tradition, but these are the only inaccuracies in Exodus 5–7.

The *additiones* have been identified as a potentially flexible part of the tradition: as the term suggests, they were not part of the main body of the text, and could therefore have been regarded as more open to change. The following tables chart the distribution and the extent of variation of the *additiones* in the books of Judges and Ruth in the *Historia scholastica*:

1.4.2 The *additiones* in the book of Judges in the *Historia scholastica*[77]

1: Hoc etiam vult Augustinus, ordine suo dictum in Josue praeoccupatum.

2: In Regum libro, ubi incipit agere de Saul, dicitur vir fortis robore (*I Reg. XVI*), ob hoc quidam putant dictum geminum, quasi binomium.

3: Qui primus infestavit Israel in deserto.

4: Sexto suscitavit Dominus spiritum Gedeonis in Israel.

5: Forte tabernaculum eorum dixit vexillum, quo ducebantur, vel habebant tabernaculum, in quo idolis suis sacrificabant.

6: Per quod conjicitur quod postea poenitentiam egerit, qui alibi quam ubi Dominus constituerat sacrificabat.

7: Nota quod Olympias dicta est a ludis, qui sub Olympo monte fiebant apud Elidem civita tem Elidis agentibus agonem, et quinquennale certamen quatuor annis mediis vocantibus, et ob hoc Elidis certaminis tempus olympiadem vocaverunt quadriennium in una Olympiade computato. Est autem Olympias spatium quatuor annorum.

8: Qua lege viverent Nazaraei require in historia Numerorum (*Num. VI*). Istud apposuit magister, ut satisfaceret Hieronymo, qui ait nomen ejus praedictum a Domino, cum praedeterminatum sit supra quot fuerint, quorum nomina praedicta sunt, quia nomen fuit ei impositum scilicet Samson. Juxta aequipollentiam horum verborum Domini, ait Hieronymus, praedictum ejus nomen.

9: Nota quod in Veteri Testamento quatuor hominum nomina per angelum nuntiata fuerunt: Ismael, Isaac, Josias, Samson; in Novo duo Joannes et Jesus.

[77] These are quoted verbatim from Migne; the punctuation is either his own or that of the edition by E. Navarro, which has not been available to me.

10: Omnis enim mulier fere naturaliter avara, et levis, unde addam: Quid levius flumine? flamen, Quid flamine? fama. Quid fama? mulier. Quid muliere? nihil.
11: Ebrium dicit non de vino, sed amore, vel satiatum, aliter legem Nazaraeorum excessisset ante tonsuram, et recessisset ab eo Dominum.
12: Decimam partem virorum intellige. Sensus est. Decimam partem virorum elegerunt, ad apportanda cibaria.
13: Petra haec excelsa fuit. Rama autem *excelsum* sonat. Unde de planctu istorum plangentium filios suos dictur in Evangelio: 'Vox in Rama,' etc. (*Matth. II*)

Migne add.	**gloss**	**in text**	**at end**	**change**	**omission**
1: Cap. 2, col. 1273	fhjlmoqrst	acd			be
2: Cap. 6, col. 1275	acdfhjlmoqrst				abcdefhjlmoqrst
3: Cap. 7, col. 1277	acdfhjlmoqrst				be
4: Cap. 8, col. 1280	acdfhjlmoqrst				be
5: Cap. 8, col. 1280	acdfhjlmoqrst				be
6: Cap. 8, col. 1280	acdfhjlmoqrst			a	be
7: Cap. 15, col. 1285	fhjlmoqrst	acd		adfmqrst	be
8: Cap. 16, col. 1286	acdfhjlmoqrst				be
9: Cap. 16, col. 1286				acdfhjlmoqrst	be
10: Cap. 19, col. 1290	acdfhjlmoqrst			acdfhjlmoqrst	be
11: Cap. 19, col. 1290	acdfhjlmoqrst				abce
9:	fhjlmoqrst	acd	acd		be
12: Cap. 22, col. 1292	acdfhjlmoqrst				be
13: Cap. 22, col. 1292	acdfhjlmoqrst				be

Table 4: Distribution and Variation of *additiones* in the book of Judges

Explanation of Table

'Migne add.' The *additiones* are numbered consecutively in the order in which they occur in Migne; chapters and columns are numbered according to his *PL* 198.

'gloss' The *additio* occurs in a smaller column, inserted into the main column of text at the relevant point of the narrative.

'in text' The *additio* is not distinguished from the main text in this way.

'at end'	The *additio* is placed at the end of the chapter.
'change'	The wording or context of the *additio* differs from Migne (but not by omission).[78]
'omission'	All or part of the *additio* is omitted.

Differences in individual additiones[79]

2: *libro*] om. abcdefhjlmoqrst
6: *sacrificabat*] *sacrificavit* a
7: *quadriennium*] *quadriennio* adfmqrst
...annotaverunt tempora iuxta numerum olimpiadum. $ Nota quod ... spacium quattuor annorum. Tandem romani florentes... inserted into *incidens* 10 in ad
9: occurs in Cap. 20 in all the editions studied.
incorporated into main text at end of Cap. 20 in acd
10: *avara*] *amara* acdfhjl
flumine] *flamma* afmoqr, *flamine* st
11: *Ebrium dicit non de vino, sed amore*] om. ac

1.4.3 The *additiones* in the book of Ruth in the *Historia scholastica*

1: Sic certum, quod cum Aaron quatuor habuit filios, duo ex eis in deserto igne perierunt; eorum qui remanserant, major natu fuit Eleazar, cui debebatur sacerdotium, quod duravit usque ad Heli, qui fuit de Ithamar fratre suo.
2: Super Paralipomenon dicit Hieronymus quod in diebus Elimelech, sol stetit ad transgressores legis. Sed quia non timuerant Deum, tanta fames invaluit, ut potior in tribu Juda fugeret cum uxore et liberis.
3: Opiniones plures ponuntur. Unde civitas, quae nunc Bethlehem dicitur, prius vocata fuit Ephrata, secundum primam opinionem dicentem, Mariam sororem Moysi translatam illuc, quia quod Caleb suscepit de Ephrata, Hur virum Mariae, et Hur genuit Bezeleel.
4: Cum terra illa calidissima sit, homines regiones illius contra remedium aestus in condimentis suis in aceto, quod frigidum est, utuntur. Contraria enim contrariis curantur, quoniam etiam calidissimus aestus mitigatur.
5: Arconium dictum est ab arcendo, quia gelimae ibi arcentur quaelibet ab alia.
6: Sensus verborum Joannis secundum unam expositionem is est: Putabatur Joannes sponsus sponsae, id est Ecclesiae, et fuit consuetudo, ut, mortuo uno sine prole, uxorem ejus duceret propinquior ejus cognatus. Quod si nollet proximus, eum discalceabat, et duxit eam. Dicit ergo Joannes: Non sum ego sponsus, sed Christus, cujus corrigiam calceamenti non sum dignus solvere, ut

[78] Variations in spelling, where the pronunciation remains unchanged, have not been taken into account.
[79] Editions b and e omit the *additiones* altogether.

ducam ejus sponsam; non tamen ipse discalceabat repudiantem ducens eam. Quod notat hic.

6a: Hec sunt generationes phares Phares genuit esron. Esron genuit aram. Aram genuit aminadab. Aminadab genuit naason. Naason genuit salmon. Salmon genuit boos. Boos genuit obeth. Obeth genuit ysai. ysai genuit david.

Migne Add.	gloss	in text	at end	change	omission
1. col. 1295	acdfhjlmoqrst			a	be
2. col. 1295	abcdfhjlmoqrst	e	f	eqrs	
3. col. 1296	acdfhjlmoqrst	be		abe	be
4. col. 1296	acdfhjlmoqrst			a	be
5. col. 1296	acdfhjlmoqrst			a	be
6. col. 1296	acdfhjlmoqrst				e
6a.	e				

Table 5: Distribution and Variation of *additiones* in the book of Ruth

Notes on individual additiones

1: *et hoc est primus* added at the end of the *additio* in a
2: *sol stetit ad terrendos transgressores* eqrs, *ut*] *vbi* b
3: *Opiniones...in deserto*] om. be (remainder incorporated into main text)
Hur virum Mariae, et Hur genuit Bezeleel] *vr virum marie et iuri ante beselebel* a, *vr virum marie. et vri auum beseleel* b, *ur virum beseleel* e
4: *vnde apud virgilium. Alia serpillum danda sunt messoribus* added in a
5: *gelimae*] *gelune* a
6a: found only in e

Here again there is some similarity between editions b and e, which both omit the *additiones* to the book of Judges altogether, and incorporate the third *additio* to the book of Ruth into the main text, omitting the first part. However, e contains some extra material such as the *additio* numbered 6a, which occurs only in e, and would appear to be an individual addition made by the editor. Editions a, c, and d correspond in their presentation: they all incorporate the same *additiones* into the main body of the text. Editions a and c both omit part of the eleventh *additio* to the book of Judges, but a is alone in containing a reference to Virgil in the fourth *additio* to the book of Ruth.

There is a consistent variation in the tenth *additio*: all the early editions have 'amara', which has been revised to 'avara', and many have 'flamma' or 'flamine' where Migne has 'flumine'. Migne's ninth *additio* to the book of Judges occurs after his eleventh in all the earlier editions studied.

The *incidentia*, short summaries of parallel events in world history, are another distinctive feature of the *Historia scholastica*. They are an integral part of the work, but their non-sacred status, and their presentation, generally in separate paragraphs at the end of chapters of biblical history, might have rendered them more liable to omission or variation. As the following table shows, this does not generally appear to have been the case in the book of Judges.

Migne Inc.	**at end**	**in text**	**change**
1: Cap. 5, col. 1271	abcdefhjlmoqrst	cde	ab
2: Cap. 6, col. 1275	abcdefhjlmoqrst	cd(e)	acdehlmoqrst
3: Cap. 7, col. 1277	abcdefhjlmoqrst	cd(e)fhjloqrs	
4: Cap. 8, cols 1280–81	abcdefhjlmoqrst	acd(e)	abcdefhjlmoqrst
5: Cap. 9, cols 1282–83	abcdefhjlmoqrst	cde	
6: Cap. 10, col. 1283	abcdefhjlmoqrst	cd(e)	abcdefhjlmo
7: Cap. 11, col. 1283	abcdefhjlmoqrst	cde	
8: Cap. 12, col. 1283	abcdefhjlmoqrst	cde	b
8a: Cap. 13, col. 1283			b
9: Cap. 14, col. 1283	abcdefhjlmoqrst	cd(e)	abcdefhjlmoqrst
10: Cap. 15, col. 1283	abcdefhjlmoqrst	acde	abcdefhjlmo

Table 6: The *incidentia* in the book of Judges in the *Historia scholastica*

Explanation of table

'at end' The *incidens* occurs at the end of a chapter.
'in text' The *incidens* is not separated from the main text of the chapter.
'change' Addition, omission or change in wording.

Differences in individual incidentia

1: *Cadmus*] *captiuus* a, *cadinus* b
color ille Phoeniceus] *color punicius* a

Corinthus] *cornutus* a
Sysipho] *sasipho* a
2: in d not given title *Incidentia*, but preceded by paragraph-mark
Aod] *ahoth* a, *aioth* cdehlmoqrst
novercales] *noverculas* m
3: not distinguished from main text in any way in cfl
d, as in Incidens 2
not separated from main text, but preceded by paragraph-mark and introduced as *Incidens est et non de biblia. Eo tempore...* moqrst
4: *uxore Cadmi*] *uxore cathmi et armonica* adfst, *uxore cathim vel cadim armonica* b, *uxore cathmi et armonice* cehjlmqr
dicitur etiam fecisse simulacra] *dicitur autem fuisse simulachra* b
Musaeus] *miseus* ad
6: *et illum vastavit*] *et ilium vastavit* abdfhjlm
Lapitas] *laphites* b
describit] *scribit* b
filius] om. b
minotaurum] *minotharum* a
7: *quam rursus receperunt fratres eius*] *quam fratres eius rursus receperunt* b
litteras Latinas] *latinas literas* b
8: *flammis*] *flamminis* b
8a: last sentence of Cap. 13 (correctly) labelled *Incidentia* in b
9: *Paris Helenam rapuit*] *alexander helenam rapuit* abcdefhjlmorst, *alerander* q
Memnon] *Mennon* bf
10: *trecenti et sex*] *ccccvi* abcdfhjlmo, *quadringenti et sex* e

As with the *additiones*, there is some variation in the presentation of the *incidentia*, although here it is editions c, d, and e that tend not to separate them from the main text of the chapter. The first *incidens* in a shows many inaccuracies, but otherwise variations are minor for the most part. Migne's version again shows standardization of names, and a corrected version of the ninth *incidens* which goes against the whole tradition. Two mistakes appear to have occurred at different times in the printed transmission: all the Lyon editions have 'trecenti sex' in the tenth *incidens* as Migne does, and Migne omits the reference to 'armonica' in the fourth *incidens*.

The general impression remains the same with all these approaches: though the text offered by Migne is not infallible, it does provide a generally accurate representation of the printed tradition of the *Historia scholastica*. The possibility of individual manuscript variants remains and can never be ignored, but it is more surprising that there should be so great a level of consistency over such a long period of transmission than that minor alterations and inaccuracies should exist. Migne's text should be used with care and checked against earlier versions where doubts arise, but it is a valid starting-point for the study of the reception of the *Historia scholastica* in the Middle Ages.

1.5 The *Historia scholastica* and Later Writers

The above sections provide a brief introduction to the transmission of the *Historia scholastica*, which testifies to the popularity of the work. Another gauge of its success is the extent to which it, in turn, is used as a source by other writers. The *Historia scholastica* was translated into many languages and was used as a source of biblical history by authors of diverse works.[80] In Morey's opinion, 'because of its comprehensive assembly of apocryphal and legendary elements, and because of its frequent translation and paraphrase, the *Historia* was the single most important medium through which a popular Bible took shape, from the thirteenth into the fifteenth century, in France, England, and elsewhere'.[81]

Vollmer sketches the reception of the *Historia scholastica* throughout Europe in the introduction to his edition of a German reworking of the text dating from approximately 1400. Morey's article concentrates in more detail on the principal works in French and in English which carried Comestor's biblical narratives into the vernacular. The present work is concerned with the German and Dutch reception of the *Historia scholastica*, and investigates the subject through detailed textual analysis of several very different works and their approach to their common source.

This book derives from studies of four texts from different literary genres and their reception of the *Historia scholastica*. The first of these studies involves the so-called *Schwarzwälder Predigten*, a thirteenth-century sermon cycle in German, as an example of this important mode of diffusion. Chapters three and four concern two further thirteenth-century works: the *Weltchronik* of Rudolf von Ems, a German verse chronicle of sacred and secular history by an influential literary author, which is known to make considerable use of Comestor, and Jacob van Maerlant's *Scolastica* (also known as his *Rijmbijbel*),

[80] Stegmüller, *Repertorium*, IV, nn. 6567–6572; Morey, 'Comestor', pp. 8–9; Vollmer, 'Einleitung', in: *Schulbibel*, pp. XVI–XXIX.

[81] Morey, 'Comestor', p. 6.

a Dutch verse-translation of the *Historia scholastica.* The final study examines the place of the *Historia scholastica* in the Dutch *Historiebijbel van 1360.*[82]

The importance of Peter Comestor as a source and authority for 'biblical' material for authors in the thirteenth and fourteenth centuries is a generally accepted but largely unexplained phenomenon. The focus of my research is the use of Comestor material within the framework of ancient or contemporary authorities consulted by a given author, and the aim of this series of studies is to investigate the position of the *Historia scholastica* relative to other sources and to examine why and how it was used at this time.

[82] This book is a reworked version of my D. Phil. thesis: 'Studies in the Reception of the *Historia scholastica* of Peter Comestor in Medieval German and Dutch Literature' (unpublished doctoral thesis, University of Oxford, 1996). Pressures of space necessitated reduction. In order to retain the comparative range of the work, I have chosen to retain discussion of all four texts, omitting a section of analysis from chapter 4 on the Tobias section of Maerlant's *Scolastica* and from chapter 5 on the Book of Judges in the *Historiebijbel van 1360.*

2 THE *SCHWARZWÄLDER PREDIGTEN*

2.1 The Reception of the *Historia scholastica* in the *Schwarzwälder Predigten*

The first of the studies in the reception of the *Historia scholastica* involves the late thirteenth-century *Schwarzwälder Predigten.*[1] At this period of limited access to the written word, the sermon holds a central position in the diffusion of information about the Bible among lay people. This particular sermon collection has been chosen both because it is very widespread, and because of its unusual manuscript tradition which permits some investigation into the various stages of composition and the consultation of source-works.[2]

It might seem initially that a collection of sermons is the 'odd one out' in a series of texts which could otherwise be classified loosely as biblical paraphrase. However, when one analyses the approach of the authors, it becomes apparent that to a certain extent the *Schwarzwälder Predigten* also fit into this category of biblical paraphrase. They have been referred to as a 'Florilegium für alttestamentliche Geschichten', and it is possible to read them as a collection of Bible stories.[3] They differ from the other works in that the stories are not recounted in 'chronological order', within a historical framework, but are rather set within a framework of spiritual exegesis with moral-didactic guide-lines.

The *Schwarzwälder Predigten* are a good starting-point for the study of the reception of the *Historia scholastica.* Since here the individual stories are divorced from their consecutive context, it is easier to attempt a classification of the types of material drawn from Comestor, and this provides a backdrop for the later studies, where the material is analysed in consecutive order. Investigating the use of Comestor within the framework of sources of biblical material available to these Franciscan authors provides an introduction to the recurring problems of identifying Comestor material in this network,

[1] See section 2.2 below for general background information, bibliography etc.

[2] Hans-Jochen Schiewer, *'Die Schwarzwälder Predigten': Entstehungs- und Überlieferungsgeschichte der Sonntags- und Heiligenpredigten,* (Tübingen, 1996).

[3] Schiewer, *Überlieferungsgeschichte,* p. 330.

where Comestor's own sources – and/or other works which themselves draw on the *Historia scholastica* – may potentially be available to the vernacular author. It demonstrates the importance of close textual analysis in this process. Finally, the manuscript tradition allows unique insights into the way such authors went about their task and used their source-works.

2.2 The *Schwarzwälder Predigten*

The *Schwarzwälder Predigten*[4] are a collection of sermons in German written by an anonymous author,[5] or group of authors,[6] in the last quarter of the thirteenth century. The collection consists of a cycle of sermons for the Sundays and feast-days of the church year, of which the first and only complete edition was furnished by Grieshaber in 1844 – 46,[7] and a cycle of sermons for saints' days, of which as yet only a partial edition exists.[8]

This study is concerned with the former, *de tempore*, cycle. It is the most widespread collection of sermons in the High-German-speaking area in the fourteenth and fifteenth centuries, surviving in thirty-three manuscripts. This manuscript tradition confirms 'daß es sich bei der Sonntagspredigtsammlung um den beliebtesten hochdeutschen Predigtjahrgang de tempore vor dem Auftreten der gedruckten Plenarien handelt'.[9]

[4] See Hans-Jochen Schiewer, 'Schwarzwälder Predigten' in: VL², VIII, cols 919–924; Gerhard Stamm, *Studien zum 'Schwarzwälder Prediger'*, (Munich, 1969); Werner Williams-Krapp, 'Das Gesamtwerk des sogenannten "Schwarzwälder Predigers"', *ZfdA* 107 (1978), pp. 50–80; Hans-Jochen Schiewer, '*Et non sit tibi cura quis dicat sed quid dicatur.* Entstehung und Rezeption der Predigtcorpora des sog. Schwarzwälder Predigers', in: *Die deutsche Predigt im Mittelalter*, ed. by Volker Mertens and H.-J. Schiewer (Tübingen, 1992), pp. 31–54; Schiewer, *Überlieferungsgeschichte*.

[5] Schiewer rejects the previously current title 'Schwarzwälder Prediger': 'Da weder der Verfasser, noch dessen geistlicher Stand bekannt sind, werde ich künftig nur noch von den 'Schwarzwälder Predigten' sprechen. Dies entspricht den Gepflogenheiten des Faches bei anonym überlieferten Werken', *Überlieferungsgeschichte*, pp. 5–6.

[6] Schiewer, *Überlieferungsgeschichte*, pp. 328–334.

[7] Franz Karl Grieshaber, *Deutsche Predigten des XIII. Jahrhundert*, 2 vols (Stuttgart, 1844–46; repr. Hildesheim/New York, 1978).

[8] Fest- und Heiligenpredigten des Schwarzwälder Predigers, ed. by Peter Schmitt, Ulla Williams, Werner Williams-Krapp, Kleine deutsche Prosadenkmäler des Mittelalters 14 (Munich, 1982); the links between the two cycles are first recognized by Williams-Krapp and explored in more detail by Schiewer, *Überlieferungsgeschichte*.

[9] Dietrich Schmidtke, Review of Stamm, *Studien*, *PBB* 92 (1970), pp. 285–290 (p. 287), quoted in Schiewer, Überlieferungsgeschichte, p. 16.

The author(s) of the *Schwarzwälder Predigten* made use of four main sources of 'biblical' material in their composition. These four: the *sermones de tempore* of Conrad of Saxony, the Vulgate, the *Aurora* of Peter Riga and the *Historia scholastica* of Peter Comestor, were used in different measure and for different purposes. The aim of the present study is to examine the use of each of these sources individually and in relation to each other, with a view to finding out more about Peter Comestor's position as one of a number of sources available to a thirteenth-century author of a handbook for preachers. General work on the sources for the cycle has been carried out by Stamm.[10] The difference between his study and mine is that whereas his focused on the sermon cycle itself and its place within the sermon tradition, mine is more concerned with the *Historia scholastica* and its reception as exemplified by the *Schwarzwälder Predigten.*

The *de tempore* cycle of the *Schwarzwälder Predigten* comprises fifty-five sermons in total. The present survey concentrates on the forty-seven sermons printed in full (or almost in full) in Grieshaber's edition;[11] the sermon for the third Sunday after Advent, of which only a fragment remains in Grieshaber's manuscript, but which is edited by Schiewer, is also included.[12] Schiewer has shown the fallacy of the view, posited by Grieshaber and perpetuated by later studies, that this manuscript (now Freiburg i. Br., U.B., Hs. 460) is an autograph, though he confirms that it is the origin of the tradition. However, of the thirty-three surviving manuscripts of the *de tempore* cycle, only four contain the original version as represented by Grieshaber's edition; the vast majority contain a revised version, the so-called 'Vulgatfassung (X)'. In the absence of an edition which is truly representative of the redaction in which the sermons were most widely diffused, it is necessary to consider the viability of Grieshaber's edition as a basis for research into the *Schwarzwälder Predigten* as a vehicle for the transmission of material from the *Historia scholastica.* Fortunately, it appears from the tendencies identified by Schiewer that the revisions to the text are unlikely to affect the Comestor material; of the sermons lost to the main tradition (T51–T65 in the table below), only two number the *Historia scholastica* among their sources.[13]

[10] Stamm, *Studien*, pp. 37–54.

[11] Grieshaber assimilates material which has been added in the margins of his manuscript into the main text without marking it; for this reason, the microfilm of his manuscript, now Freiburg im Breisgau, U.B., MS 460, was consulted where necessary.

[12] Schiewer, *Überlieferungsgeschichte*, pp. 356–369.

[13] Schiewer, *Überlieferungsgeschichte*, pp. 99–106.

2.3 The Sources of the *de tempore* cycle of the *Schwarzwälder Predigten*

The primary, though never acknowledged, source for the *Schwarzwälder Predigten* for Sundays and feast-days is the *sermones de tempore* of Conrad of Saxony.[14] Only two sermons in the cycle (those intended for Easter and Pentecost) are not based on one or more of Conrad's sermons.[15]

Conrad Holtnicker of Saxony was a Franciscan friar, lector in theology in Hildesheim and Provincial of the province of Saxony between 1247 and 1262, and from 1272 until his death in 1279. His works include commentaries on the Bible and the *Sentences* of Peter Lombard, expositions of the Ave Maria and the Lord's prayer, and various collections of Latin sermons.[16]

Within the structure furnished by Conrad's sermons other sources are used to expand or provide examples to illustrate certain points. The main source of illustrative material is Jerome's Vulgate. Other sources of 'biblical' illustrative or explanatory material include the *Historia scholastica* of Peter Comestor, and the *Aurora* of Peter Riga, a versified Bible which itself draws heavily on Comestor.[17] Here though, the emphasis is very much on the spiritual rather than the literal or historical meaning of the Scripture. The version used by the author of the sermons includes the Acts of the Apostles and must thus be either Peter Riga's third and last edition (c. 1200) or one of the two revised versions produced by Aegidius Parisiensis between 1200 and 1209, the year of Peter's death.[18]

Other sources are consulted for individual pieces of information or narrative. These are listed by Stamm and will be discussed briefly in so far as they are relevant to the *Historia scholastica.*[19]

[14] Falsely attributed to Bonaventure and interpolated into his *sermones de tempore*: Bonaventura, *Opera Omnia* III (Mainz, 1609); a list of the incipits of Conrad's sermons is given in: Schneyer, *Repertorium*, I, pp. 748–791.

[15] Stamm, *Studien*, p. 39.

[16] Adolf Franz, *Drei deutsche Minoritenprediger aus dem 13. und 14. Jahrhundert* (Freiburg i. Br., 1907), pp. 9–46; *LThK*, VI, col 471; *DSAM*, II, col 1548; Jean Longère, *La Prédication médiévale* (Paris, 1983), p. 101; David L. d'Avray, *The Preaching of the Friars. Sermons diffused from Paris before 1300* (Oxford, 1985), pp. 100–101.

[17] *Aurora Petri Rigae. Biblia versificata. A Verse Commentary on the Bible*, ed. by Paul E. Beichner, (Notre Dame, Indiana, 1965); Stegmüller, *Repertorium*, IV, nn. 6822–6827.

[18] For the successive editions of the *Aurora* see Beichner's Introduction, pp. XVII–XX.

[19] Stamm, *Studien*, pp. 39–46, 49.

Temp	Grieshaber	Conrad	OS
T29	In Oct. Pasche: 'Affer manum tuam'; vol. 1, pp. 1–6	T29; B III, p. 104 = Schn. 131	O.T., H.S., Aur.
T30	Dom. II post Pascha: 'Ego sum pastor bonus'; vol. 1, pp. 6–12	T30; B III, p. 106 = Schn. 133	O.T., H.S.
T31	Dom. III post Pascha: 'Tristicia vester vertetur'; vol. 1, pp. 12–19	T31; B III, p. 110 = Schn. 137	O.T., Aur.
T32	Dom. IV post Pascha: 'Cum autem venerit'; vol. 1, pp. 19–25	T32; B III, pp. 111–112 = Schn. 141, 142	O.T., N.T., H.S., Aur.
T33	Dom. V post Pascha: 'Petite et accipietis'; vol. 1, pp. 25–29	T33; B III, p. 115 = Schn. 143	O.T., N.T.
	(Dom. VI post Pascha?); vol. 1, p.30 (fragment)	T34; see Stamm, p. 39	
T39	De Sancto Spiritu: 'Spiritus sanctus hodierna die'; vol. 1, pp. 30–37		O.T., N.T.
T41	Dom. I post Pentecosten: 'Mortuus est autem et dives'; vol. 1, pp. 37–43	T41; = Schn. 182	O.T., H.S.?
T42	Dom. II post Pentecosten: 'Homo quidam fecit coenam'; vol. 1, pp. 43–49	T42; B III, p. 145 = Schn. 184	O.T., N.T.
T43	Dom. III post Pentecosten: 'Inveni ovem meam'; vol. 1, pp. 49–55	T43; B III, p. 147 = Schn. 187	O.T., N.T., H.S.
T44	Dom. IV post Pentecosten: 'Estote misericordes'; vol. 1, pp. 55–62	T44; BIII, p. 142 = Schn. 191	O.T., N.T.
T45	Dom. V post Pentecosten: 'Ascendens iehsus in unam navim'; vol. 1, pp. 62–68	T45; B III, p. 150 = Schn. 195	O.T.
T46	Dom. VI post Pentecosten: 'Si offers munus'; vol. 1, pp. 68–74	T46; B III, p. 155 = Schn. 197	O.T., N.T., H.S.?
T47	Dom. VII post Pentecosten: 'Misereor super turbam'; vol. 1, pp. 74–79	T47; B III, p. 158 = Schn. 200	O.T.
T48	Dom. VIII post Pentecosten: 'Omnis arbor que non fecit'; vol. 1, pp. 79–81	T48; B III, p. 161 = Schn. 203	N.T.
	(Dom. IX post Pentecosten); vol. 1, pp. 82–83 (fragment)		O.T.
T51	Dom. X post Pentecosten: 'Publicanus a longe stans'; vol. 1, pp. 83–90	T51; B III, p. 168–169 = Schn. 211	O.T., N.T., H.S.?
T52	Dom. XI post Pentecosten: 'Solutum est vinculum lingue eius'; vol. 1, pp. 90–94	T52; B III, p. 173 = Schn. 215	O.T.
T53	Dom. XII post Pentecosten: 'Beati oculi'; vol. 1, pp. 94–99	T53; B III, p. 174–175 = Schn. 217	O.T., N.T.
T54	Dom. XIII post Pentecosten: 'Cum ingrederetur iehsus'; vol. 1, pp. 99–104	T54; B III, p. 178 = Schn. 220	O.T., N.T., H.S.
T55	Dom. XIV post Pentecosten: 'Scit enim pater vester'; vol. 1, pp. 104–109	T55; B III, p. 182 = Schn. 224	O.T., N.T.

Table 7: Main Sources of Biblical Material in the *Schwarzwälder Predigten*

Temp	Grieshaber	Conrad	OS
T56	Dom. XV post Pentecosten: 'Resedit qui erat mortuus'; vol. 1, pp. 109–114	T56; B III, p. 185 = Schn. 227	O.T.
T57	Dom. XVI post Pentecosten: 'Idropicus erat ante illum'; vol. 1, pp. 114–118	T26; B III, p. 88 = Schn. 108, 109?	O.T.
T58	Dom. XVII post Pentecosten: 'Diliges dominum deum tuum'; vol. 1, pp. 118–123	T58; B III, p. 192 = Schn. 234	O.T., N.T., Aur.
T59	Dom. XVIII post Pentecosten: 'Tolle lectum tuum'; vol. 1, pp. 123–129	T59; B III, p. 195 = Schn. 237	O.T., N.T.
T60	Dom. XIX post Pentecosten: 'Simile est regnum'; vol. 1, pp. 129–135	T60; B III, p. 197 = Schn. 238	O.T., N.T.
T61	Dom. XX post Pentecosten: 'Domine descende'; vol. 1, pp. 135–141	T3?; B III, p. 14? = Schn. 12?	O.T., N.T., Aur.
T62	Dom. XXI post Pentecosten: 'Serve nequam'; vol. 1, pp. 141–147	T62; B III, p. 203 = Schn. 244	O.T., N.T., Aur.
T63	(Dom. XXII post Pentecosten): 'Ostendite mihi numisma'; vol. 1, p. 148 (fragment)	T63; B III, p. 107 = Schn. 248	
T65	Dom. XXIV post Pentecosten: 'Tunc apparebit signum'; vol. 1, pp. 148–155	T65; B III, p. 214 = Schn. 256	N.T., H.S., Aur.
T1	Dom. I in Adventu Domini: 'Emitte manum'; vol. 1, pp. 155–160	T1; B III, p. 4 = Schn. 1	O.T.
T3		T3; B III, p. 14 = Schn. 12	O.T., N.T.
T4	Dom. IV in Adventu Domini : 'Dirigite viam'; vol. 1, pp. 161–167	T4; B III, p. 17 = Schn. 15	O.T., N.T.
T7	Dom. infra Nativitatem Domini: 'Puer autem crescebat'; vol. 2, pp. 1–8	T7; B III, p. 28 = Schn. 40	O.T., N.T.
T11	Dom. I post Epiphaniam: 'Pater tuus et ego'; vol. 2, pp. 9–15	T11; B III, p. 37 = Schn. 52	O.T.
T12	Dom. II post Epiphaniam: 'Nuptie facte sunt'; vol. 2, pp. 15–22	T12; B III, pp. 38–39 = Schn. 54	O.T., H.S.
T13	Dom. III post Epiphaniam: 'Domine si vis potes me mundare'; vol. 2, pp. 22–30	T13; B III, pp. 41–42 = Schn. 57	O.T., N.T., H.S., Aur.
T14	Dom. IV post Epiphaniam: 'Ecce motus magnus'; vol. 2, pp. 30–37	T14; B III, pp. 45–46 = Schn. 61 + 62?	O.T., N.T.
T15	Dom. V post Epiphaniam: 'Simile est regnum celorum'; vol. 2, pp. 37–44	T15; B III, pp. 47–48 = Schn. 63	O.T., N.T., Aur.
T16	Dom. in Septuagesima: 'Ite et vos in vineam'; vol. 2, pp. 45–51	T16; B III, p. 52 = Schn. 66	O.T., N.T.
T17	Dom. in Sexagesima: 'Aliud cecidit in terram bonam'; vol. 2, pp. 51–58	T17; B III, pp. 56–57 = Schn. 71, 69?	O.T., H.S.?
T18	Dom. in Quinquagesima: 'Tradetur enim gentibus'; vol. 2, pp. 59–65	T18; B III, p. 59 = Schn. 72, 73?	O.T., N.T.

Table 7: continued.

Temp	Grieshaber	Conrad	OS
T18/4	In Capite Jejunii: 'Confitemini alterutrum'; vol. 2, pp. 66–73	T34; B III, p. 118 = Schn. 150	O.T., N.T., H.S.
	Sermo "Convertimini": 'Convertimini ad me'; vol. 2, pp. 74–82	T18/4; B III, pp. 62–63 = Schn. 77–79	O.T., N.T.
T19	Dom. I in Quadragesima: 'Cum ieiunasset'; vol. 2, pp. 82–90	T19; B III, p. 67 = Schn. 83	O.T., N.T.
T20	Dom. II in Quadragesima: 'Dimitte eam qui clamat'; vol. 2, pp. 90–98	T20; B III, p. 69 = Schn. 87	O.T., N.T., H.S.
T21	Dom. III in Quadragesima: 'Beatus venter'; vol. 2, pp. 98–106	T21; B III, p. 74 = Schn. 91	O.T., N.T.
T22,	Dom. IV in Quadragesima: 'Est puer unus hic'; vol. 2, pp. 106–114	T22; B III, pp. 76–77 = Schn. 93	O.T., H.S.
T23	Dom. in Passione: 'Si sanguis hircorum'; vol. 2, pp. 114–126	T23; B III, p. 78 = Schn. 95	O.T., N.T., H.S., Aur.
T24	Dom. in Palmis: 'Cum apropinquaret'; vol. 2, pp. 127–137	T23; B III, p. 82 = Schn. 98	O.T., N.T., H.S., Aur.
T28	In Resurrectione Domini: 'Jehsum queritis nazarenum'; vol. 2, pp. 137–150	T28; B III, p. 96 = Schn. 118	O.T., N.T., H.S., Aur.

Table 7: continued.

Abbreviations used in Table 7:

Temp	Day for which sermon was intended, in Schneyer's notation[20]
Grieshaber	Heading, incipit and page-no. in Grieshaber's edition[21]
Conrad	Source sermon by Conrad of Saxony, with page-no. in Bonaventura, *Opera Omnia*, vol III, and number in Schneyer's *Repertorium*
OS	Other sources of biblical material
H.S.	*Historia scholastica*
Aur.	*Aurora*

[20] The manuscript on which Grieshaber's editon is based (Freiburg i. Br., U.B., Hs. 460) mistakenly assigns the sermon intended for the eleventh Sunday after Pentecost (T51 in Schneyer's notation) to the *tenth* Sunday, with the result that the remaining 13 sermons for the Sundays after Pentecost are numberered incorrectly. The numbers T51 to T65 in the table are adjusted to compensate for this fault, and refer to the day for which the sermon was *originally* intended; this will facilitate cross-reference to an eventual new edition of the sermon collection. These numbers are given in italics.

[21] Only a fragment remains in Grieshaber's manuscript of the sermon for the third Sunday in Advent. An edition is provided by Schiewer, *Überlieferungsgeschichte*, pp. 356–369.

2.3.1 The Interaction of the Four Main Sources in the *Schwarzwälder Predigten*

The following sections will each examine the use of one of the four main sources in the *Schwarzwälder Predigten*. This preliminary section is concerned with their interaction in the sermon for Passion Sunday (T23),[22] chosen because it demonstrates many of the characteristic features of the authors' approach to their sources and is a good example of the difficulties in distinguishing between them.

The sermon begins with a quotation from Conrad of Saxony's first sermon for the same day.[23] Both *thema* (Hebrews 9:13–14) and *dispositio* (the four effects of the shedding of Christ's blood) are quoted exactly, though the word-order in these versions of the German and Latin sermons varies slightly.[24] In line eight of the German sermon 'operacionem' is an error caused by contamination with 'operatus' in the same line and is later translated as 'erloeset'.[25]

After the characteristic greeting 'Saligen kint' and placing the sermon in its context within the church year, the author gives the context of the *thema*, both within the church service and the Bible itself, and translates it into German.[26] This is one of seven sermons in the collection in which the *thema* is not drawn from the gospel for the day, but from the Old Testament or, as here, from the epistle for the day.[27] The author returns to the beginning of the epistle, quotes the first few words in Latin and translates the first two verses that lead into the *thema*. He again cites the first words in Latin, then repeats his translation of the two verses. The translation of the following and last verse of the epistle is also preceded by the citation of the first few words in Latin. The translation closely follows the Vulgate,[28] which could have been found in a lectionary. The author recalls the context with the formula 'Dc sint diu wort der hailigen epistel als man si hat ze der messe gelesen'. This part of the sermon concludes with the repetition yet again of

[22] T23 'Si sanguis hircorum', Grieshaber II, pp. 114–126.

[23] Conrad's sermon is printed in full at the end of section 2.3.1.

[24] For terminology see section 2.3.2.

[25] Grieshaber II, p. 125.

[26] This greeting is a defining characteristic of the 'sammlungstypische Ausdrucksweise' discussed by Schiewer, *Überlieferungsgeschichte*, pp. 99–101 (p. 100), which is intensified in the later revisions of the collection.

[27] Stamm, *Studien*, p. 66.

[28] Hebrews 9:11–15.

the first words of the *thema*, and the indication to the user of the sermon manual to repeat the translation: 'hic repete thema vulgariter'.[29]

The German author then translates Conrad's *dispositio*, the remainder of the Latin quotation with which he opened his sermon, adding a phrase which gives both the cause and the duration of man's banishment from Heaven. He gives Conrad's first *distinctio* – 'dc got [...] mit sinem hailigen blůte die welt hat gerainet' –, but then diverges from the earlier sermon and illustrates the point with an account the high priest's sacrifice of atonement in the tabernacle and the associated rite of the scape-goat (Lv 16) rather than building on Conrad's example of the purification of a house which harbours leprosy (Lv 14:51). The word 'tabernacle' requires further explanation for the eventual recipients of the sermon he anticipates: 'dc ier wissent waz dc tabernacel sîge. uñ och wissent wie der bischof in der alten .ê. dar in si gegangen. so wil ich ez mit kurzen worten überlöfen.'[30] There follow four pages of detailed description of the tabernacle and the rites performed there, based on the book of Exodus, but for which the direct source is probably the *Historia scholastica* of Peter Comestor. The reason for the divergence from Conrad here is not clear, but the detail in which the tabernacle and the associated rites are described suggests that this was a focus of considerable interest for the authors.

It is often difficult to distinguish material taken from the *Historia scholastica* from that taken directly from the Bible, particularly when dealing with a description which in the Bible encompasses eight chapters,[31] and in the *Historia scholastica*, twenty-four columns in Migne.[32] The possibility of contamination between similar descriptive elements (colours, materials, dimensions etc.) within one source is considerable. Nevertheless in the German sermon's description there are passages which can be definitively traced back to Comestor, and as there is nothing in the account which is not mentioned by him it seems reasonable to suppose that the *Historia scholastica* is the only source for this material. The different ways in which the authors of the *Schwarzwälder Predigten* introduce material from Comestor will be discussed elsewhere.

The dimensions of the tabernacle correspond in all three descriptions, though the wording of the German is closer to that of the *Historia scholastica*

29 Grieshaber II, p. 115.
30 Grieshaber II, p. 116.
31 Exodus 25–28; 35–40.
32 *PL* 198, cols 1169–1193.

than to the Vulgate, in which one has to calculate the dimensions of the whole object from the size and number of the planks used to build it. The colours and materials of the tabernacle curtains too could come from either source. But in the description of the curtains surrounding the courtyard, the German author follows Peter Comestor in giving the purpose of the system of rings and cords : 'uñ dar zů waren an den umbehaͤngen uñ an den tuͤchern scloͮsa und ringga dc man si mit saillin moͤhte zement geziehen' is based on Comestor's 'Super hoc vero dicit, aliam cortinam lancam superpositam [...] funibus per annulos eam ducentibus et retrahentibus', and not the Vulgate, where the emphasis is on size and materials.[33]

The candle-stick is made, in the Vulgate version, 'de auro mundissimo'; the sermon states 'die arme waren iseni. uñ waren uͥberguͥldet', in accordance with the *Historia scholastica*, which gives preference to Josephus' assertion that it was gold-plated:

> Praecepit quoque Dominus fieri candelabrum ex auro purissimo ductile (Exod. XXV). Tamen Josephus fusile dicit. Cujus hastile basi infixum erat, et ferreum super vestimentum calamis aureis [...].[34]

The account of the use of the incense altar and the dispute about its position (ll. 30–36) is also drawn from Peter Comestor:

> Hoc altare dicebatur incensi, vel thymiamatis, quia singulis diebus mane et vespere ad consumendum juge sacrificium [...] super illud thymiama incendebatur, sanctificatum Domino. [...] Caeterum utrum hoc altare esset intra sancta sanctorum, an in sanctuario cum candelabro et mensa, sancti videntur dubitare. Nec est putandum in dubium venisse quin esset in sanctuario; cum Hebraeus hoc dicat, et Josephus plane, et prima positio tabernaculi facta a Moyse innuit, nisi quia Paulus, ad Hebraeos, thuribulum ponit aureum intra sanctum sanctorum solummodo (Hebr. IX).[35]

The Vulgate again concentrates on materials and dimensions rather than function.[36]

The details in the description of the legs of the table, and the name 'aureola' for the smaller crown do not occur in the Vulgate.[37] The source for

[33] Grieshaber II, p. 116; *PL* 198, col. 1176; Exodus 38:9–17 (description of tabernacle curtains, Ex 37:10–18).

[34] Grieshaber II, p. 116; *PL* 198, col. 1172; Exodus 37:17; Josephus, *Ant.* III, VI, 7 (Blatt, *Latin Josephus*, p. 236).

[35] *PL* 198, col. 1187.

[36] Exodus 37:25–29.

[37] Grieshaber II, p. 117; Exodus 37:10–15; *PL* 198, col. 1171.

the description of the twelve loaves of bread on the table too, is not the Bible, but the *Historia scholastica*:

> Et ponebatur super eam duodecim panes azymi de simila, mundi valde, et ponebantur altrinsecus seni, et constabant singuli de duabus decimis ephi (Exod. XXV), quas Josephus duos assarios vocat. Et singulis superponebatur patena aurea, et super patenam pugillis thuris. [...] Hi diluculo Sabbati recentes et calidi imponebantur mensae, et erant ibi immoti usque ad Sabbatum sequens. Tunc illis sublatis, et toto thure incenso super altare, novi cum altero thure substituebantur. [...] Dicebantur etiam panes propositionis [...].[38]

The account of the contents of the ark of the covenant originates in the same chapter of Hebrews from which the epistle for the day is taken. However the German author did not refer directly to the Bible at this point, but to the *Historia scholastica*, as is indicated by the inclusion of the book of Deuteronomy among the contents and the explanation of the name of the ark: 'uñ da waz och dc fiumfte bůch der alten .ê. dc da haizet Deutronomius uñ da von. do hiez diu arche. archa testamenti.' The passage in the Vulgate reads: '[...] arcam testamenti [...] in qua urna aurea habens manna et virga Aaron quae fronduerat et tabulae testamenti', and the source must thus be Comestor: 'Posita est ibi urna aurea [...], Tabulae [...], Virga Aaron [...], Deuteronomium, in testimonium pacti [...]. Ob hoc dicta est arca testamenti, vel testamonii'.[39] Similarly, the different names for the mercy seat and their explanations are also taken from the *Historia scholastica* :

> Responsum autem divinum oraculum dicitur, quia orantibus datur. Dicebatur etiam propitiatorum; quia exinde loquens Dominus propitiabatur populo, vel quia die propitiationis dicebant gloriam Domini semper ibi descendere.[40]

The description of the golden cherubims could, for the most part, stem from either source. However, their position 'vornan an der tavelon oerten' and height 'fiumf ellen hôch' are found in the *Historia scholastica*. Here the German author refers to an *additio* in Comestor's text: '*Additio 1.* Possunt etiam dici, ad terram juxta arcam positi quinque cubitis alti [...]'.[41] The remainder of the description of the tabernacle too is mainly common to both sources, but the

[38] Grieshaber II, p. 117; *PL* 198, cols 1171–1172.

[39] Grieshaber II, p. 117; Hebrews 9:4; *PL* 198, col. 1170.

[40] Grieshaber II, p. 118; *PL* 198, col. 1170; (Exodus 37:6).

[41] Grieshaber II, p. 118; *PL* 198, col. 1171; Exodus 37:7–9. For further discussion of the *additiones* in the *Historia scholastica*, see section 1.4 above.

reference to the hanging sacrifice tray is not in the Bible and is based on Peter Comestor's account:

> [...] in quibus quatuor catenae annulis inserebantur, de quibus dependens craticula aerea, in modum retis facta, usque ad medium altaris intus descendebat, super quam cremanda in odorem Domino ponebantur [...].[42]

In the German author's description of the tabernacle there is no material which is contained exclusively in the Vulgate, whereas there are some details from the *Historia scholastica* which do not occur in the biblical account. There is no evidence to suggest that the Bible was consulted directly, despite the introduction above: 'Wir lesen also in der alten .ê. an dem andern bůche dc ist in Exodo'.[43] The *Historia scholastica* would appear to be the immediate source for the account.[44] However, the earliest manuscript of the sermons shows that there are several stages of composition, and that some (but not all) of the extra details from the *Historia scholastica* are added, by the same hand as the main text, in the margins.[45] These additions are incorporated into Grieshaber's edition without comment. The first occurs in the description of the candelabra discussed above: 'uñ zer andron siton och drige arme. uñ die arme waren iseni. uñ waren übergúldet'; in this case, it is precisely this detail which Comestor has added to his account from Josephus. Some of the varying names for the mercy seat are also added in the margin: 'diu tavel hiez propitiatorium alder oraculum [i. templum. vel responsum. vel vaticinium.] si hiez ain antwurte', as is the height of the two golden angels: 'dc wâren zwen guldin engel. [uñ wâren fiumf ellen hôch.]'.[46] In these cases it would appear that the scribe has added in extra details from his own reading of the *Historia scholastica.* The remaining parallels with Comestor discussed above all occur in the main body of the text in the manuscript.

Once he has explained what a tabernacle is, the German author introduces

[42] Grieshaber II, p. 118; *PL* 198, col. 1180.

[43] Grieshaber II, p. 116.

[44] Comestor's commentary is mainly a compilation from earlier works, so that one cannot entirely discount the possibility that the non-scriptural details in the description of the tabernacle found their way into the sermons via other routes. However, the occurrence of details which Comestor has drawn from the accounts of Josephus in combination with his own interpretative commentary means that there is a high probability that the *Historia scholastica* is the direct source.

[45] Freiburg i. Br., U.B., Hs. 460, ff. 222^{r}–223^{r}.

[46] Grieshaber II, p. 118; I use brackets to mark the additions from the margin, which are not distinguished from the main text in Grieshaber's edition.

the next section: 'so sont ier och hören wie der bischof in dc tabernacel sölte gân'. Here no source is mentioned initially, but it becomes apparent that the *Historia scholastica* is again in use, despite the author's assertion at the end of the section that 'dc ist diu alte .ê.'[47] The differences between the sermon account and that in Leviticus 16 are, however, very minor at this point and mainly consist in added details.

The day on which the high priest is allowed to enter the inner sanctum is not specified in Leviticus, but in the *Historia scholastica*.[48] The sacrificed calf is red; this too is a detail supplied by Peter Comestor.[49] Comestor and the German author omit the ram which Aaron sacrifices for himself (Lv 16:3). There are many such minor additions and omissions to the Bible account, all of which are in accordance with the *Historia scholastica.* Some borrowings are more substantial. The author of the sermon includes Comestor's description of the priest 'ponens etiam, ut tradunt quidam, cartham inscriptam peccatis populi super caput ejus [...]'.[50] He does acknowledge that his source for this material is not the Bible, using the formula with which he often introduces material from Comestor: 'als sümeliche maister scribent'. The account of the making of purifying liquid from the ashes of the sacrifice is also taken from the *Historia scholastica* and is not in Leviticus: 'Ex his cineribus fiebat aqua aspersionis, qua per totum annum purificabantur immundi'.[51]

The German author concludes his account of the ritual of the high priest with a repetition of the translation of the *thema* of the sermon, and then proceeds with the exegesis of the allegorical meaning of the tabernacle and the rites associated with it. This gradually leads back to Conrad's sermon, which is the source for the discussion of the sevenfold shedding of Christ's blood (lines 16–21).[52] Where Conrad merely lists the occasions on which Christ's blood was shed, the German author paints in the details, comments on and explains each instance, and relates it to its biblical context and to the eventual audience of the sermon. He indicates that even this may not be enough and invites the priest, the intended user of the handbook, to extemporize if he wishes: 'Hic enumera plures passiones domini si tibi placuerit'.

47 Griehaber II, p. 120.
48 Grieshaber II, p. 118; *PL* 198, col. 1209.
49 Grieshaber II, p. 118; *PL* 198, col. 1209.
50 Grieshaber II, p. 119; *PL* 198, col. 1210.
51 Grieshaber II, p. 119; *PL* 198, col. 1210.
52 Line-references to Conrad's sermon in the appendix at the end of section 2.3.1.

The second *distinctio*, the account of the Harrowing of Hell, and the quotation of Zachariah 9:11 are both taken from Conrad (lines 27–43). The German author translates the quotation and paraphrases Conrad's discussion of it, interspersing elements from Conrad's sermon with his own exegesis: 'sich waz betůtet der sê in dem da kain wazzer waz? dc ist anders niht wan diu helle. in der waz kain wazzer. dc ist kain erbermherzekait'.[53] He summarizes the story of Lazarus and Dives, but does not include any direct quotations from Luke 16. He omits Conrad's quotation from St. Bernard, but includes the account of the ostrich and Conrad's exegesis of it in conjunction with psalm 21, which he also quotes. He follows Conrad in giving the Old Testament as the source of the ostrich story, which must originate from the Physiologus. However, he then again diverges from Conrad and expands his second *distinctio* with a second allegory of Christ breaking open Hell, the story of Samson and the honey in the lion's mouth. The equivalent Bible passage is found in Judges 14:5–9, but the story is narrated freely, evidently from memory. The German author adds details to suit his exegesis (the Bible does not mention that Samson left the bees behind, for example), but there is no evidence of another source at this point.

The German author remains within Conrad's structure and keeps his third *distinctio*, Christ's opening Heaven to man (lines 44–57), but illustrates it with a different example, taken from 'der alten .ê. an dem vierden bůche. dc ist in Numero'. This is the basic source for this section, but the author of the sermon refers sometimes to others for comment or extra information. The idea that manna took on the taste desired for each individual is rejected by Comestor: 'Quod vero dicitur, quia sapiebat in ore cujusque quod desiderabat non multum authenticum est'; however, the authors of the *Schwarzwälder Predigten* are not alone in overruling Comestor's doubts, and the idea is espoused by, among others, Peter Riga: 'Internum mentis designat manna saporem'.[54] The German author emphasizes it: 'sic dicas de singulis cibariis'.[55] In line 35 f. the words of the Israelites are quoted first in Latin from the Vulgate (Nm 21:5) and then translated. Stamm notes that this

[53] Grieshaber II, p. 121.

[54] *PL* 198, col. 1160; *Aurora*, Liber Numeri, l. 219. It is possible that the *Aurora* is the direct source here, but this is relativized by the fact that Comestor's objections are ignored also in Rudolf von Ems' *Weltchronik*, ll. 11234–11238 and Jacob von Maerlant's *Scolastica*, ll. 4362–4364, where there is no further evidence for contamination from the *Aurora*; see also Andersson-Schmitt, 'Die Verwendung', pp. 15–16.

[55] Grieshaber II, p. 123.

technique is a convention of the Middle High German sermon tradition.[56]

The source of the extra details about the fiery serpents and their bite is unclear, but it is not one of the four with which this study is principally concerned. The allegorical interpretation of the healing brass snake of the Israelites in the desert as a prefiguration of Christ on the cross is either based on, or supported by, a quotation from Peter Riga's *Aurora*.[57] Like many of the quotations from this work throughout the sermon collection, it is not translated verbatim by the German author(s), but it is part of the main body of the text in Grieshaber's manuscript.[58] The question of the manner in which material from the *Aurora* is incorporated will be discussed in more detail in section 2.3.5 below.

The German author draws the implications of his allegorical example in a call to repentance and confession, and indicates that this point can be emphasized by the contemplation of Christ's passion: 'hic facias plures exhortaciones de passione domini'.[59]

In the fourth *distinctio* too Conrad supplies only the point to be illustrated: Christ's saving mankind from eternal Judgement by his blood (lines 57–end). The German author ignores his examples and turns to St. John's gospel for his own illustration. He quotes John 3:16–18, translating each sentence before quoting the next. He then briefly discusses the section before quoting and translating James 2:26. This verse is quoted in Conrad's second sermon for the day in question, which could thus have been the source at this point. The German sermon finishes with an exhortation to prayer and a detailed exegesis of the allegory of the tabernacle.

This sermon is one of five in the *de tempore* cycle in which all four of the main sources of biblical material are consulted.[60] It demonstrates that though in some cases a particular source is associated with a certain feature (e.g. Conrad with structure, *Aurora* with exegesis), there is a certain amount of variety in the use made of these sources. Though Conrad always provides the basic structure, it is impossible to predict which further elements of his sermon will be used. There is little evidence that the *Aurora* provides anything but exegetical material, but the situation as regards the *Historia scholastica* and the Vulgate, which both provide illustrative material in the form of historical

56 Stamm, *Studien*, p. 52.

57 Grieshaber II, p. 124; *Aurora*, Liber Numeri, ll. 425–430.

58 Freiburg i. Br., U.B., Hs. 460, f. 228v.

59 Grieshaber II, p. 125.

60 The five sermons in which all four sources are consulted are: T32, T13, T23, T24, T28.

narrative, is less straightforward. In this sermon it appears that the author turns to the Bible for stories and to the *Historia scholastica* for more factual information. In other sermons this distinction is not applicable. The problems in determining the reasons for the choice of a particular source will be discussed in the section on each individual source concerned.

Appendix: Conrad of Saxony, Sermones de tempore : Dom. in passione, S I[61]

[Hebr. 9. d] *Si sanguis hircorum, & taurorum, & cinis vitule aspersus, inquinatos sanctificat ad emundationem carnis, quanto magis sanguis Christi?* & caetera. Commendatur in hac epistola pretiosus sanguis Christi, per quem ipse Pontifex noster Christus caelum, tamquàm sancta sanctorum intravit, & mundum inquinatum sanctificavit. Considerandum est ergò quòd Pontifex noster per sanguinis suum operatus est mundi purgationem, inferni spoliationem, caeli referationem, [Levi. 14. g] iudicij evasionem. De primo dicitur hic: *Si enim sanguis hircorum, & taurorum*: & omnia penè in sanguine mundantur, secundum legem miser mundus leprosus fuit: vnde per sanguinem mundari debuit. Sacerdos autem ipsum mundans, est Christus, de quo: Asperget domum septies, purificabitque; eam in sanguine passeris, quàm in aquis viuentibus. Domus leprosa mundum, passer carnem Christi, [Septem effusiones sanguinis Christi] aquae viuentes baptismum, septem aspersines, septem sanguinis Christi effusiones significare possunt. Prima effusio fuit in circumcisione. Secunda in oratione: Factus [Luc. 2. c] est sudor eius, &c. Tertia in flagellatione. Quarta in corona- [Luc. 22. e] tione. Quinta in manuum perforatione. Sexta in pedum [Ioan. 19. f] confixione. Septima in lateris apertione. Ecce quando Christus in terra, & in aëre commissa immunda mundaret. Vnde Ionnes Chrysostomus: Non sub tecto, sed sub caelo Christus immolabatur, vt vniversus aër in excelso immolatae ouis odore à tetro mundetur. Sed terra simile beneficium sentiebat, decursi de later sanguinis stillatione mundata. [Zach. 9. c] De secundo: Tu quoque in sanguine testamenti emisisti vinctos de lacu, in quo non erat aqua. Glossa: Nulla refri- [Luc. 16. f] gerans misericordia, quà diues petijt, cum dicit: Mitte Lazarum, &c. Quaere ergò misericordiam Dei non in inferno, sed dum vivis in mundo. Ibi enim aquam negat, hic

[61] Bonaventura, *Opera Omnia*, III, p. 78.

sanguinem dat, ibi misericordiae guttam aquae negauit, hic plurimas guttas, immò fluuios sanguinis ministrat. [Ber. in Cant. ser. 22 circa med.] Bernardus: Apud Dominum misericordia, & copiosa apud eum, &c. [Ps. 129. a] Quia non guttam, sed vndam sanguinis largitur, quae per quinque partes corporis emanauit. Hoc ergò sanguine liberauit infernum, sicut legitur, quòd struthio, cuius pullum Salomon vitro incluserat, tulit vermiculum, cuius sanguine vitrum liniuit, & fractum est, & pullus liberatus est: sic Christus electos suos liberauit fracto inferno per sanguinem vermiculi carnis suae. [Psal. 21. a] Psalmus: Ego vermis & non homo, &c. Infernus enim Christo frangenti fuit quasi vitreus, sed damnato est quasi ferreus. [Apo. 22. c] De tertio: Beati qui lauant stolas suas in sanguine agni, vt sit potestas eorum in ligno vitae, & per portas intrent in ciuitatem, foris autem, &c. Lignum vitae est Christus, per quem spiritualiter, & aeternaliter animae nostrae viuunt, quae mortuae erant in peccatis. Vnde Christus benè ait in [Ps. 101. b] Psalmo: Similis factus sum pelicano. Pelicanus enim, sicut Glossa dicit, est pullos suos triduo lugens, & tunc rostro sanguinem suum fundens, & reuiuiscunt: ita Christus sanguine suo nos reuiuicauit. Sed ecce ad ligna vite per portas ciuitatis supernae nullus potest intrare, nisi lotus Christi sanguine, solus .n. sanguis agni aperire portas potuit. Bernardus: Sanguis Christi est clauis paradisi. Vnde clauiger noster primus per proprium sanguinem introiuit semel in sancta. [Rom. 5. b] De quarto: Commendat suam charitatem Deus in nobis, &c. vsq; iustificati in sanguine ipsius, salui erimus ab ira per ipsum. Sicut electi per sanguinem Christi iram iudicij euadunt, ita reprobi per sanguinem habebunt grauius iudicium, quia sanguis Christi clamat contra eos. [Job. 16. d] Terra ne operias sanguinem meum, ne inueniat in te locus latendi clamor meus. Tunc quidem contra, sed nunc pro [Heb. 12. f] peccatoribus sanguis Christi clamat: Accessistis ad sanguinem aspersinis meliùs loquentem quàm Abel. Gregorius: Sanguis Abel mortem fratricidae petijt: sanguis Domini vitam persecutoribus impetrauit. Quia ergò sanguis Christi in iudicio saluat electos, & confundit reprobos: ideò dicitur [Apoc. 19.c] quòd Ioannes vidit vestitum veste apersa sanguine, habentem diademata multa in capite, & gladium in vtraque parte acutum in ore. Diademata ad coronandum electos, gladium ad refellendum reprobos. Caput Christi diuinitas est. In capite ergò diademata habuit, quia in contemplatione, & fruitione deitatis, honor, coronaque beatorum erit.

2.3.2 Conrad of Saxony

All but two of the sermons in the *de tempore* cycle of the *Schwarzwälder Predigten* are based on one or more of Conrad's sermons.[62] A detailed account of the influence of the Latin sermon-cycle on the German one is given by Stamm in his chapter 'Bauformen der Predigten'.[63]

Conrad offers a selection of sermons, generally four, for each Sunday and feast-day in the church year. These begin with a few words of a quotation from the Bible, the *thema*, which is followed by the *dispositio* in which Conrad sets out the way in which he intends to approach this *thema* in the sermon. On ordinary Sundays the *themata* are taken from the gospel for the day, on feast-days frequently from the epistle or the Old Testament reading for the day.[64] Conrad's *dispositio* most often takes the form of *distinctio*: an idea suggested by the *thema* is approached from four different angles which bring to light different meanings or implications. These *distinctiones* form the backbone of the sermon and a section is devoted to the exploration of each. The *dispositio* can also take other forms, among which the emblematic approach where an image suggested by the *thema* is explored in various contexts.

The authors of the German sermons begin by quoting the *thema* and *dispositio* of one of Conrad's sermons for the day.[65] Ruh points out the German authors' preference for *dispositiones* which are directly related to the meaning of the *thema* as a whole, rather than those based on more arbitrary, verbal links.[66] The *dispositio* determines the structure of the new sermon, though it is succeeded in most cases by an additional element, the narration of the gospel for the day. This will be discussed in the section on the Bible as a source. The gospel ends with the repetition of the *thema* and its translation, and is followed by a translation of the *dispositio*. The framework of Conrad's sermon, determined by this *dispositio*, is retained, though the illustrative

[62] These exceptions are the sermons for Easter Sunday (T28) and Pentecost (T39); see Stamm, *Studien*, p. 39.

[63] *Studien*, pp. 55–72; I have followed his use of technical terms relating to the structure of the sermons. The terms which occur in the different 'Artes praedicandi' of the Middle Ages and their applications are by no means uniform. For this reason modern critical works sometimes apply diverse terminology or give slightly different definitions of the same term.

[64] Stamm, *Studien*, pp. 55–56.

[65] For the three exceptions see Stamm, *Studien*, p. 39.

[66] Ruh, 'Deutsche Predigtbücher', pp. 19–20.

material in individual *distinctiones* may differ considerably from the original. Unlike the Latin sermons, where the *distinctiones* in a particular sermon are of approximately equal length, the German sermons tend to illustrate the earlier *distinctiones* in greater detail than the later ones.

Conrad most frequently illustrates the point of each section of his sermon by a chain of quotations from the Bible and the Church Fathers which provide an example, not in themselves, but in the associations which they evoke for the recipient, who must therefore be well versed in the Scriptures to understand the implications of the sermon in full. The authors of the German sermon handbook, on the other hand, favour a more narrative approach, so that they tend to enlarge upon one or two of Conrad's instances. An example of this can be seen in the sermon for the second Sunday in Lent (T20) in the first *distinctio*:[67] Conrad illustrates the point, that one should pray to God to overcome obstacles, by a series of references to the Bible. The first of these, a reference to Jonah, serves as a cue for the later author to tell the story of Jonah's salvation through prayer, and he omits Conrad's subsequent references to Psalms 68 and 129 and Luke 16.

The method employed most often by the authors of the German sermons is to take their cue from Conrad, to turn to the Vulgate or the *Historia scholastica* for a detailed account of the story, and then to follow Conrad's interpretation in their exegesis. This technique can be observed throughout the *de tempore* sermon cycle. An apt example occurs in the sermon for the first Sunday after Easter (T29) in the second *distinctio*.[68] Here Conrad's quotation from Genesis 2:18 leads the German author to the story of the creation of Eve. He then paraphrases Conrad's exegesis in a simplified form, omitting the parallel between the sacraments and blood from the wound in the dying Christ's side and not mentioning St. Augustine, Conrad's authority for this interpretation. In other instances his exegesis, though still based on Conrad, lays different emphasis than the earlier sermon. This is generally in line with the attempts of the author in the vernacular to simplify his approach for the eventual lay recipient.[69] An example of this is found in the same sermon in the first *distinctio*.[70] Conrad's emphasis is on the learned analogy between Christ's wound and the door of Noah's ark; the German author, on the other

[67] Grieshaber II, pp. 92–93; Bonaventura, III, p. 69, Sermo 3 (Schn. 87, p. 753).
[68] Grieshaber I, p. 4; Bonaventura III, p. 104, Sermo 3 (Schn. 131, p. 756).
[69] Stamm, *Studien*, pp. 73–106: 'Prediger und Publikum'; Schiewer, *Überlieferungsgeschichte*, pp. 8–9.
[70] As above, Grieshaber I, p. 3.

hand, is more concerned with the general allegorical meaning of the ark. Here too Conrad's reference to St. Augustine is omitted.

Conrad provides links, not only with the Bible, but also with such authorities as St. Augustine, St. Bernard and Gregory the Great. Frequently these are omitted entirely, as in the above allegory of Noah's ark, but more often they are absorbed unattributed into the main body of the exegesis. Examples of the latter can be found in the sermon for the fifth Sunday after Pentecost (T45) in the first *distinctio*, where Conrad names the *Glossa Ordinaria* as his source and the later author does not mention it,[71] and in the twenty-fifth Sunday after Pentecost (T65; Gr 24 p. Pent.), where the same occurs with a reference to John Chrysostomus.[72] Conversely, in his sermon for the first Sunday in Advent (T1) the German author attributes to St. Augustine a passage which in fact he quotes from Conrad.[73]

Sometimes such references are both included and attributed as is the case with the reference to St. Bernard in the sermon for the Sunday after Epiphany (T11). This is also an example of another use of Conrad by the author of the *Schwarzwälder Predigten*: it occurs in the fourth *distinctio* of a sermon based on Conrad's fifth sermon for the day in question, but is in fact taken from his sixth sermon for that day.[74]

This is one of the instances where the later author diverges completely from his model, and though the point illustrated is Conrad's, the material used to illustrate it is not. For Conrad the search is worthwhile because if one seeks God he in turn will seek one out, and he gives examples of this from the Bible and from Gregory the Great. The author of the German sermon is concerned more with the value of the act itself of searching for God to the seeker, and illustrates the usefulness of the search with a series of six reasons why God hides himself. It is in this context that he includes the quotation from St. Bernard from Conrad's next sermon.

In the sermon for the Sunday after Christmas, the German author seems deliberately to omit the first element of Conrad's *dispositio*, 'sicut pueri cum matre', both in the Latin introduction and in his translation. In the main body of the sermon too, he treats Conrad's second section as his first and so on, but then returns and makes the omitted reference his fourth *distinctio*. Here he takes up Conrad's reference to Solomon's wisdom in judging the

[71] Grieshaber I, p. 64; Bonaventura III, p. 150, Sermo 1 (Schn. 195, p. 760).
[72] Grieshaber I, p. 153; Bonaventura III, p. 214, Sermo 4 (Schn. 256, p. 764).
[73] Grieshaber I, p. 155; Bonaventura III, p. 4, Sermo 3 (Schn. 1, p. 748).
[74] Grieshaber II, p. 9; Bonav. III, p. 37, Sermones 5 & 6 (Schn. 52, p. 751).

true mother and narrates the story in great detail, then again returns to Conrad for the allegorical interpretation. This re-ordering of the elements of a sermon is unusual, and would seem, in conjunction with the sermon's conclusion in a prayer to the Virgin Mary, the mother of Christ, to be motivated by a desire to emphasize her importance.[75]

The general picture which emerges of the German authors' attitude to their source is one of great diversity in methods of approach. Though the *thema* and *dispositio* are retained and the structure they determine adhered to, in all other respects the authors of the German sermons pick and choose elements from Conrad at will, following him closely when it suits them, only to abandon him completely when they prefer another approach. They clearly do not feel bound by Conrad's interpretation, but generally seem to find it sound, if sometimes too complicated for the recipients whom *they* have in mind. In this one can observe the use made of such sermon handbooks, the process of transmission in action. The Latin directions which the German authors give to the intended users of their own handbook, and the further development of the collection in the later redactions, are an indication of the continuation of the process.[76] The question of the position of the *Historia scholastica* in this development will be discussed in section 2.3.4 below.

2.3.3 The Vulgate

After Conrad of Saxony the most significant source for the *Schwarzwälder Predigten* is the Vulgate. This is used most frequently in conjunction with material taken over from Conrad, to fill in the framework provided by his sermon, but is sometimes used independently when the German author selects a different biblical example to illustrate a point.

The general procedure is that which has been seen in the sermon for Passion Sunday (T23), where the Latin *thema* and *dispositio*, taken over from Conrad, are followed by a translation into German of the gospel for the day. This closely follows the Vulgate, usually taken from the pericope for the day in question. The translation generally proceeds verse by verse and the author frequently quotes part of the verse in Latin before translating it.[77] The function

[75] Grieshaber II, pp. 1–8; Bonav. III, pp. 28–29, Sermo 4 (Schn. 40, p. 750). Schiewer, *Überlieferungsgeschichte*, p. 104, notes a 'stärkere Betonung der Marienfrömmigkeit' among the characteristic tendencies of the later redaction.

[76] See Schiewer, 'Et non sit tibi cura', pp. 46–49.

[77] The term 'verse' is used here for ease of reference, although numbering of Bible verses

of this is not entirely clear: Stamm remarks that the Latin quotations are usually direct speech, and attributes this to a convention of the vernacular sermon tradition designed to render the account more direct and thus more credible.[78] However, in some cases the quotations are purely narrative. The use of Latin, one of the three sacred languages, reinforces the links with the liturgy and perhaps contributes a certain sense of awe-inspiring mystique.

In the sermon for the twenty-fifth Sunday after Pentecost (T65; Gr 24 p. Pent.), where the verses are not translated in consecutive order, the Latin quotations mark the beginning of each new section.[79] The sermon for the fourteenth Sunday after Pentecost (T54; Gr 13 p. Pent.) too quotes narrative passages of the gospel in Latin before translating them. Here, though, the author specifically refers to his translation as 'dc hailige ewangelium nach dem bůchstaben'.[80] Sometimes the authors of the German sermons interrupt the translation of the gospel to comment on its literal or allegorical meaning. An example of this occurs in the sermons for the third Sunday in Advent (T3) and the second and third Sunday in Lent (T20 & T21), where after several verses the author adds a few lines of his own interpretation, introduced by the formula: 'als ob er spreche...'.[81]

Stamm points out that this gospel-paraphrase is not an integral part of the sermon but provides background information.[82] It is omitted, for example, in the sermons for the first Sunday in Advent (T1), Passion Sunday (T23) and the Sunday after Christmas (T7). In the latter a substantial part of the gospel for the day, Luke 2:33–40, is narrated in the third *distinctio*.[83] The Passion Sunday sermon (T23) has already been discussed: here, as in several sermons for feast-days, the *thema* is taken from the epistle, which is then translated in place of the day's gospel.[84] The sermon for the first Sunday in Advent (T1) is one of only two sermons in the *de tempore* cycle to have an Old Testament *thema*. The other, 'Convertimini', is a general sermon, prefaced

---

was not common until the sixteenth century; see Loewe, 'The Medieval History of the Latin Vulgate', in: *Cambridge History of the Bible*, II, pp. 147–148.

[78] Stamm, *Studien*, p. 52.

[79] Grieshaber I, p. 149.

[80] Grieshaber I, p. 100.

[81] T3: Schiewer, *Überlieferungsgeschichte*, pp. 356–369; T20: Grieshaber II, pp. 90–98; T21: Grieshaber II, pp. 98–106.

[82] Stamm, *Studien*, p. 66.

[83] Maura O'Carroll, 'The Lectionary for the Proper of the Year in the Dominican and Franciscan Rites', *Archivum Fratrum Praedicatorum* 49 (1979), pp. 79–103, here pp. 85–103.

[84] Stamm, *Studien*, p. 66, foot-note 45.

with the instruction: 'etiam est communis quandocumque volueris', and thus has no gospel for the day.[85] There is no apparent reason why, in the case of the Advent sermon (T1), from the six sermons offered by Conrad for this day the German author selects one in which the *thema* (Ps 143,7: 'Emitte manum tuam de alto') is not taken from the gospel.

After translating Conrad's *dispositio*, the authors of the German sermons generally illustrate each *distinctio* with one or more examples from the Bible. These are most often suggested by what in the Latin sermon is a long string of references designed to call up the right associations in the clerical reader. It is unclear whether the user of Conrad's handbook was intended to choose and elaborate as the authors of the *Schwarzwälder Predigten* do, or to assume knowledge on the part of his listeners. The German authors, at any rate, assume no such knowledge, and are always careful to point out explicitly the implications of each example. Though the narrative technique and the length of each instance may vary, it always forms a neat whole.

The German authors approach the Vulgate in conjunction with Conrad's sermon in a variety of ways. Most frequently, Conrad provides the cue for the later author to consult the Bible for the details to narrate the story in full. These examples are usually taken from the Old Testament and are referred to as 'urkůnden'. Within this basic pattern there is considerable variety in the treatment of material.

Sometimes the author remains very close to the original text in his paraphrase. In the second *distinctio* of the sermon for the first Sunday in Advent (T1), for example, there are close syntactic parallels in the translation of Genesis 27:7–17 and 20–23, the story of Jacob's deception of Isaac, which Conrad evokes with the brief reference: 'sicut significatum est in Isaac sene et caeco, qui manum Jacob sibi ministrantem non nouit, quia pellicula circumdata fuit'.[86] Similarly, in the sermon for the fourth Sunday in Advent (T4), the account, in the second *distinctio*, of the angel feeding Elijah, is a close re-narration of I Kings (III Regum) 19:4–8.[87]

Sometimes Conrad's reference to the Bible prompts a freely narrated account, loosely based on the Vulgate. An example of this can be seen in the sermon for the third Sunday after Easter (T31), in the first *distinctio*, where the story of Moses and the waters of Marah is a summary of Exodus 15:22–25, and the story of Samson and lion is a summary of Judges 14:1–9.[88] It is

[85] Grieshaber II, p. 74.

[86] Grieshaber I, pp. 158–159; Bonaventura III, p. 4, Sermo 3.

[87] Grieshaber I, p. 164; Bonaventura III, p. 17, Sermo 4.

[88] Grieshaber I, pp. 14–15; Bonaventura III, p. 104, Sermo 4.

in cases such as these that inaccuracies or contaminations tend to occur, which can obscure the question of the source in use at a given point. Thus in second *distinctio* of the sermon for the third Sunday in Lent (T21),[89] the story of Abimelech's attack on the town of Shechem so loosely follows the original, Judges 9:22–49, with three thousand men where the Bible has one thousand, that it is possible to speculate whether another source may have been used here. However, comparison with the relevant passage in the *Historia scholastica*, the most frequent alternative to the Vulgate as a source of narrative material in the *Schwarzwälder Predigten*, shows that, though much of this account is also found there, it does not share the free renderings of the German text, and is missing several details, such as the name of the mountain, Selmon.[90] Though this, of course, does not preclude the use of yet another, unidentified, source, it seems more likely that the author was at this point working from his memory of the Vulgate.

This would seem the probable solution too, to the question of the provenance of the 'quotation' from Esther in the sermon for the second Sunday in Lent (T20), in the third *distinctio.*[91] The story of the whole book of Esther, which in the Bible comprises ten chapters, is condensed into about forty lines in German, which incorporate a Latin 'quotation' of King Ahasuerus' comforting words to his wife, Esther, who has fainted at her own audacity in defying his commands and approaching him unbidden. The form used by the German author is: 'Pete quod vis hester et dabo tibi'. The Vulgate has: 'quid vis Hester regina / quae est petitio tua / etiam si dimidiam regni partem petieris dabitur tibi' and 'quid petis ut detur tibi'.[92] The *Historia scholastica* has: 'Quid vis, Esther? Quidquid petieris dabo tibi' and 'Pete quod vis, Esther, et impetrabis', which is nearest to the sermon's version.[93] The *Aurora*, another occasional source for such quotations, contains yet another slight variation: 'Quod cupis ergo pete' and 'Hester, que cupis, illa pete', and is thus also not in use here.[94] It appears that the German author has 'reconstructed' a vaguely remembered quotation from the Bible or the *Historia scholastica.*

The authors of the *Schwarzwälder Predigten* tend to give more detail and

[89] Grieshaber II, pp. 104–105.
[90] *PL* 198, col. 1282.
[91] Grieshaber II, pp. 96–97.
[92] Est 5:3, 5:6; as in *Glossa ordinaria*, II, p. 364.
[93] *PL* 198, col. 1492.
[94] *Aurora*, Liber Hester, l. 175.

follow the Vulgate more closely in those cases where they diverge from Conrad of Saxony's sermon and select their own examples from the Bible. Thus in his sermon for the fifth Sunday after Pentecost (T45), in the second distinction, where the German author rejects Conrad's references to Job, Acts, Lamentations, the Psalms and St. Ambrose in favour of the story of the dove from Noah's ark, Genesis 8:8–12 is translated verbatim and in full.[95] Similarly, in the sermon for the third Sunday of Advent (T3), where the author rejects all of the second half of the Latin sermon except the titles of the *distinctiones*, both stories about Elisha are translated closely from the Vulgate.[96] However, here too there is considerable variety of approach: the story of David and the Amalachites in the sermon for the third Sunday after Easter (T31) is narrated freely, despite its having no basis in Conrad,[97] and in the sermon for the third Sunday in Lent (T21), the first three chapters of Jonah are much summarized, but Jonah 4:5–10 is translated verbatim with some Latin quotations.[98]

In their choice of examples, both from, or in conjunction with, Conrad of Saxony, and directly from the Bible, the authors of the *Schwarzwälder Predigten* show a marked preference for the Old Testament.[99] Every single sermon which survives in full contains Old Testament material.[100]

Leaving aside the translations of the gospel for the day which begin most of the sermons, New Testament material occurs in 34 of the sermons. It most frequently takes the form of a brief quotation, generally based on Conrad and supplemented from the Vulgate. Only two sermons rely predominantly on examples from the New Testament: the sermon for the Resurrection (T28), with its account of the appearances of Christ to his disciples, and the one for the Sunday after Christmas (T7).[101] In the latter, four of the five examples are taken from the New Testament and are narrated, for the most part, in detail, with close translation of the Vulgate.[102] The only other longer examples based on stories from the New Testament are the

[95] Grieshaber I, p. 65; Bonaventura III, p. 150, Sermo 1.

[96] Schiewer, *Überlieferungsgeschichte*, pp. 361–365; IV Regum 4:1–7, 2:8–14.

[97] Grieshaber I, p. 16; I Regum 30.

[98] Grieshaber II, pp. 102–103.

[99] Stamm, *Studien*, pp. 112–115; Schiewer, *Überlieferungsgeschichte*, p. 330.

[100] In the case of the 25th sermon after Pentecost (T65; Gr 24 p. Pent.), the direct source of the story of the Antichrist may be the *Historia scholastica*, but the material originates in the book of Daniel.

[101] Grieshaber II, pp. 139–143; Grieshaber II, pp. 1–8.

[102] Mt 2:13–16; Apc 14:1–4; Mt 2:19–23; Lc 2:22–28.

account of two of Christ's miracles in the fourth Sunday after Epiphany (T14), the parable of the prodigal son in the all-purpose sermon 'Convertimini', and the detailed translation of John 3:16–18 in the sermon for Passion Sunday (T23).[103] The latter two sermons have in common the fact that neither is based on a gospel-reading, and that their New Testament examples take the format of the gospel-paraphrase of the other sermons, with each verse quoted in Latin and then translated. However, the other sermons in the collection which do not take their *thema* from the gospel of the day, those for the first Sunday in Advent (T1) and the Lenten sermon 'In Capite Jejunii' (T18/4), do not contain extensive New Testament examples.

It is most frequently Old Testament stories which are designated as 'urkuͥnde'. Thus in the above-mentioned sermon for the Sunday after Christmas (T7), the first four examples are introduced with some variation of the formula 'dc wirt uns bewêret an...', but the last with 'Und dez vinden wier ain urkuͥnde in der alten .ê.'. The inevitable exceptions can be found in the sermon for the fourth Sunday in Advent (T4) and the fourth Sunday in Epiphany (T14): 'und dez vinden wir ain urkuͥnde an dem hailigen ewangelio'.[104]

The whole question of what precisely is meant by the term 'urkuͥnde' in the *Schwarzwälder Predigten* is problematic. Stamm states that it is applied only to biblical material and defines it: 'Mit dem Begriff 'Urkunde' bezeichnet der Schwarzwälder ganz bestimmte Predigtstoffe, die die Funktion haben, Glaubenswahrheiten und moralische Forderungen zu beweisen oder zu begründen'.[105] He comments on the author's particular preoccupation with the truth and credibility of his teaching, but can find no intrinsic reason for the special status accorded to the Old Testament in this context.[106] He justifies this emphasis on the Old Testament by highlighting the difference in attitude to it before the Reformation, but the exact meaning of the word

[103] Grieshaber II, pp. 35–36; Grieshaber II, pp. 77–79; Grieshaber II, pp. 125–126.

[104] Grieshaber I, p. 163; Grieshaber II, pp. 35, 36.

[105] Stamm, *Studien*, p. 110; Ruh defines 'urkuͥnde', in this specific context, as 'biblisches Wahrheitszeugnis in Gestalt einer Geschichte', 'Deutsche Predigtbücher', p. 20.

[106] The predominance of Old Testament material is all the more striking when one compares the number of stories and the range of Old Testament books included in the sermon collection with the very limited space accorded to the Old Testament in the mass. Only five Old Testament epistles or lessons from four books were ordained for reading in the Franciscan rite throughout the entire year: Is 40:1–6 (T10, Epistle), Joel 2:12–19 (T18/4, Epistle), Ex 15:27 – 16:7 (T24, Lesson 1), Hosea 6:1–6 (T26, Lesson 1), Ex 12:1–11 (T26, Lesson 2); O'Carroll, 'Lectionary', pp. 85–103.

'urkünde' in these sermons remains unclear, and will be discussed later in conjunction with the status of the *Historia scholastica* as a source.

For the authors of the *Schwarzwälder Predigten* the Bible is a source of material to illustrate various points in a sermon. Though they usually use it in conjunction with Conrad, they are selective in their approach and choose those stories which emphasize their own favoured interpretation. They prefer Old Testament examples to New Testament ones. Their narrative technique varies from highly summarized and freely narrated accounts of the events covered by several chapters of the Bible, to close translations of a few verses. Their references are imprecise; they seldom specify more than the book of the Bible involved. The frequent use of the term 'urkünde' seems to indicate a concern for their examples to be accurate, credible documents, weighed down by the authority of the Old Testament.

Where Conrad of Saxony gives examples from the Old Testament, or when they occur in the liturgy, the interest in them is mainly typological, and thus confirms the higher status of the New Testament events which they prefigure. Though this typological interest is undoubtedly also a feature of the *Schwarzwälder Predigten* (see particularly section 2.3.5), the length and detail in which the Old Testament examples are narrated far exceeds that required by their role as 'sign-posts'. Perhaps this different balance of biblical reference can be seen as indicative of a new comprehensive view of the Bible which is encouraged by the *Historia scholastica.*

2.3.4 The *Historia scholastica*

The analysis of the interaction of the four main sources of the *Schwarzwälder Predigten* in the Passion Sunday sermon has shown that the Bible is not the only source of 'biblical' illustrative material in the *de tempore* cycle. In that sermon the *Historia scholastica* was a much more significant source. Though the sermon was chosen for this reason, and thus cannot be taken as representative of the general frequency of Peter Comestor material, it nevertheless demonstrates the intricacies of the use of sources by the authors of the sermons.

Stamm discusses the difficulties in distinguishing between use of the *Aurora* and the *Historia scholastica*, concluding: 'Sicher ist jedenfalls, daß nicht alle Inhalte der "SP-Sammlung", die auf Petrus Comestor zurückgehen, über die "Aurora" Eingang in die Predigten gefunden haben'.[107] He points

[107] Stamm, *Studien*, p. 48.

to four instances where he detects direct use of the *Historia scholastica*, but does not explore the issue in any depth or give examples or reasons for his assertions. He also does not address the more important question of the position, amongst the sources of the sermons, of the *Historia scholastica* in relation to the Vulgate. These questions cannot be solved conclusively, but they are central to the interest of the present study on the relevance of Peter Comestor in this context.

Stamm lists four examples for which he believes Comestor is the source: the historical information about donkeys in Jerusalem in the sermon for Palm Sunday (T24), the account of Miriam's leprosy in the sermon for the fourteenth Sunday after Pentecost (T54; Gr 13 p. Pent.), the description of the tabernacle in the sermon for Passion Sunday (T23), and the death of the Antichrist in the sermon for the twenty-fifth Sunday after Pentecost (T65; Gr 24 p. Pent.). Of these only the former two are regarded as definitely based on the *Historia scholastica*; for the latter two, this is merely said to be a possibility.[108] Though the identity of a medieval source can seldom be definitively proven, detailed investigation points to fifteen instances where one can say with a high degree of certainty that the material is taken from Peter Comestor, and several further examples of significant parallels in detail or wording.

The situation is schematized in Table 8 below.

As has been discussed before, the main difficulty in examining use of the *Historia scholastica* in the *Schwarzwälder Predigten* (and elsewhere) is distinguishing between material taken from it and material taken from the Vulgate. Many features of this process remain constant from work to work, but others may be determined by the genre. In all the works studied, one can identify use of Comestor most easily by the occurrence of non-scriptural details and interpretation, but sometimes also, though less conclusively, through similarities in wording between the vernacular and Latin texts. One feature, though, which is characteristic of the sermon collection and does not occur in the other works, is the presence of quotations in Latin. In some cases it is only the wording of a 'quotation from the Bible' which introduces the possibility that the *Historia scholastica* may be the direct source, although generally this evidence is corroborated in other ways.[109]

It is the 'misquotation' of certain sentences from the Bible in the sermon

108 Stamm, *Studien*, p. 48.

109 Sermons which contain quotations which are more similar to the *Historia scholastica* than to the Vulgate: T17, T18/4, T24, T28, T30, T65.

Sermon		HS	Subject	Assessment
T30	I, p. 10	Genesis, col. 1117	Laban & Jacob	probable
T32	I, p. 23	I Regum, col. 1301	Philistines & the ark	probable
T41	I p. 42	Genesis, col. 1058	Firmament/dew	probable
T43	I, pp. 52–53	III Regum, col. 1373	Jeroboam & calf	highly probable
T46	I, p. 71	Evangelia, col. 1602	Gazophilacium	tenuous
T51	I, pp. 89–90	IV Regum, col. 1412	Ezechias	tenuous
T54	I, p. 101	Exodus, col. 1144	Moses & Ethiopian	probable
T65	I, p. 151	Daniel, col. 1465	Antichrist	probable
T12	II, pp. 17–18	Tobias, col. 1434	Tobias & fish	possible
T13	II, pp. 25–26 II, pp. 27–28	Exodus, col. 1157 II Regum, col. 1346	Crossing of Red Sea David's deliberations	highly probable highly probable
T17	II, p. 57	Josue, col. 1269	Caleb's daughter	tenuous
T18/4	II, p. 70 II, p. 71	Josue, col. 1264 I Regum, col. 1309	Stoning of Achor Amalechites' animals	possible probable
T20	II, p. 94	Judicum, col. 1279	Gideon attacks camp	tenuous
T22	II, p. 111	Exodus, col. 1143	Birth of Moses	possible
T23	II, pp. 116–119 II, p. 117	Exodus, col. 1169–93 Exodus, col. 1170	Tabernacle Contents of the Ark	highly probable highly probable
T24	II, p. 128 II, pp. 130–131 II, p. 134 II, p. 136	Evangelia, col. 1598 Numeri, col. 1237 Genesis, col. 1126 Genesis, col. 1085	Donkeys in Jerusalem Balaam & ass Joseph & his brothers Raven after flood	highly probable highly probable probable highly probable
T28	II, p. 140	Evangelia, col. 1638	Mary Magdalen	probable

Legend

Sermon	Sermon no. in Schneyer's notation (see table 7, above), volume and page-no. in Grieshaber's edition
HS	Parallel in *Historia scholastica*, book, column in Migne, PL 198
Subject	Subject of parallel passage
Assessment	Probability of direct consultation

Table 8: The *Historia scholastica* as Source in the *Schwarzwälder Predigten*

for Palm Sunday (T24) which first alerts one to the probability that the Vulgate is not, in fact, the direct source for the story of Balaam here:[110]

T24 'Dom. in Palmis'	*Historia scholastica* – Nm	Numeri 22
do sprachеr ze in. *Si dederit mihi Balach plenam domum suam auri. non potero mutare verbum domini.*	Cap. XXXII. *De itinere Balaam, et quod ei locuta est asina.* [...] Quibus ait Balaam: 'Si dederit mihi Balac domum suam plenam auri, non potero mutare verbum Domini. (cols 1236–1237)	[18]respondit Balaam si dederit mihi Balac plenam domum suam argenti et auri non poteri inmutare verbum Domini Dei mei
[...] Do sprach der engel ze im. (233[a]) *Perversa est mihi via tua. et nisi asina declinasset occidissem te.*	[...] Cui angelus: 'Perversa est mihi via tua,' et nisi asina declinasset, occidissem te. (col. 1237)	[32]cui angelus cur inquit tertio verberas asinam tuam ego veni ut adversarer tibi quia perversa est via tua mihique contraria [33]et nisi asina declinasset de via dans locum resistenti te occidessem et illa viveret
[...] *Quomodo maledicam populo. cui benedixit dominus.*'	Cap. XXXIII. *De ariolathesi Balaam, et ejus prophetia.* [...] 'Quomodo maledicam populo, cui benedixit Dominus?' (col. 1238)	Numeri 23 [8]Quomodo maledicam cui non maledixit Deus

Comestor's paraphrase characteristically incorporates much direct quotation from the Vulgate, but sometimes in an abbreviated form. The author of the German sermon here quotes Comestor's amended version of the Scriptures.

The supposition that the *Historia scholastica* is the direct source for this account is borne out by the fact that the German author also includes some of Comestor's interpretative commentary on the motivation of the protagonists. Balaam, who is renowned for the effectiveness of his curses, has been promised a substantial reward if he will curse the Israelites. God initially orders him not to go with the enemy messengers, then seems to change his mind:

T24 'Dom. in Palmis'	*Historia scholastica* – Nm	Numeri 22
Also kom unser herre in der naht. uñ hiez in mit in varen. uñ ferbot im. dc er niht anders redeti wan als er in hiezi. Enmornon do sateloter sine eselinon uñ fůr mit in. uñ do er also fůr ûf dem wege. sich do hâter sinen munt ferkeret. von der gabe uñ von dez kůnegez	Et ait Dominus ad eum nocte: 'Surge, vade cum eis; ita duntaxat, ut quod praecepero tibi facias.' Mane strata asina profectus est cum eis: 'Et iratus est Dominus ei, stetitque angelus Domini, gladio evaginato, in via contra Balaam.' Mutaverat enim propo-	[21]surrexit Balaam mane et strata asina profectus est cum eis [22]et iratus est Deus stetitque angelus Domini in via contra Balaam qui sedebat asinae et duos pueros habebat secum

[110] Grieshaber II, pp. 130–131; *PL* 198, cols 1236–1238; Nm 22:12–22, 32–33; Nm 23:8.

gehaizen. uñ trahtot wider sich selber wie er dc volk môhte ferflůchen. swie dc wêre dc ims got hête ferboten. Uñ do got den gedanch sach in sinem herzen. do santer ainen engel. uñ der stůnt fůr in in den weck mit ainem blôzen swerte.

situm, et captus cupiditate promissorum, disponebat quomodo populo malediceret, licet prohibuisset Dominus. Josephus videtur velle quod Dominus iratus, quasi ironice dixerit ei: 'Vade cum eis.' Quod quia non intellexit obstitit ei angelus. (col. 1237)

Here the reason for God's sudden anger is not clear from the account in the Bible; Balaam is surely just obeying God's revised orders? Comestor offers two possible explanations for this apparent 'volte face': either God has become aware of a change of heart in Balaam, who has been corrupted by the promise of reward, or, the interpretation ascribed to Josephus, Balaam has failed to notice that God's contradictory command was intended ironically.[111] The author of the German sermon chooses to include the first explanation, rejecting the alternative explanation based on the idea of an ironic God.

Another example of direct quotation from the *Historia scholastica* can be found in the story of Jacob and Laban, as recounted in the third *distinctio* of the sermon for the second Sunday after Easter (T30). Comestor's summarizing paraphrase, which combines Genesis 30:25 and 30:26, is quoted by the German author, and the wording of the surrounding lines is similar:[112]

T30 'Dom. II p. Pasch.'
da lesen wir. dc herre Jacob dem herren Laban vierzehen iar hat gedienet durch siner tôchtero willen. dc er aines tages sprach zem herren Laban. *Da mihi uxores meas et liberos meos ut revertar ad terram meam.* Er sprach gib mir min wirtinna. uñ miniu kint. dc ich hain var in mines vater lant. Also bater in. dc er im dannoch sůben iar dienete. so wôlter im ze lône geben swaz er selbe wôlti. uñ sprach. ich waiz wol. dc mir got sinen segen durch dinen willē hat gegeben.'

Historia scholastica – Gn
Cap. LXXXVIII.
De diversicoloribus virgis et fetibus.
Finitis ergo annis quatuordecim servitii pro uxoribus, Jacob dixit socero suo: *Da mihi uxores, et liberos meos, ut revertar ad terram meam. Et ait Laban: Inveniam gratiam in conspetu tuo, ut adhuc servias mihi septem annis, et constitue mercedem, quam dem tibi. Scio enim, quia propter te benedixit mihi Deus* (Gen. XXX). (col. 1117)

Genesis 30
25 nato autem Ioseph dixit Iacob socero suo
dimitte me ut revertar in patriam et ad terram meam
26 da mihi uxores et liberos meos pro quibus servivi tibi ut abeam tu nosti servitutem qua servivi tibi
27 ait ei Laban inveniam gratiam in conspectu tuo
experimento didici quod benedixerit mihi deus propter te
28 constitue mercedem tuam quam dem tibi

[111] The term 'ironice' is introduced here by Comestor himself; Josephus reads: 'tunc ille studens aliquid viris illis praestare denuo consuluit deum, qui volens eum rem experimento probare, iussit ne legatis in aliquo contradiceret, sed cum eis iret. qui arbitratus deum haec ei non pro deceptione iussisse cum legatis mox ibat'. Blatt, *Latin Josephus*, p. 275.

[112] Grieshaber I, p. 10; *PL* 198, col. 1117; Genesis 30: 25–28.

The German version is marginally closer to that of the *Historia scholastica*, so that it seems likely that this is the direct source. However, here, unlike in the story of Balaam, there are only verbal parallels; the detailed discourse on Jacob's method of genetic engineering, which is, at this point, Comestor's only supplement to the information contained in the Bible, is not used by the German author.

There are some instances where parallels in wording may be the main indication of the influence of the *Historia scholastica*.[113] One such example is the account of the expedition of Tobias the younger, in the sermon for the second Sunday after Epiphany (T12). Both Peter Comestor and the author of the sermon provide a summarized version of the story which is told in four chapters in the Bible, and both quote Tobias 5,23–27 with the same omission from verse 26.[114] The focus and order of their summaries are the same, and there are many verbal parallels. The most striking example of this occurs in the discussion of the salting of the fish which Tobias catches:

T12 'Dom. II in Epiph.'	*Historia scholastica* – Tb	Tobias 6
do brieter ain stucke dez vischez uñ dez âzen si. dc ander dc sielzen si. uñ trůgen ez mit in ûf dem wege. (II, p. 18)	Cap. I. *De Tobia.* [...] Tunc Tobias partem piscis assavit, et comederunt, partem vero salsam secum tulit. (col. 1435)	6quod cum fecisset assavit carnes eius et secum sustulerunt in via cetera salierunt quae sufficerent eis quousque pervenirent in Rages civitatem Medorum

The German version corresponds closely to Comestor's slight variation of the Vulgate. However, despite the many similarities between the accounts in the *Schwarzwälder Predigten* and the *Historia scholastica*, the latter cannot be the sole source for this story, since the German version also includes a close translation of Tobias 6,17, which is not quoted by Comestor. It is difficult to reconstruct the manner of composition of passages like this one; it is possible that memory and a detailed knowledge of the Bible are playing a role here, or that these are traces of earlier stages of additions to the text. This will be discussed later in this section.

A somewhat similar situation can be found in the sermon for Palm Sunday (T24), where the German author tells the story of Joseph and his brothers. Here the account appears to be based on the Vulgate, but there are several

113 Sermons where verbal parallels are the main indication of influence of the *Historia scholastica*: T12, T20, T23, T24, T29, T43, T46, T51.

114 Grieshaber II, pp. 17–19, here p. 18; *PL* 198, cols 1434–1436, here col. 1434; Tb 5–8.

details, generally of an explanatory nature, which are added from the *Historia scholastica*.[115] Comestor gives an alternative explanation for Jacob's particular affection for Joseph: 'tum quia praestantior corpore, et sapientior caeteris erat', which is translated exactly by the German author as 'do waz er och schoͤner uñ wîser et si'; Comestor's explanation for the absence of Ruben, that he went looking for better pasture, is also included. Though the account of Ruben's reaction to the discovery that Joseph is no longer in the pit does not differ substantially from the Vulgate, the wording is more like that in the *Historia scholastica*:

T24 'Dom. in Palmis'	*Historia scholastica* – Gn	Genesis 37
Do nu Ruben hin wider kom ze sinen brůdern. uñ er Josephs niht vant in der cistern. do zersnaider sin gewant uñ wainot uñ sprach. *Puer non comparet. et ego quo ibo?* Er sprach. Wê mir ich vinde dc kint niht. wa sol ich armer man hin gân. wan er wânde si hêten dc kint ersclagen do er sin niht vant. do si aber im saiton ez lebti noch. do geschwaiger.	Cap. LXXXVII. *De venditione Joseph.* [...] Reversus autem Ruben ad cisternam, non invenit puerum, et credens eum interemptum, scissis vestibus ejulabat. Sed accepto quod viveret, quievit. (col. 1126)	29reversusque Ruben ad cisternam non invenit puerum 30et scissis vestibus pergens ad fratres ait puer non conparet et ego quo ibo

The Vulgate does not mention that Ruben calms down once his brothers assure him that Joseph is not dead, but the German text and the *Historia scholastica* concur in this detail. However, there are other passages in the account which translate verses of the Vulgate which have no parallel in Comestor's paraphrase. Here, as in the story of Tobias discussed above, it is impossible to say which direct source is being supplemented with material from the other.[116]

Perhaps the most striking parallels with the *Historia scholastica* in the *Schwarzwälder Predigten* occur where the German author incorporates material which Comestor has derived (sometimes by way of Josephus) from the apocryphal Jewish legends of the Midrash.[117] There are four examples in the *de tempore* collection, three of which relate to the life of Moses.[118] The first occurs in the second *distinctio* of the sermon for the fourteenth Sunday after

115 Grieshaber II, pp. 133–134; *PL* 198 cols 1125–1126; Gn 37.

116 The earliest manuscript, Freiburg i. Br. U.B., Hs. 460, offers no solution in either of these cases; the parallels with Comestor occur in the main body of the text.

117 See section 1.2 above on the sources of the *Historia scholastica*.

118 Sermons which contain non-scriptural details from the *Historia scholastica*, mainly derived from Midrash: T13, T22, T24, T32, T54.

Pentecost (T54; Gr 13 p. Pent.), as background for the story of Miriam's affliction with leprosy. The reference, in Numbers 12:1, to Moses' marriage with an Ethiopian woman, who is not mentioned elsewhere in the Bible's account of his life, gave rise to the midrashic legend of an early campaign to the kingdom of Saba and a marriage of convenience with the princess, which Comestor takes from Josephus for his account of the events of the book of Exodus. The circumstances of this marriage are narrated by the German author.[119]

The *Glossa ordinaria* also quotes a brief version of Josephus' story, but close analysis of the passage shows that the *Historia scholastica* is the more likely direct source:

T54 'Dom. 13 p. Pent.'	*Historia scholastica* – Ex	*Glossa ordinaria*
da besaz er si inne. ainer stat. do er lange vor der stat lach. uñ dc er ier niht moht gewinnen. do ersach in dez kuͥneges (84a) tohter. wan er do ain schôn man waz. do leget si mit im an dc er si nême ze der .ê. so wôlte si im die stat antwuͥrten. Also nam si herre Moyses ze der .ê.	Cap. VI. *De uxore Moysi Aethiopissa.* [...] Quam cum, quia inexpugnabilis erat, diutius obsedisset, oculos suos injecit in eum Tarbis filia regis Aethiopum, et ex condicto tradidit ei civitatem, si duceret eam uxorem, et ita factum est. (col. 1144)	Cum ergo venisset ad ciuitatem quam expugnaturus erat adamauit eum ethiopum regina et secundum condictum ciuitatem ei tradidit et nupsit.

At this point the two possible sources are very similar, but there are several details which are common only to the sermon and the *Historia scholastica*, such as the reference to a siege and the exact status of the Ethiopian woman. There is also the strong visual attraction exerted by Moses, although his beauty is not mentioned by Comestor here.[120]

The account of the birth of Moses, in the sermon for the fourth Sunday in Lent (T22), is also amplified with elements which derive, through the same channel of Josephus, from the Midrash.[121] These include the name of the Pharaoh's daughter, 'Tremuht', and the detail that the child Moses refused

[119] Grieshaber I, p. 101; *PL* 198 cols 1144 and 1227; Nm 12; *Glossa ordinaria*, I, p. 115; Blatt, *Latin Josephus*, pp. 202–203; Mark Balfour, 'Moses and the Princess: Josephus' *Antiquitates Judaicae* and the *Chansons de Geste*', *Medium Aevum* 64 (1995), pp. 1–16.

[120] The author of the sermon does not distinguish this apocryphal anecdote from the scriptural material which forms the basis for the remainder of the 'urkuͥnde'. However, fifteenth-century marginal annotations in a manuscript (Karlsruhe, Bad. LB, Lichtental 64) of the later redaction of the sermon collection (X) show a different awareness: 'Desz ist nit usz bewerter schrifft. lasz blyben', Schiewer, *Überlieferungsgeschichte*, p. 182.

[121] Grieshaber II, p. 111; *PL* 198, col. 1143; *Glossa ordinaria*, I, p. 114; Blatt, *Latin Josephus*, p. 199.

the breast of a heathen. In this case it is impossible to determine whether the *Historia scholastica* or the *Glossa ordinaria* is the source for the German author, as all these details occur in both accounts. The names of Moses' parents, which are not mentioned at this point in the Bible, though they are in the *Historia scholastica*'s account of Moses' birth and in the *Glossa interlinearia*, have been added in the bottom margin of the manuscript by the same hand as wrote the rest of the sermon.[122] The implications of the different stages of composition of the sermons are discussed below.

The last story from the life of Moses to contain details which Comestor has derived from the Midrash is the Crossing of the Red Sea, in the sermon for the third Sunday after Epiphany (T13).[123] Here it is the non-scriptural detail that the sea was divided into twelve columns, one for each of the tribes of Israel, which points towards the *Historia scholastica* as the probable source for this passage. The supposition that Comestor is the direct source is confirmed by parallels in wording in the earlier description of the terrain and the way in which the Israelites are hemmed in on all sides:

T13 'Dom. III p. Epiph.'	*Historia scholastica* – Ex
Also was dc volk von israel komen an dc rôte mêr. uñ mohte weder hinder sich noch fúr sich. wan die vigende wâren hinder in. do waz dc röte mêr vor in. do wâren hôhe berge neben in. úber die vor hôhe nieman mohte komen. (p. 25)	Cap. XXX. *De ducatu columnae, et mari Rubro.* [...] et posuerunt castra super mare Rubrum. [...] Sane ibi coarctati sunt filii Israel. Ex una parte erant montes asperrimi et immeabiles, ex altera parte mare. (col. 1157)

In the above examples from the life of Moses, the Midrashic elements were merely an incidental part of the illustrative narrative of the sermon. In the third *distinctio* of the sermon for Palm Sunday (T24), however, the non-scriptural story of the return of the raven after the flood has an important function.[124] Comestor quotes Josephus' theory that the raven from Noah's ark returned with nothing to show for its journey, and this provides the German author with part of his exegesis, the raven representing the sinner who has no good works to show for his life on earth. Unlike the case of the *Aurora*, which is often used as a source of allegorical interpretation of the Bible, here it is literal information which is taken from the source and used as part of the author's own exegesis.

The Midrash is narrative interpretation of the Old Testament, and as such it forms a link between the narrative and commentary components of the

[122] Freiburg i. Br., U.B., Ms 460, f. 218r.
[123] Grieshaber II, pp. 25–26; *PL* 198, cols 1157–1158; no parallel in Josephus.
[124] Grieshaber II, p. 136; *PL* 198, col. 1085.

Historia scholastica. Sometimes, as in the above example from the story of Balaam in the sermon for Palm Sunday, the author includes some of Comestor's interpretative commentary. Another example of this can be found in the Lenten sermon 'In Capite Jejunii' (T18/4), where the German author explains the reason for the apparently gratuitous command to slaughter the herds of the Amalechites:[125]

T18/4 'In Capite Jejunii'	*Historia scholastica* – I Sm/Rg
wan ez waren sůmeliche under in. die sich kundon machon ze rindern alder ze schâfen. uñ da von dc si iht hin kômen in rindez bilde alder in schâfez bilde. do hiez der wissage Samuel dc veh mit den lůten ferderben.	Cap. XV. *Quod Saul vicit Amalec.* [...] Jumenta quidem voluit Dominus interfici, ut nec in aliquo memoria Amalec superesset. Sunt qui dicant illos maleficos fuisse, et in pecudes se vertendi habuisse peritiam; et ideo ne sub forma pecudum evaderent, etiam pecudes periisse. (col. 1309)

Comestor offers two possible explanations, of which the author of the sermon includes only the second and more exotic: the Amalechites might be sorcerers, who could survive by transforming themselves into animals. The wording of the German is not very similar to the Latin at this point, so that it is possible that the detail was added from memory or from a different direct source.[126]

The inclusion of purely factual background information is rare in the *Schwarzwälder Predigten*, though this type of approach might conform better to our modern perception of the purpose and potential applications of Comestor's work. However, there are a few instances where this type of material is included.[127]

One example of this use of the *Historia scholastica* can be found in the discussion of the creation of the firmament, in the sermon for the first Sunday after Pentecost (T41).[128] The phrase 'wan dc sůmeliche maister wen. dc dc tǒ daruz werde in dem sumer', which corresponds to Comestor's 'nisi quod quidam autumant inde rorem descendere in aestate', has been added, by the main hand, in the top margin of the manuscript.[129] Here there is no pressing reason to regard the *Historia scholastica* as the source for the remainder

[125] Grieshaber II, p. 71; *PL* 198, col. 1309.

[126] The *Glossa ordinaria*, a possible source for such commentary, does not contain this material at this point.

[127] Sermons which include literal commentary material from the *Historia scholastica*: T24, T41, T18/4.

[128] Grieshaber I, p. 42; *PL* 198, col. 1058.

[129] Freiburg i. Br., U.B., Hs. 460, f. 37r.

of the discussion, so that it seems likely that the adding of the extra detail constitutes a revision of the text by the scribe. The implications of this will be discussed below.

Another example occurs in the gospel-paraphrase of the sermon for Palm Sunday (T24). In narrating the story of Christ's entry into Jerusalem on a donkey, the author mentions, with the introduction which often denotes this particular use of Comestor in the sermons: 'Nu wen die maister...', that communally owned donkeys were available in Jerusalem for the use of those too poor to have their own, and explains that these were purely beasts of burden and had never been ridden. Peter Comestor had added this background information into his account of the happenings of Palm Sunday. There is no apparent reason for the inclusion here of information which is not intrinsically relevant to the development of the gospel story or the sermon as a whole. The situation is further complicated when one studies the manuscript, as part of the commentary from Comestor has been added in the margin.[130]

T24 'Dom. in Palmis'	*Historia scholastica* – In Evangelia
Nu wen die maister. dc der selbe esel wêre gemain den armen lůten. uñ swer kainen moht umbe lôn gedingon ze arbaitende. dc der hin gie. uñ den esel nam uñ da mit worhte swez er bedorfte. uñ im denne gab ze essende. uñ fůrte in denne hin wider da er in hât genomen. [Uñ swie dc wêre. dc vil uñ vil wêre gewůrket mit dem esel. doch do waz kain mensch dennoch nie ûf in gesessen. wan dc got der erste waz. der ûf in sas uñ in rait.] So scribet denne S. Marcus. uñ S. Lucas. uñ S. Johannes dc unser herre niuwan sêze ûf der eselinon fůli. Aber S. Matheus. der scribet (231^b^) dc er sêze ûf in baiden. ûf der eselinon uñ ûf dem fůli. uñ er seze zem ersten ûf dem fůli. uñ wan ez do ungestům were uñ wilde. do sezer dar ab uñ sêze ûf die eselinon.	Cap. CXVII. *De maledictione ficus, et sessione super asellum.* [...] Asina haec dicitur fuisse communis pauperibus, qui propria jumenta non habebant. Cumque quis in ea operatus fuerat pabulum dabat ei, et pullo qui pariter ad opera communia nutriebatur. Nondum enim quisque ascenderat eam,[...]. Marcus, Lucas et Joannes non dicunt eum sedisse, nisi super pullum. Zacharias quoque propheta dixit: 'Sedens super pullum asinae (*Zach.* IX).' Matthaeus dicit eum sedisse super asinam et pullum. Quod licet brevis esset via, fieri tamen potuit, ut primo insedisset pullo, et forte quia nondum domitus et lascivus erat, descendit, et insedit asinae [...]. (col. 1598–1599)

This again raises questions about the stages of composition of the German text. Stamm cites the passage as evidence that Grieshaber's manuscript ('Gr': Freiburg i. Br., U.B., Hs. 460) is an autograph: 'Wäre der Schreiber der Handschrift nicht identisch mit dem Verfasser des Zyklus, so müßte man voraussetzen, daß er die Quelle erkannt und daraufhin das Werk des Petrus

[130] Grieshaber II, p. 128; *PL* 198, cols 1598–1599; Freiburg i. Br., U.B., Hs. 460, ff. 231^r^–231^v^; I have marked the additions from the margin with brackets.

Comestor nachgeschlagen hat, um die Ergänzung vorzunehmen. Mit einer solchen Möglichkeit wäre aber selbst dann kaum zu rechnen, wenn jener Schreiber in seiner Vorlage an der genannten Stelle einen fehlerhaften oder unvollständigen Text vorgefunden hätte. Wie all die übrigen zahlreichen Ergänzungen zur Palmsonntagspredigt in Gr fügt sich auch diese in einen Zusammenhang ein, der ohne die Ergänzung weder in inhaltlicher noch in formaler Hinsicht Anlaß zu Beanstandungen und Korrekturen gäbe'.[131] Although it is certainly difficult to reconstruct the circumstances of composition here, Schiewer has demonstrated convincingly that the manuscript is the work of four contemporary scribes, and that the scribe of this sermon, the main hand in the manuscript, makes too many mistakes for one to credit him with the authorship of the collection, though he may have written at the dictation of the author(s).[132]

The study of the earliest extant manuscript is important for the study of the sources in what it reveals about the way in which a group of medieval authors of a series of sermons approach their task. It is clear that there were several stages in the composition of the sermons; as Stamm and Schiewer have pointed out, the additions in the margins are not merely scribal corrections or annotations, but constitute a revision of the text. From Gr one can see that material from the *Historia scholastica* (and other sources, such as the *Aurora*) entered the work at different stages; most Comestor material is already present in the main body of text in Gr, but some is added, by the main scribe, in the margins. If one assumes, with Schiewer, that this manuscript preserves 'work in progress',[133] then one can speculate that just as these marginal additions were incorporated into the later redaction (and Grieshaber's edition), earlier annotations from the *Historia scholastica* had already been incorporated into the main text of Gr. This would explain the existence of explanatory details from Comestor in accounts which seem otherwise to be closer to the Vulgate. In any case, it is clear that a copy of the *Historia scholastica* was present in the workshop of the Franciscan monastery in which the *Schwarzwälder Predigten* were composed, that it was consulted repeatedly, and that in this way Comestor's interpretation of the Scriptures was passed on to a new, vernacular, audience.[134]

This pattern will account for the passages which appear to mingle material

[131] Stamm, *Studien*, p. 16.
[132] Schiewer, *Überlieferungsgeschichte*, pp. 52–63.
[133] Schiewer, *Überlieferungsgeschichte*, p. 62.
[134] Whether this contained the *Historia scholastica* in full, or merely in extracts, is not clear; see Andersson-Schmitt, 'Die Verwendung', p. 19.

from both the Vulgate and the *Historia scholastica*; the function of the latter in these instances is clearly that of an ancillary source, supplying extra details, background information and interpretation. However, as the above examples show, the majority of parallels with Comestor are found in passages which appear to be based entirely on his work, where the wording throughout shows his influence.[135] In these cases the *Historia scholastica* fulfils a role very similar to that of the Vulgate: it provides narrative information to illustrate points of the sermon. Here the *Historia scholastica* would seem to be preferred for its conciseness and clarity.

The characteristic term 'urku̍nde', discussed above, does not appear to discriminate between the Vulgate and the *Historia scholastica* as source. Of the examples discussed above, for which Comestor appears to be the main source, six are introduced as 'urku̍nde'.[136] The terms 'alte ê' or 'hailige ewangelie' are applied to all the narrative examples which contain material from the *Historia scholastica*, regardless of whether this material is scriptural or apocryphal;[137] the non-narrative commentary material is introduced by the phrase 'nu wen die maister' (or a variant such as 'su̍meliche maister wen'). This term is used frequently to introduce commentary, and is thus also associated with the nature of the material rather than a specific source. It is difficult to identify a sense of hierarchy of authority in the authors' approach to their sources, but rather a striving for conciseness and comprehensiveness, both of which aims are served by the *Historia scholastica*. The work is used to supplement the Vulgate where it can supply extra details, and as a substitute where its simplicity and brevity are preferred. It does not replace the Vulgate entirely; its importance as a source of biblical material for the *Schwarzwälder Predigten* remains secondary to 'the original', but is nevertheless considerably greater than has previously been supposed.

2.3.5 The *Aurora*

The *Aurora* of Peter Riga is also a source of biblical material in the *Schwarzwälder Predigten*;[138] it is quoted twelve times in the sermons studied.[139]

[135] T13, T17, T18/4, T20, T23, T24, T30, T32, T43, T54.

[136] T13, T17, T20, T30, T43, T54.

[137] The only exception to this is T65, where the Comestor material referring to the Antichrist is introduced with the phrase 'Wir lesen aber an herren Daniels bůche anders', Grieshaber I, p. 151.

[138] See section 2.3 for background and bibliography.

[139] The discussion in this chapter mentions only passages in which the *Aurora* is quoted

Sermon	Aurora	Subject	Category
T29 I, p. 5	Josue, ll. 13–16	Raab	S (t)
T31 I, p. 13	Evangelia, ll. 2881–2884	Five Wounds of Christ	S (t)
T32 I, p. 25	Genesis, ll. 835–838	Lot's wife	S (t)
T58 I, p. 122	Exodus, ll. 331–332	Moses and victory	LS (t)
T61 I, p. 137	Judicum, ll. 111–112	Gideon's fleece	LS (t)
T62 I, p. 146	Leviticus, ll. 613–614	Flying Fish	S (t)
T65 I, p. 151	Daniel, ll. 257–258	Antichrist	L (t)
T13 II, p. 27	II Regum, ll. 361–378	David's options	L (m/t)
T15 II, pp. 43–44	Daniel, ll. 301–302	Writing on Wall	S (m)
T23 II, p. 124	Numeri, ll. 425–430	Brazen Serpent	S (t)
T24 II, p. 131	Numeri, ll. 509–520	Israelites' Corruption	L (t)
T28 II, p. 138	Evangelia, ll. 2881–2884	Five wounds of Christ	S (t)

Legend

Sermon Sermon no. in Schneyer's notation (see table 7 above), volume and page-no. in Grieshaber's edition

Aurora Parallel in *Aurora*, book, line-numbers

Subject Subject of parallel passage

Category Spiritual (S) or Literal (L) sense of the Bible; 'SL' designates passages where the quotation itself can be characterized as literal, but occurs in the context of spiritual exegesis. Quotations occurring in main body of text are marked 't', those added in margin are marked 'm'.

Table 9: The *Aurora* as Source in the *Schwarzwälder Predigten*

The main function of the *Aurora* for the authors of the *Schwarzwälder Predigten* is to provide, or illustrate, their exegesis of a particular anecdote, generally according to the spiritual sense of the Bible. Stamm views the *Aurora* as a more important source than the *Historia scholastica*, and attributes this preference on the part of the German authors to the allegorical nature of the work. 'Man erkennt, aus welchem Grund der Schwarzwälder die

---

in Latin. It is possible that close analysis might reveal further influence of this work in the *Schwarzwälder Predigten*, but this is not the main interest of the present study, which is concerned with the *Aurora* only in its relation to the *Historia scholastica* as a source for the sermons. In this context it will suffice to note that the *Aurora* is **not** the source of the material attributed to the *Historia scholastica* in Table 8 above.

'Aurora' häufiger benutzt als die 'Historia scholastica', die er offensichtlich auch kennt. Wie bereits der Titel seines Werkes deutlich macht, bemüht sich Petrus Comestor durchweg nur um eine kritische Darstellung der historischen Sachverhalte.'[140] Within the general context of the reception of the *Historia scholastica*, one can dispute this rather narrow assessment of the meaning of the title, of Comestor's aims in writing the work, and of its applications as a source. Morey suggests that 'readers liked the *Historia* because it is indeed a book of *stories*',[141] and this is backed up by the above observations about the use of this source in the sermon-collection, that 'deutschsprachige[s] Florilegium für alttestamentliche Geschichten'.[142]

The fact that the *Aurora* is itself based largely on the *Historia scholastica* leads Stamm to view the process of identifying Comestor material mainly in terms of distinguishing between these two sources. In this he overlooks the very issue of the essential difference in the nature of the two works which he himself had emphasized, which means that the *Aurora* fulfils a completely different role to the *Historia scholastica* and the Vulgate. Where the latter works supply the narrative material for the 'urkünden', the literal sense of the Bible, the *Aurora* tends to be used to draw out the spiritual meaning of the examples, for allegorical or tropological exegesis.

An example of this, the most common, function of the *Aurora* can be found in the sermon for the Sunday after Easter (T29), in the third *distinctio*, where the German author, illustrating the point of this section with a different biblical example than Conrad of Saxony, includes a quotation from the *Aurora* as part of his allegorical interpretation of the story of Raab:[143]

> Wer ist nu dc venster. in dc dc rôt sail gehenchet ist. sich dc ist anders niht wan diu sîte dez zarten gotes. ûz der ist gerunnen sin roseuarwes blůt. mit dem hat er uns alle unser sünde abgeweschen. uñ hat uns mit dem fersůnet sinẽ vater eweclichen uñ rehte gelicher wise. als dc rôt sail vron Raab waz ain zaichen. dc si sicher waz vor den vigenden. uñ vor herren Josues zorn. als ist uns dc blůt unsers herren ain sicherhait. dc wir och sicher sîgen vor dem zorn dez almehtigen gotes. uñ och aller unser vigende. Uñ da von stat da gescriben in aurora. *Funis coccineus pendens herensque fenestre. Servat ab hoste raab resque genusque suum. Ecclesiam servat cristi cruor in cruce fusus. Quem mundo lateris sacra fenestra pluit.*

[140] Stamm, *Studien*, p. 47.
[141] Morey, 'Peter Comestor', p. 7.
[142] Schiewer, *Überlieferungsgeschichte*, p. 330.
[143] Grieshaber I, p. 5; *Aurora*, Liber Iosue, ll. 13–16.

The *Aurora* sets the story of Raab within its context in Salvation History: Peter Riga traces a link between the Old Testament and the historical present which hinges on the Redemption, the parallels between the saving power of Christ's red blood and of the red rope used by Raab in her escape. This passage of verse is not translated directly by the author of the sermon, but he expands on it to bring home the point of this *distinctio*: 'Diu dritte gůttete die wir enphangen haben von der siton unsers herren. dc ist dc wir da mit gehailet sigen von der schulde. uñ dc (3b) wir da mit fersůnet sigen got dem ewigen vater.' The author heightens the affective impact of the parallel, and emphasizes the direct, personal relevance of Christ's Passion with his repetition of 'uns'.

The majority of examples of use of the *Aurora* in the *Schwarzwälder Predigten* conform to this pattern, as is demonstrated by the above table. There are two examples which differ slightly, where the passage from the *Aurora* quoted in the sermon does not fit into the category of 'spiritual exegesis', but where it is inserted into a German passage which can be classified in this way. One such example occurs at the end of the account of Moses' prayers for Joshua's victory in the sermon for the 18th Sunday after Pentecost (T58; Gr 17 p. Pent.).[144] The lines quoted by the author of the sermon merely summarize the story: 'Moyse levante manus iosue victoria cedit. Dumque remittit eas victus ab hoste redit'. But the interpretation of this event, which relates Moses' gestures to the ceremonial of the Mass, draws on the continuation of this passage in the *Aurora*:

T58 'Dom. XVII post Pent.'	*Aurora*
Wer ist nu herre Moyses der da hat gebeten fůr sin volk. dc ist din êwart uñ din lêrer. der bittet och fůr dich in der messe swenne er sin hende zerbraitet en cruces wise ob dem altêr. sich mit dem bittende fertribet er och din vigende. dc sint die bősen gaiste.	'Liber Exodi' Sic pro plebe manu, lacrimis, prece sidera pulsans, Presbyter instanti munit ab hoste suos; At si dormitet uictus torpore sacerdos, Subdita plebs uitiis insidiisque patet. (ll. 333–336)

The situation in the other example of this type, the discussion of Gideon's fleece in the sermon for the twenty-first Sunday after Pentecost (T61; Gr 20 p. Pent.), is less straightforward. Here, as above, the quotation is historical and the context allegorical, but the German author does not base his spiritual exegesis on the surrounding lines in the *Aurora*. Where Peter Riga interprets the fleece in terms of the old and new covenant, the author of the sermon once again relates it specifically and graphically to the Passion of Christ.[145]

[144] Grieshaber I, p. 122; *Aurora*, Liber Exodi, ll. 331–336.
[145] Grieshaber I, p. 137; *Aurora*, Liber Judicum, ll. 107–116.

In all the examples discussed above, it is difficult to assess the exact function of the Latin quotation from the *Aurora*, but it would seem to purvey authority rather than information.

Three of the quotations from the *Aurora* occur in a narrative, rather than exegetical context. It is here that there is most overlap between material found in this work and in other possible sources such as the Vulgate, the *Historia scholastica*, and the *Glossa ordinaria*. In two of the three cases, part or all of the quotation has been added in the margin of the manuscript.[146] This allows the possibility, which will be investigated here, that the *Aurora* is not the source of the passage as a whole, but that the quotation has been added in the later redaction and has a purely illustrative function.[147]

The first of these examples occurs in the discussion of David's punishment in the sermon for the third Sunday after Epiphany (T13).[148] The narrative contains three quotations from the same passage in the *Aurora*, the first of which has been added in the margin of the manuscript. David has sinned in attempting to ascertain the number of fighting men in the tribes of Israel and Judah, and is offered the choice of three punishments:

T13 'Dom. III p. Epiph.'	*Historia scholastica* – II Sm/Rg
do erzuͥrnder got als sêre. dc got hinz im sante. ainen wissagen der hiez Gad. uñ der gab im driu sweriu getailten. uñ sprach also. [Aurora. *Ecce trium rerum tibi rex datur optio. septem Annis. vexabit teque tuosque fames. Aut tribus instantes patiuntur mensibus hostes. Aut per tres currit pestis ubique dies.* Er sprach.] kuͥnech du hast got mit diner hochvart vaste erzuͥrnet. uñ dez wil dich got enbůz sezzen. Nim dier under drin dingen swelez du wellest. Ainweder dc der groͦste hunger kom suͥben iâr in allez din riche der ie kom. Alder dc die vigende dier rîten mit gewalte drîge mânode in dc lant. uñ dc wůsten (155b) mit rǒbe uñ mit brande. Alder wilt der zwaiger niht. so nim aber. dc ain grôzer sterbe kom under dc hêr dri tage.	Cap. XXIII. *De numero populi, et altari erecto a David.* [...] Peccavit autem David in duobus, quod superbe numeravit, et quia quisque numeratorum non reddidit pecuniam Domino, quinque scilicet siclos argenti, sicut scriptum est in lege Moysi. [...] Diluculo misit ad eum Dominus Gad prophetam tres supplicii conditiones portantem. Qui ait: 'Aut septem annis veniet tibi fames in regno tuo, aut tribus mensibus fugies adversarios tuos, aut tribus diebus erit pestilentia in populo tuo.' (col. 1346)

The three alternatives are stated in the Bible, and Comestor quotes the entire passage verbatim from the Vulgate. There is no pressing reason to see the

[146] Freiburg i. Breisgau, U.B., Hs. 460, ff. 155r–155v and f. 233r.

[147] That this is not necessarily the case, is demonstrated by T15, where the quotation from the *Aurora* is added in the margin, but where the work is clearly the source for the passage as a whole.

[148] Grieshaber II, pp. 27–28; *Aurora*, Liber II Regum, ll. 361–364, 372, 377–378; *Glossa ordinaria*, II, p. 87; *PL* 198, col. 1346.

Aurora as the direct source for the main text of the sermon at this point, since the wording of the German shows no more similarity to it than to the Vulgate. The explicit reference to David's 'hochvart' might perhaps point to the *Historia scholastica*, but this is the standard interpretation of David's sin, and Comestor's more unusual alternative is not mentioned.

The continuation of the story, in which David deliberates about which of the three options to choose, has no equivalent in the Vulgate or in the *Aurora*, but echoes a passage from Josephus, which is quoted in both the *Historia scholastica* and the *Glossa ordinaria*:

T13 'Dom. III p. Epiph.'	*Historia scholastica* – II Sm/Rg	*Glossa ordinaria*
Do herre David dc horte do erscrack er. uñ enwisse waz er soͤlte tůn. uñ gedahte also. Nim ich den hunger. so sterbent die armen. ich gener aber wol. wan ich han vil kornez. uñ vil wînez. uñ oͤlez. Nim ich denne dc die vigende in dc lant rîten drige manôde. die ersclahent mier dc hêr. ich genêre aber wol. wan ich han gůte buͥrge uñ gůte veste. dar ûf ich mich wol beschierme. der zwaiger wil ich niht wellen. ich wil rehte den sterben uñ den tôt. dc ist ain gemainez dinch. der erbîzet mich als schier als ainen armen.	Cap. XXIII. *De numero populi, et altari erecto a David.* [...] Et ait David: 'Coarctor nimis.' Quasi dicat: Si famem eligo, pauperum erit supplicium, non divitum. Si victoriam hostium, supplicium erit exercitus, et non meum, qui circumvallor fortissimis. Eligam ergo communem plagam regi et plebi. 'Melius est enim ut incidam in manus Domini misericordis, quam in manus hominis. (col. 1346)	Cogitans rex. quia si famem eligeret. contra alios hoc facere videretur. cum ipse multa frumenta haberet nec inopiam sustineret: reliquis vero angustia esset. Si vero eligeret trium mensium victoriam hostium. ipse habens circa se viros fortissimos et custodes nihil timeret: sed neci exercitus subiaceret. communem potius passiones et omnibus equalem elegit dicens: Multo melius est in dei quam hostium manus incidere.

In its mention of corn, the German version is closer to the *Glossa ordinaria*, which gives more detail than Comestor; however, the author of the sermon elaborates considerably throughout the passage, and the other details have no parallel in either source, so that it is possible that the similarity is merely coincidental.

Comestor gives an alternative version of the duration of the pestilence, which is quoted by the German author:

T13 'Dom. III p. Epiph.'	*Historia scholastica*	*Glossa ordinaria*
Nu hoͤre ain clageliche dinch. waz beschach. ez kom ain sterbe under dc hêr. der wêrot von morgen. hinz enbis. aber suͥmeliche maister die wen. dc er wereti hinz vesperzît. uñ in der wîle do sturben under den driuzehen hundert tûsenden. suͥbenzech tûsent manne. uñ da von ist ge-	[...] Misit ergo Dominus pestilentiam in Israel de mane usque ad tempus constitutum,' id est usque ad horam prandii, secundum Josephum, vel usque ad horam sacrificii vespertini, secundum alios, 'et mortui sunt de populo extra Jerusalem septuaginta millia virorum.' In Paralipomenon (*I*	Incipiente pestifero languore ab hora matutina usque ad horam prandij consumpta sunt septuaginta milia.

scriben in aurora. *Milia multa ru-unt. terque quaterque decem.*	*Paral.* XXI) legitur 'fere trecenta millia.' (col. 1346)

The possibility that the Israelites were afflicted until the evening does not occur in the other potential source-works. The quotation from the *Aurora*, which again duplicates material that can be found in the Vulgate and the *Historia scholastica*, this time forms part of the main body of text in the manuscript.[149] As in the examples discussed above in section 2.3.4, it is clear that there were several stages of composition; the *Aurora* cannot be the source of the entire passage, but quotations from it have been added on two separate occasions. The *Historia scholastica* is the only source-work which shows parallels throughout, but at some points the sermon shows closer similarities with other works, so that it is possible that the reference to the duration of the pestilence – the only detail which is exclusive to Comestor – could have been added at an interim stage.

The other example where narrative material from the *Aurora* has been added in the margin occurs in the sermon for Palm Sunday (T24), where the author includes the apocryphal story that Balaam advised Balak that his best policy for defeating the Israelites would be to corrupt them, thus losing them God's favour.[150] Here too there are parallels in the *Glossa ordinaria* and the *Historia scholastica*, but close analysis confirms that the *Aurora* is probably the direct source for at least part of the German passage, as neither of the other Latin works gives a detailed strategy with specific instructions to dress the girls in fine clothing and to encourage them to sing and dance seductively. However, the *Aurora* does not mention that the women lead the Israelites to worship their idol, Beelphegor and to eat of their sacrifices to it; this detail must be included by the German author from the Vulgate or another source.[151]

The above analysis has confirmed that the *Aurora* is occasionally used as a source of literal, narrative material by the authors of the *Schwarzwälder Predigten*, though its predominant role is spiritual exegesis. As in the case of the *Historia scholastica*, the work is consulted at several stages in the composition of the sermons, and existing references and quotations are augmented with marginal additions during this reworking of the text.

[149] Freiburg i. Breisgau, U.B., Hs. 460, f. 155v.

[150] Grieshaber II, p. 131; *Aurora*, Liber Numeri, ll. 509–520; *Glossa ordinaria*, I, pp. 340–341; *PL* 198, col. 1239; Blatt, *Latin Josephus*, pp. 278–280.

[151] Since the *Historia scholastica* is the source for the preceding example from the life of Balaam in this sermon, it is possible that it is also the direct source here; however, there are no particularly close parallels in detail or wording to confirm this speculation.

2.3.6 Conclusion: The Position of the *Historia scholastica* among the Sources

The above analysis of the main sources of biblical material in the *Schwarzwälder Predigten* focuses on the *Historia scholastica* and seeks to situate it with relation to the other works consulted by the authors. This is illuminating not only with regard to the reception of the *Historia scholastica*, but also in what it reveals about the manner in which a group of Franciscan monks went about their task of composing a sermon handbook, and the resources which were available to them. Although one cannot speculate about whether they had a complete copy of the Bible at their disposal, or whether the source works consulted were actually owned by the monastery in which the sermons were composed, one can state with a high degree of certainty that at some stage the authors had access to the *Historia scholastica*, the *Aurora* and a large part of the Vulgate.[152] The fact that, as is demonstrated by the manuscript tradition, these works were consulted repeatedly, at different stages in the composition of the sermons, suggests that they were present in the monastery for a long period and were not merely borrowed for a short while.

One can highlight various trends in the approach of this group of authors to the *Historia scholastica* which will be borne in mind in the subsequent studies:

- Peter Comestor is never mentioned by name in the sermon collection. The nearest to this is the formula 'sůmeliche maister', which introduces commentary material in general and is not used exclusively of Comestor.
- The *Historia scholastica* is never mentioned by name, and no distinction is made, where narrative material is concerned, between it and the Vulgate, or between apocryphal and canonical stories.
- The *Historia scholastica* is used mainly as a source of narrative material, where it seems to be preferred for its brevity and extra detail. It appears to be perceived more as a repository of Bible stories than an exegetical tool or a source of authority.
- The *Historia scholastica*'s main 'rival', as source, is the Vulgate, and the main problem in identifying use of Comestor in the sermon collection is distinguishing between these two potential sources.

The various points highlighted here lead to two general conclusions about the study of the reception of Peter Comestor in medieval literature. The

[152] Old Testament books consulted in the *Schwarzwälder Predigten*: Gn, Ex, Lv, Nm, Ios, Iud, I–IV Rg, Tb, Idt, Est, Iob, Ps, Prv, Is, Ier, Dn, Ion, I–II Mcc,

overlap between the *Historia scholastica* and the Vulgate as sources of biblical narrative, which gives rise to the difficulty in identifying use of Comestor by later authors, may explain the fact that the reception of the work is so badly documented. It also determines the methodology of the present study: close textual analysis is frequently the only way to distinguish between Comestor and other possible sources, and to attempt to characterize the approach of a later author.

3 THE *WELTCHRONIK* OF RUDOLF VON EMS

3.1 Introduction: The *Weltchronik* of Rudolf von Ems

Between 1250 and 1254 Rudolf von Ems wrote the work which is known as the *Weltchronik*, in which he set out to narrate the history of the world from its creation until his own time.[1] The work remains unfinished and breaks off, after over thirty-six thousand lines, in the middle of its account of the life of the prophet Elisha.[2] Thus the work as it stands, and as it appears in Ehrismann's edition, comprises the story of the Old Testament from Genesis to II Kings, with accounts of parallel events from the history of other, heathen, races inserted into the main narrative at irregular intervals.[3]

Rudolf uses many sources in the composition of his *Weltchronik*, and it has long been recognized that the *Historia scholastica* is among them. However, the exact extent of the material from Comestor, the position of the work with regard to the other sources, and the manner in which it is used, has not yet been assessed. This is the aim of the present study, which is the first to concentrate specifically on Rudolf's use of the *Historia scholastica*, and to investigate it within the broader context of the reception of Comestor's work.

Rudolf's *Weltchronik* stands at the beginning of a long tradition of universal histories in German and is incorporated into later chronicles, surviving in some form in 103 manuscripts, the highest number of any poetical work in Middle High German.[4] It can thus be seen as an important vehicle for the

[1] For life and works of Rudolf von Ems, see: Wolfgang Walliczek, 'Rudolf von Ems', in: *VL*², VIII, cols 322–345.

[2] *Rudolfs von Ems Weltchronik* ed. Gustav Ehrismann (Berlin, 1915). This, the only edition, is of München, Cgm 8345, formerly known as the Wernigerode manuscript and held to be the best. This supremacy is challenged by Hubert Herkommer, *Der St. Galler Kodex als literarhistorisches Monument. Die 'Weltchronik' Rudolfs von Ems* (Luzern, 1987), p. 142, but the manuscript is still acknowledged as one of the most reliable. Ehrismann's introduction outlines his principles of edition (p. XXXVI) and gives details of the two other manuscripts consulted in cases of doubt.

[3] A brief overview of the contents of the work and the occurrence of these *incidentia* is given by Herkommer, *St. Galler Kodex*, p. 188, a more detailed one by Helmut Brackert, *Rudolf von Ems. Dichtung und Geschichte* (Heidelberg, 1968), pp. 174–175.

[4] Max Wehrli, *Literatur im deutschen Mittelalter* (Stuttgart, 1984), p. 25.

transmission of Comestor material in the vernacular, and an important contribution to the medieval popular conception of the Bible in the German-speaking area.

The previous chapter examined the use of the *Historia scholastica* by the authors of the *Schwarzwälder Predigten.* There it appeared that Comestor's work was consulted mainly in its capacity of compendium of Bible stories, rather than for its literal-historical exegesis of the Scriptures. The present chapter will investigate the approach of Rudolf von Ems, the author of a historical narrative, in an attempt to evaluate to what extent and how it differs from that of the authors of the sermon collection.

3.2 The Sources of Rudolf's *Weltchronik*

As one would imagine even from the above cursory description of the contents of the *Weltchronik* of Rudolf von Ems, his main source for this work is the Vulgate. But, as has been seen in the case of the *Schwarzwälder Predigten*, this is not as obvious a choice as the direct source of biblical material for a medieval author as it might appear to a modern reader. Other works treating of the same events were available and might be preferred, either for their brevity, their explanations of difficult points, their emphasis on history or on the symbolic meaning of the Old Testament or perhaps merely for their accessibility. One such work is the *Historia scholastica* of Peter Comestor.

The *Historia scholastica* is never mentioned by name in the work, but the presence of material from Comestor was pointed out by Vilmar as early as 1839.[5] He suggests two further sources for the *Weltchronik*: Godfrey of Viterbo's *Pantheon*, and Julius Solinus' 'Polyhistor' (= *Collectanea rerum memorabilium*), though he regards them as very minor. 'Auch wird der erstere nur zur weiteren Ausführung solcher Erzählungen, welche, nur kürzer, auch in der Historia scholastica enthalten sind, der andere bloß bei dem geographischen Abschnitte benutzt, wenn überhaupt, was ich fast bezweifle, Rudolf wirklich unmittelbar aus Solinus und Gotfrid schöpfte'.[6]

Doberentz's detailed work on the geographical passages of the *Weltchronik* dismissed Solinus as a possibility and demonstrated that it was the *Imago*

[5] A.F.C. Vilmar, *Die zwei Recensionen und die Handschriftenfamilien der Weltchronik Rudolfs von Ems* (Marburg, 1839).

[6] Vilmar, *Recensionen*, p. 13.

Mundi of Honorius Augustodunensis which was Rudolf's direct source for this part of the work.[7]

There is then a gap of nearly one hundred years before the next study of the sources of the work by von Tippelskirch.[8] She examines the possibility that three further sources which share material with the *Historia scholastica* might have been consulted directly by Rudolf. These are the *Revelationes* of Methodius and the *Antiquitates Judaicae* of Josephus, both used by Comestor, and the chronicles of Bishop Otto of Freising, which themselves draw heavily on Josephus. She concludes that it is very unlikely that Methodius was used directly, but fails to reach a satisfactory conclusion in the case of the Josephus material: 'Daß Rudolf seine Josephus-Zitate direkt aus einer lateinischen Übersetzung der "Jüdischen Altertümer" geschöpft hat und nicht auf die Vermittlung des Petrus Comestor angewiesen war, ist nicht unwahrscheinlich, aber keineswegs mit Sicherheit zu bejahen'.[9] The fact that she herself relies on a German translation of the original Greek version, from which the medieval Latin translation varies considerably in some cases, leads to further uncertainty. This question is of obvious importance in discussing Comestor's position as a source in the *Weltchronik*, and will be addressed in detail in section 3.3.2.

Von Tippelskirch devotes much of her discussion of sources to the demonstration that the twelfth-century Otto of Freising's *Chronica sive historia de duabus civitatibus* is used by Rudolf for his account of the story of Semiramis and that he influences Rudolf's general conception of history. However, this suggestion is questioned by Herkommer: 'Die von TIPPELSKIRCH, S. 58 vertretene These, daß Rudolf die Chronik Ottos von Freising "'auf seinem Schreibtisch' liegen hatte" stützt sich im wesentlichen auf "Übereinstimmungen" (S. 49) beider Werke in der Behandlung der Semiramis-Episode und der Trierer Gründungssage (S. 49–60). Angesichts der weiten Verbreitung dieses Stoffes, der zum historischen Bildungswissen der Zeit gerechnet werden darf, erscheinen die beigezogenen Parallelen jedoch für eine so weitreichende Folgerung nicht beweiskräftig genug'.[10]

This assimilation of 'Bildungswissen', which makes the *Weltchronik* a

[7] Otto Doberentz, 'Die Erd- und Völkerkunde in der Weltchronik des Rudolf von Hohen-Ems', *ZfdPh* 12 (1881), pp. 257–301, 387–454; *ZfdPh* 13 (1882), pp. 29–57, 165–223.

[8] Ingrid von Tippelskirch, *Die Weltchronik des Rudolf von Ems. Studien zur Geschichtsauffassung und politischen Intention* (Göppingen, 1979).

[9] Von Tippelskirch, *Geschichtsauffassung*, p. 197.

[10] Herkommer, *St. Galler Kodex*, p. 183, n. 276.

product of a long tradition of historical and exegetical scholarship, is a further aspect of the study of Rudolf's sources. Herkommer warns repeatedly of the complicated nature of the 'Quellenlage'.[11] He points to the use of another German medieval chronicler, Frutolf von Michelsberg, who wrote a record of contemporary events at the end of the eleventh century. However, Rudolf's use of this chronicle would appear to be minimal. He also points to Rudolf's knowledge of Augustine.[12]

This then is the state of research into Rudolf's sources. Some have been studied in sufficient detail; others require more attention. The aim of the present study, as has been stated, is to examine the position of the *Historia scholastica* among these sources. As in the case of the *Schwarzwälder Predigten*, and all such discussions of sources, one can only speak in terms of 'strong similarity' and 'high probability' rather than of 'proof', but at least it should be possible in this way to add more definition to the picture of Comestor's position within the traditions of medieval scholarship.

3.2.1 The *Historia scholastica* and the Sources of the *Weltchronik*: Distinguishing between Comestor and other material

The main problems involved in assessing the reception of Peter Comestor's *Historia scholastica* remain constant from work to work. The analysis of part of his account of the book of Exodus (section 1.2.1) shows his own approach to his sources: he gathers raw materials from a wide variety of texts, then refines and processes them to produce a fabric so finely woven that it is a problem to find criteria to permit the separation of individual strands. The result of this process, the *Historia scholastica*, is in turn used by the later authors. But they also have direct access to some of the raw materials of Comestor's work; his compilation is seldom used in isolation, but rather in combination with the other authorities, which are, naturally, frequently the very sources he himself consulted.

The problem is compounded, as time goes by, by the fact that these later works, which contain material from the *Historia scholastica*, may in turn be added to the array of available sources. The authors of the *Schwarzwälder Predigten* made use of the Vulgate, the *Historia scholastica* and the *Aurora*, as well as their main source, the sermons of Conrad of Saxony. Rudolf von

[11] Herkommer, *St. Galler Kodex*, p. 198, nn. 341 & 342; p. 206, n. 383[a]; p. 221.

[12] Herkommer, *St. Galler Kodex*, p. 206; the immediate source for the passage discussed by Herkommer would seem to be the *Glossa ordinaria*, II, p. 12.

Ems, the historian, consults the *Historia scholastica* in conjunction with the Bible, the prime source for universal history, and possibly also the *Antiquitates Judaicae* of the Jewish historian Josephus, both major sources for Comestor, though in this case there is no evidence for his using works which themselves draw on Comestor.

The difficulties encountered even in a merely quantitative evaluation of the use of Comestor's work in the *Weltchronik* will be apparent from the following analysis of a few lines from Rudolf's narration of the birth of Moses, as related in the book of Exodus and the *Historia scholastica*'s 'Historia de Libri Exodi'.[13]

The events of Exodus are covered in the *Weltchronik* in lines 8406 to 12,910. The beginning of the section follows the Vulgate:

Exodus 1	*Weltchronik*
5 Ioseph autem in Aegypto erat	Do Joseph in Egipte starp
6 quo mortuo et universis fratribus	und des geslehtes stam virdarp
eius omnique cognatione illa	und Josebes brůdir gar,
	die mit ir vater kamen dar
	und sidir nah dén jaren
	in dem lande ir wachsen waren, [...].

Rudolf recapitulates with a paraphrase of the end of verse 5 and verse 6, before translating verse 7:

Exodus 1	*Weltchronik*
7 filii Israel creverunt et quasi germinantes multi-	do wůchs dú fruht der kúnneschaft
plicati sunt	an lúten und an grozer kraft
ac roborati nimis impleverunt terram	so sere das si tegelich
	wahsende so mertin sih
	das si das lant irfulten do.

Here, though due to the verse format of the German the word order is different, the translation is very accurate, with great attention to detail. The theme of organic growth is rendered in the German with the words 'fruht' and 'wůchs'; 'multiplicati sunt' becomes 'mertin sih', and the idea of 'roborati' is taken up in the phrase 'an grozer kraft'; and 'impleverunt terram' is directly translated by 'das lant irfulten'.

The above lines have no equivalent in the *Historia scholastica*, so that determining the source is thus far not problematic. With lines 8417–8425, however, where Comestor draws from the Vulgate, the situation becomes more complex:

[13] *PL* 198, cols 1141–1142, quoted in full; see section 1.2 for Comestor's sources.

Exodus 1

8 surrexit interea rex novus super Aegyptum qui ignorabat Ioseph

Weltchronik

nu wart ein núwir Pharao
herre und kúnig ubirs lant,
dem was Joseph vil umbekant
und al dú gůtat die er ie
an dem lande begie.
des wart an sinen nah komen
von im vil kleine war genomen,
wand er der gůtat virgaz;
und gwan des kúnnis solhin has
das er sih tegelich beriet
wie er virdarpte also die diet
das er an angest were gar
von der uf genden schar.

Historia scholastica

'Surrexit igitur rex novus in Aegypto' longo tempore post mortem Joseph (Exod. 1). Ab illo enim sub quo fuit Joseph, qui proprio nomine dictus est Nephres, octavus regnavit Ammonaphis, sub quo natus est Moyses. Regno autem translato ad aliam domum, rex ille ab hoc quasi novus, ignoravit beneficia Joseph, quae contulerat Aegypto, et odiebat Israel maxime, ut ait Josephus, quia [...] (col. 1141)

The German text first translates the verse from the Vulgate, then adds more information from Comestor. But he only takes from Comestor that which corroborates the Vulgate, the phrase 'ignoravit beneficia Joseph, quae contulerat Aegypto, et odiebat Israel maxime', omitting the extra details about the succession of the Pharaohs. He translates Comestor's phrase and then clarifies and expands it with his own reference to Joseph's descendants. And where Comestor goes on to give Josephus' interpretation of the cause of the Pharaoh's hatred, Rudolf, at this point, gives the result, returning to the cause in lines 8491–8497.

In the following passage Comestor is again very similar to the Vulgate, but a close analysis reveals details which point to the Vulgate as Rudolf's direct source here:

Exodus 1

9 et ait ad populum suum ecce populus filiorum Israhel multus et fortior nobis
10 venite sapienter opprimamus eum ne forte multiplicetur et si ingruerit contra nos bellum addatur inimicis nostris expugnatisque nobis egrediatur e terra

Weltchronik

er sprah zen sinen: 'diz lút ist
irwahsen so in kurzer vrist
das si sint sterchir danne wir.
nu ratih iuh das unde mir,
wie wir si in disem riche
so rehte wisliche
virderbin uf dirre erde,
das ir iht mere werde:
wan beginnin wir urlúge han
und wil ieman úns bestan,
si helfent widir úns zehant
und rument danne hie dú lant,
so si úns hie virtribint:
unlange si hie blibent.'

Historia scholastica

Et ait rex ad populum suum: 'Populus Israel fere fortior est nobis; sapienter opprimamus eum, ne multiplicatus, vel ipse contra nos insurgat, vel addatur hostibus nostris, et egrediatur liber.' (col. 1141)

The linking of number and strength in the Bible is rendered causally in Rudolf's text, but omitted altogether in Comestor's, and the fear of a possible insurrection, which the *Historia scholastica* suggests as an alternative reason for the Pharaoh's decision to oppress the Israelites, is not mentioned by Rudolf.

The following passage is another example of how both sources can be used simultaneously, with elements from each in the German text which do not occur in the other.

Exodus 1

11 praeposuit itaque eis magistros operum ut adfligerent eos oneribus

Weltchronik

Des kúnegis wort in allen
began so wol gevallen
das si rieten im also
das man si hieze wrcken do
an sinen wercken tag und naht
ubir kraft und ubir maht,
das man alsus virdarpte ir lebin.
in wrdin werch meistir gegebin,
die si mit slegin ze wercke tribin:
so si mit rů̊we belibin,
si slů̊gen si vil sere.
mit ungů̊tlicher lere
namen die werch meister hie
undir meistir ubir sie,
die ir geslehtes waren:
swenne in die rů̊we baren
und si ze wúrckenne twungin niht,
so arneten si die geschicht
mit unrebermeclichen sitin,
wand si vil slegen drumbe liten.

Historia scholastica

Imposuit ergo eis graves angarias operum, quibus fracti non vacarent amplexibus, et magistros operum praefecit eis Hebraeos, sed magistris operum praefecit Aegyptios, ut durius affligerent eos. (col. 1141)

The verse from the Vulgate is translated in lines 8451–8452, but the idea of Hebrew sub-foremen, with Egyptian foremen to afflict the Israelites still further, is taken from the *Historia scholastica*.

Thus far it has only been a question of distinguishing between use of the Vulgate and the *Historia scholastica*. The following section of the *Weltchronik* describes the building of the two cities Phiton and Ramesses. The relevant verse in the Vulgate (Ex 1:11) reads merely: 'aedificaveruntque urbes tabernaculorum Pharaoni Phiton et Ramesses' and does not give any further details. Comestor's main source at this point is the *Antiquitates Judaicae* of Josephus, which is possibly also an occasional source for the *Weltchronik*.[14] Did Rudolf take this material directly from Josephus or via the *Historia scholastica*?

[14] See section 1.2 for Comestor's sources, and section 3.3.2 for discussion of Rudolf's possible use of Josephus.

Historia scholastica

Coxerunt ergo lateres ex quibus 'aedificaverunt regi civitates tabernaculorum, Phithon et Ramessen.' Civitates quidem prius erant, sed non erant *tabernaculorum*, erantque in finibus Aegypti, et ideo muravit eas Pharao, ut ibi poneret armatos, quasi in tabernaculis semper excubantes, ne quis posset ingredi, vel egredi sine regis nutu: vel 'tabernaculorum,' id est pauperum prius, et opere illorum illas dictavit; vel, ut alia littera habet, 'positionum,' ubi scilicet fiscus reponeretur. Aliud etiam opus, non tam grave quam servile, imposuit eis, ut lutum platearum et sordes vicorum cophinis exportarent [...] Tertium etiam addidit opus, secundum Josephum, ut fluvium per multas derivationes dividerent, et circumdarent civitates fossatis, ne eas inundare fluvius valeret, [...] (cols 1141–1142)

Weltchronik

si můsten werchen ane lon
Ramassen und Phyton,
zẘ stete groz, da Pharao
bi dén ziten wolte do
sine besten houbit veste han
und sine riterschaft da lan,
swenne in not ane gienge,
und das man da empfienge
die zinse von dem lande,
die man dem kúnege sande.
ein andir not mit erbeit
wart in da bi noh uf geleit:
das si her, hin unde dar
dú wazer zerleiten gar
durh dú gevilde hie und da;
zehant dabi můsten si sa
die stete umbegrabin und drin
dú wazer schone wisen hin;
darzů můstens inir pflege
han mit subirckeit die wege
und das hor ab dén strazen
tragen.

Antiquitates

fluvium namque per multas derivationes eos dividere murosque civitatibus fabricare et fossata circumducere, ut eas inundare fluvius non valeret er pyrimidas aedificare praecipiebant, ut nostrum hoc modo genus attererent.

It is clear in this case from the inclusion in the *Weltchronik* of details from the *Historia scholastica* which are not in the *Antiquitates Judaicae*, that Josephus is not Rudolf's direct source here. As Comestor here takes details from a variety of sources, and it is unlikely that Rudolf would have mentioned exactly the same details if he consulted the individual works independently, one can say with a high degree of certainty that this was indeed Rudolf's direct source. Other instances where material from Josephus occurs in the *Weltchronik* will be discussed in section 3.3.2.

The above analysis of a short section from the beginning of the *Weltchronik*'s account of Exodus provides an introduction to Rudolf's main sources and the methods used in determining the direct source for a given passage. Table 10 summarizes the findings of a similar analysis of the work as a whole.

Vulgate	*Weltchronik*	*Hist. Schol./os*
	1–60: prologue	
	61–188: 'Weltalter'	
Gn 1	189–252	
Gn 2	253–338	
Gn 3	339–401	Gn 21
Gn 4	402–540	Gn 27
(Gn 4, 23)	541–564	Gn 28
Gn 4,25–26 (end)	565–585	
Gn 5	586–670	Gn 30
Gn 6	671–733	Gn 29
Gn 7	734–799	
Gn 8,1–11	800–828	
	829–831	Gn 34
Gn 8,13–end	832–845	
Gn 9,11–17	846–866	
	867–900: 2nd prologue	
Gn 9,18–end	901–971	
	972–1007	(Gn 37)
Gn 10	1008–1161	
	1162–1215	Gn 37
	1216–1245	Gn 38
	1246–1305	Gn 37
Gn 11,5–8	1306–1324	Hon. Aug.
	1325–1335	(Gn 41)/ Hon. Aug.
	1336–1344	(Gn 38)/ Hon. Aug.
	1344–1360	(Gn 37)/ Hon. Aug.
	1361–2249, 2394–3065	Hon. Aug.
	2249–2394 not Rudolf	
	3066–3093 auth. comment	
Gn 11,20	3094–3129	Gn 41
	3130–3165	Gn 37
	3166–3247	Greek Gods (source unknown)
	3248–3259	Cicia (source unknown)
Gn 11,22–28	3260–3270	
	3271–3278	Gn 41
(Gn 17,4–8)	3279–3292	(Gn 50)
Gn 11,29–end	3293–3321	Gn 41, 42
	3322–3390	(Gn 37,38)
	3391–3745	(Gen 39/40)/ Otto v. Freis
	(3422–3496)	Gn 40
	3746–3793	(Otto v. Freis)
	3794–3877 3rd prologue	
Gn 12,1–6	3878–3927	(Gn 43,44)
Gn 21,20–end	3928–3953	Gn 58
Gn 12,7–end	3954–4010	Gn 45
Gn 13	4011–4078	Gn 45
Gn 14	4079–4377	Gn 46
	(4291–4294)	Gn 46
	(4317–4347)	Gloss Ord
Gn 15	4378–4501	Gn 48
Gn 16	4502–4571	Gn 49
Gn 17	4572–4677	Gn 50
Gn 18	4678–4754	Gn 51–52
Gn 19	4755–4967	Gn 52–54
	(4822–4847)	
(Gn 20,1–2)	4968–4977	(Gn 55)
Gn 21	4978–5120	Gn 56–57
	(5029–5044)	Gn 56

Table 10: The Sources of the *Weltchronik* of Rudolf von Ems

Vulgate	*Weltchronik*	*Hist. Schol./os*
Gn 22	5121–5197	Gn 58
Gn 23	5198–5218	Gn 59
Gn 24	5219–5272	Gn 60
	5273–5292	
Gn 25	5293–5525	Gn 56
	5526–5565	Gn 68
Gn 26	5566–5639	Gn 69
	5640–5659	(Gn 71)
Gn 27	5660–5947	Gn 72–73
	(5852–5883)	(Gn 72)
Gn 28	5948–6103	Gn 73
Gn 29	6104–6264	Gn 74–75
	6265–6275	
Gn 30	6276–6407	Gn 75–78
Gn 31	6408–6561	(Gn 78–79)
Gn 32	6562–6642	Gn 80–81
Gn 33	6643–6735	Gn 82
Gn 34	6736–6798	Gn 83
Gn 35	6799–6908	Gn 83–85
	(6909–6918)	
Gn 36	6909–6990	
	6991–7028	
Gn 37	7029–7132	Gn 87
Gn 38	7133–7149	Gn 89
Gn 39	7150–7215	Gn 90
Gn 40	7216–7287	Gn 91
	7288–7313	
Gn 41	7314–7509	Gn 92–93
Gn 42	7510–7611	Gn 93–94
Gn 43	7612–7745	Gn 94–95
Gn 44	7746–7828	Gn 95
Gn 45	7829–7999	Gn 96
Gn 46	8000–8067	Gn 97–98
Gn 47	8068–8268	Gn 98–100
Gn 48	8269–8314	Gn 101
Gn 49	8315–8324	Gn 102–114
Gn 50	8325–8405	Gn 114–115
Ex 1,6–14	8406–8505	Ex 2
Ex 1,15–end	8506–8587	Ex 3
	8587–8777	Hon. Aug.
	8778–8797 auth. com.	
	8798–8867 4th prologue	
(Ex 2)	8877–9185	Ex 5
Ex 2,9	(8999–9007)	
	(9074–9167) not Rudolf	
	9168–9271	Ex 6
(Ex 2,11–22)	9272–9366	Ex 7
Ex 2,23–25 (end)	9367–9383	Ex 8
(Ex 3)	9384–9530	Ex 8
Ex 4	9531–9628	Ex 9
Ex 4, 20–26	9629–9645	Ex 10
Ex 4, 27–end	9646–9679	Ex 11
Ex 5, 1–6	9680–9733	Ex 11
Ex 5,7–end	9734–9795	Ex 12
Ex 6,1–27	9796–9870	Ex 12
Ex 6,28–30 (end)	9871–9887	Ex 13
Ex 7,1–12	9888–9936	Ex 13
Ex 7,13–end	9937–10003	Ex 14 & 15
Ex 8,1–15	10004–10068	Ex 16
Ex 8,16–20	10069–10105	Ex 17
Ex 8,21–32 (end)	10106–10176	Ex 18
Ex 9,1–7	10177–10202	(Ex 19)
Ex 9,8–12	10203–10225	Ex 20
Ex 9,13–35 (end)	10226–10285	Ex 21

Table 10: continued.

Vulgate	*Weltchronik*	*Hist. Schol.*/os
Ex 10,1–20	10286–10370	Ex 22
Ex 10,21–29 (end)	10371–10409	Ex 23
Ex 11	10410–10435	
	10436–10499	Ex 24
	10500–10503 auth. com.	
Ex 12	10606–10531	
Ex 12,29–41	10532–10606	Ex 26
	10607–10651	Ex 27
Ex 12,37	10652–10654	Ex 27
	10655–10681	
	10682–10693	Ex 27
(Ex 13)	10694–10717	Ex 28
(Ex 13,17–20)	10718–10750	Ex 29
(Ex 13,21–22) (end)	10751–10764	Ex 30
Ex 14,1–2	10765–10767	(Ex 30)
Ex 14,5–31 (end)	10768–10954	Ex 31/ Josephus
Ex 15,1–21	10955–11027	Ex 31
	11028–11089	
	11090–11095 recap.	
(Ex 15,22–25)	11096–11127	Ex 32
Ex 15,27	11128–11133	(Ex 33)
Ex 16	11134–11251	Ex 34
Ex 17,1–7	11252–11277	(Ex 35)
Ex 17,8–16 (end)	11278–11336	
	11337–11347	Ex 35
Ex 18	11348–11488	
Ex 19	11489–11634	Ex 39
Ex 20	11635–11752	
Ex 24	11753–11827	
	11828–11834	Ex 45
Ex 25–27	11835–12000	Ex 46–62
(Ex 28)	12001–12041	Ex 66
Ex 32	12042–12245	Ex 73
Ex33	12246–12326	
Ex 34	12327–12419	Ex 77
Ex 35	12420–12458	Ex 78
Ex 36–39	12458–12486	
	12487–12635	Ex 58
	12636–12654	
Ex 40	12655–12677	
Lv 1–7	12678–12705	Lv 2
Lv 8	12706–12775	Lv 13
Lv 9	12776–12811	Lv 15
Lv 10	12812–12854	Lv 16
Lv 11	12855–12875	
	12876–12909	
Lv 24	12910–12945	
Nm 1	12946–13030	Nm 1
Nm 3	13031–13047	
Nm 2–3	13048–13198	
	13199–13211	Nm 2
Nm 5	13212–13220	
Nm 6,22–27	13221–13234	
(Nm 10,1–10)	13235–13247	Nm 12
(Nm 7–9)	13248–13252	
Nm 10,11–	13253–13309	Nm 13
Nm 11,1–30	13310–13427	Nm 14
Nm 11,31–35 (end)	13428–13454	
Nm 12	13455–13513	Nm 16
Nm 13	13514–13610	Nm 17
Nm 14	13611–13755	Nm 18
Nm 15,32–36	13756–13770	Nm 19
Nm 16,1–40	13771–13909	Nm 20

Table 10: continued.

Vulgate	*Weltchronik*	*Hist. Schol./os*
Nm 16,41–50 (end)	13910–13945	Nm 21
	13946–13992	Nm 22
Nm 17	13993–14045	Nm 22
	14046–14073	
	14074–14096	Nm 23
Nm 20,1–13	14097–14158	Nm 24
	14159–14175 auth. com.	
Nm 20,14–22	14176–14216	Nm 25
Nm 20,23–29 (end)	14217–14235	Nm 26
	14236–14242	Nm 26
Nm 21,1–3	14243–14263	Nm 27
Nm 21,4–9	14264–14325	Nm 28
	14326–14359	
(Nm 21,12–15)	14360–14394	Nm 29
Nm 21,20–35	14395–14441	Nm 31
	14442–14469	
Nm 22,1–35	14470–14672	Nm 32
	(14481–14499)	
Nm 22,35–41	14673–14689	Nm 33
Nm 23	14690–14731	Nm 33
Nm 24	14732–14791	Nm 33
Nm 24	14792–14794	Nm 34
(Nm 25,1–5)	14795–14878	Nm 34
(Nm 25,6–18)	14879–14970	Nm 35
Nm 26,1–4; 51–65	14971–15012	Nm 36
Nm 27,1–11	15012–15033	Nm 37
Nm 27,12–23	15034–15069	Nm 38
(Nm 28–30)	15070–15080	(Nm 39–48)
Nm 31	15081–15161	Nm 49
(Nm 32)	15162–15223	Nm 50
(Nm 34–35)	15224–15259	Nm 52

Vulgate	*Weltchronik*	*Hist. Schol./os*
(Dt 1–4)	15260–15289	Dt 2
Dt 4,41–43; 19,6; Iosu 20,6	15290–15334	Dt 3
Dt 8,1–4; 11	15335–15395	Dt 4
Dt 12–15	15396–15426	Dt 5
Dt 16,18–19; 17,8–12	15427–15450	Dt 6
	15455–15471	Dt 6
Dt 17,14–20	15472–15505	Dt 7
Dt 18,10–15	15506–15525	Dt 8
Dt 19,18–21	15526–15532	Dt 9
Dt 20,1; 20,8	15533–15539	Dt 10
Dt 23,17–18	15540–15556	Dt 13
Dt 25,13–16	15557–15573	
Dt 25,17–19; 20,16–18	15574–15586	Dt 17; Dt 11
Dt 26	15587–15592	
Dt 28,68	15593–15613	Dt 17
Dt 31,9–13	15614–15626	Dt 18
Dt 31,27–29	15627–15650	Dt 18
Dt 31,30; 32,1	15651–15660	Dt 19
	15661–15666	Dt 19
Dt 32,48–49	15667–15672	Dt 20
Dt 33,1; 34,1–5	15673–15681	Dt 20
Dt 34,6	15682–15694	Dt 20 / Glossa ordinaria
Dt 34,7	15695–15706	Dt 20
Dt 34,8–12	15707–15721	Dt 20
	15722–15787	Hon. Aug.
Ios 1	15788–15842	Ios 1
Ios 2	15843–15998	Ios 2
Ios 3,5–17	15999–16047	Ios 3
Ios 4	16048–16072	Ios 3
Ios 5,1–12	16073–16098	(Ios 4)
Ios 5,13–15	16099–16116	Ios 5

Table 10: continued.

Vulgate	*Weltchronik*	*Hist. Schol./os*
Ios 6	16117–16168	Ios 5
Ios 7,1	16169–16179	(Ios 6)
	16180–16186	(Ios 5 add.)
Ios 7,2–26	16187–16239	Ios 6
Ios 8	16240–16334	Ios 7
	16335–16354	(Ios 7)
Ios 9	16355–16489	Ios 8
Ios 10	16490–16659	(Ios 9)
Ios 11	16660–16802	Ios 10
(Ios 12)	16803–16812	
	16813–16831	
Ios 13	16832–16869	Ios 13
Ios 14,6–13	16870–16893	Ios 12
Ios 15,14–17	16894–16914	Ios 14
Ios 18?	16915–16943	(Ios 13)
Ios 18?	16944–16959	
Ios 17,14–18	16960–16976	Ios 13
(Ios 18 – 21)	16977–17057	Ios 13
(Ios 21)	17058–17064	
Ios 22	17065–17187	Ios 15
(Ios 23 & 24)	17188–17222	Ios 16
Ios 24,29–33 (end)	17223–17240	Ios 17
	17240–17249	
Idc 1	17250–17385	Idc 2
Idc 1	17386–17454	Idc 3
	17455–17491	Idc 3
Idc 2	17492–17585	Idc 4
Idc 3,1–11	17586–17629	Idc 5
Idc 3,12–31 (end)	17630–17844	Idc 6
	(17821–17837 auth. com.)	
Idc 4	17845–18095	Idc 7
Idc 5	18096–18143	Idc 7
Idc 6	18144–18429	Idc 8

Vulgate	*Weltchronik*	*Hist. Schol./os*
Idc 7	18430–18718	Idc 8
Idc 8	18719–18967	Idc 8
Idc 8	18968–18995	Idc 9
Idc 9	18996–19323	Idc 9
Idc 10	19324–19353	Idc 10 & 11
Idc 10	19354–19400	Idc 12
Idc 11	19401–19588	Idc 12
Idc 12	19589–19627	Idc 12
Idc 12	19628–19655	Idc 13 – 15
	19656–20381 Greek myths	Frutolf von Michaelsberg
Idc 13	20382–20508	Idc 16
Idc 14	20509–20679	Idc 17
Idc 15,1–8	20680–20777	Idc 17
Idc 15,9–20 (end)	20778–20917	Idc 18
Idc 16,1–3	20918–20946	Idc 18
Idc 16,4–31 (end)	20947–21195	Idc 19
	21196–21225 sets scene	
Idc 19	21226–21294	Idc 22
Idc 20	21295–21442	Idc 22
Idc 21	21443–21485	Idc 22
Ruth 4,13–22 (end)	21486–21497	Idc 23
	21498–21517 auth. com.	
	21518–21555 5th world	
	21556–21740 Konrad IV	
I Sm 1,1	21741–21747	I Rg 2
I Sm 1,2–19	21748–21854	I Rg 3
I Sm 1,20–28 (end)	21855–21927	I Rg 4
(I Sm 2)	21928–21938	I Rg 4

Table 10: continued.

Vulgate	*Weltchronik*	*Hist. Schol.*/os
I Sm 2,12–36 (end)	21939–22032	I Rg 5
I Sm 3	22033–22126	I Rg 6
I Sm 4	22127–22239	I Rg 7
I Sm 5	22240–22316	I Rg 8
	(22248–22260)	
I Sm 6	22317–22400	(I Rg 8)
I Sm 7	22401–22569	(I Rg 9)
I Sm 8	22570–22694	I Rg 10
I Sm 9	22695–22749	I Rg 11
I Sm 10	22750–22907	I Rg 11
	(22777–22787)	
I Sm 11	22908–23071	I Rg 12
I Sm 12	23072–23154	I Rg 12
I Sm 13	23155–23282	I Rg 13
I Sm 14	23283–23563	I Rg 15
I Sm 15	23564–23735	I Rg 15
I Sm 16	23736–23935	I Rg 16
	(23862–23886)	attrib. to Josephus
(I Sm 14,49–51)	23936–23961	(I Rg 14)
I Sm 17	23962–24261	I Rg 17
I Sm 18,1	24262–24276	I Rg 17
I Sm 18,2–end	24277–24449	I Rg 18
I Sm 19,1–7	(24340–24389)	I Rg 18
I Sm 19,9–end	24450–24490	I Rg 19
I Sm 20	24491–24623	I Rg 19
I Sm 21	24624–24717	I Rg 20
I Sm 22	24718–24856	I Rg 22
	24857–24875	(I Rg 22) / Josephus (attrib.)
I Sm 23	24876–25034	I Rg 22 & 23
	25035–25042	(I Rg 23)
I Sm 24	25043–25176	I Rg 23
I Sm 25	25177–25386	I Rg 24
	25387–25400	
I Sm 26	25401–25569	(I Rg 25)
I Sm 27	25570–25632	I Rg 25
I Sm 28	25633–25878	I Rg 26
	(25682–25700)	
	(25727–25736)	Gloss (false attr. to Jose.)
	25879–25910	Josephus (attrib.)
	25911–25946 auth. com.	Gloss (ref. to Augustine)
I Sm 29	25947–26010	I Rg 27
I Sm 30	26011–26324	I Rg 27 & 28 (attr. Jose.)
I Sm 31	26325–26342	I Rg 28
I Par 10,13	26343–26372	I Rg 28 (false attr. to Jose.)
	26373–26378 auth. com.	
	26379–26804	source unknown
II Sm 1	26805–26956	II Rg 1 (false attr. to Jose.)
II Sm 2	26957–27286	II Rg 2–4 (false attr. to Jose.)
II Sm 3	27287–27524	II Rg 5
II Sm 4	27525–27642	II Rg 6
II Sm 5	27643–27879	II Rg 6, 7 & 8 / Josephus
	(27793–27820)	
(II Sm 5)	(27851–27865)	(Josephus) (attrib.)
II Sm 6	27880–28105	II Rg 9 / Josephus (attr.) / Gloss

Table 10: continued.

Vulgate	*Weltchronik*	*Hist. Schol./os*
	(27990–27996) auth. com.	
II Sm 7	28106–28174	II Rg 10
II Sm 8	28175–28348	II Rg 10 / Josephus (attrib.)
II Sm 9	28349–28410	II Rg 11
II Sm 10	28411–28592	II Rg 11
	28593–28627	
II Sm 11	28628–28855	II Rg 12
II Sm 12	28856–29100	II Rg 12
II Sm 13	29101–29221	II Rg 13
II Sm 14	29222–29349	II Rg 14
II Sm 15	29350–29555	II Rg 15
II Sm 16,1–4	29556–29583	II Rg 15
II Sm 15,32–37 (end)	29584–29595	II Rg 15
II Sm 16,5–23 (end)	29596–29756	II Rg 15 & 16
II Sm 17	29757–29949	II Rg 16 & 17
II Sm 18	29950–30211	II Rg 17
	(30121–30143 auth. com.)	
II Sm 19	30212–30402	II Rg 18
	30403–30432	(ebreyschú warheit)
II Sm 20,3–26 (end)	30433–30564	II Rg 19
(II Sm 21)	30565–30820	(II Rg 20) / (Jose.)
(II Sm 22)	30821–30856	(II Rg 21)
II Sm 23,8–39 (end)	30857–31037	II Rg 22
II Sm 24	31038–31350	II Rg 23 / Josephus (attrib.)
	(31046–31072 auth. com.)	II Rg 23

Vulgate	*Weltchronik*	*Hist. Schol./os*
I Par 22 ?	31351–31380	Jos
III Rg 1	31381–31569	III Rg 1
(I Par 22–27)	31570–31698	III Rg 2
III Rg 2,1–11	31699–31851	III Rg 3 / Josephus (attrib.)
	31852–31858 auth. com.	
III Rg 2,12–35	31859–32090	III Rg 4
III Rg 3	32091–32318	III Rg 5 & 6 / Josephus
III Rg 4	32319–32440	III Rg 7
III Rg 5	32441–32632	III Rg 8 / (Jose.)
III Rg 6,1–2	32633–32664	III Rg 9
	32665–32688 (abbreviatio)	
III Rg 8	32689–32867	III Rg 21 / Josephus
III Rg 9,1–10	32868–32970	III Rg 22
III Rg 9,11–21	32971–33064	(III Rg 24) / Josephus
III Rg 10,27	33065–33078	
III Rg 10,16–23	33079–33106	
III Rg 9,26–28	33107–33160	III Rg 25 / (Jose.) (attrib.)
III Rg 9,22–23	33161–33222	III Rg 25 / Josephus
III Rg 10,1–13	33223–33320	III Rg 26 / Josephus (attrib.)
	33321–33346	III Rg 26
III Rg 11	33347–33472	III Rg 27 / Josephus (attrib.)
	33473–33478	III Rg 27 (incidentia)

Table 10: continued.

Vulgate	*Weltchronik*	*Hist. Schol.*/os
	33479–33496 Nachruf	
III Rg 12,1–20	33497–33608	III Rg 28
III Rg 12,21–	33609–33694	III Rg 29
III Rg 13	33695–33806	III Rg 29
III Rg 14	33807–33970	III Rg 30
III Rg 15,1–2	33971–33976	III Rg 31
III Rg 15,3–8 & II Par 13	33977–34044	
III Rg 15 & II Par 14	34045–34144	III Rg 32
III Rg 16 & II Par 16	34145–34238	III Rg 32
III Rg 16 & II Par 16	34239–34304	III Rg 33 & 34
III Rg 17	34305–34418	III Rg 34
III Rg 18	34419–34680	III Rg 35
III Rg 19	34681–34828	III Rg 36
III Rg 20	34829–35096	III Rg 37 & 38
III Rg 21	35097–35218	III Rg 39
III Rg 22 & II Par 19–21	35219–35559	III Rg 40
	35560–35562 auth. com.	
	35563–35574	IV Rg 1
IV Rg 1,2–end	35575–35672	IV Rg 1 (probable)
IV Rg 2	35673–35854	IV Rg 2 & 3 (probable)
IV Rg 3	35855–36052	IV Rg 4 (probable)
IV Rg 4	36053–36339	IV Rg 5–7 (probable)
IV Rg 5	Anhang I: 1–172	IV Rg 8 (probable)
	Anhang II: 1–69 prayer	

Explanation of Table

The **first column** shows the equivalent chapters of the Bible, regardless of whether it was the *direct* source of the section in the *Weltchronik* to which it corresponds.

The **second column** gives the lines of the *Weltchronik* in Ehrismann's edition. The number of lines per section varies. Generally it corresponds to a chapter of the Vulgate; sometimes to a chapter of the *Historia scholastica* where this subdivision seems more in keeping with the structure of the *Weltchronik*.

The **third column** shows parallels with the *Historia scholastica* and/or other possible sources. The abbreviations used to refer to books of the *Historia scholastica* are as those for the Vulgate, except that the books of Kings are numbered throughout as I–IV Rg.

The abbreviations used to refer to other works are:

Hon. Aug. Honorius Augustodunensis, *De imagine mundi*
Gloss Glossa ordinaria
Jose. Josephus Flavius, *Antiquitates Judaicae*
Otto Otto von Freising, *Chronica sive historia de duabus civitatibus*
Frutolf Frutolf von Michelsberg, *Chronicon Universale*

Where there is a close correspondence which indicates probable direct consultation of a work other than the Vulgate, the source reference has been underlined. Where the variation is so great that direct consultation seems very unlikely, the reference has been placed in parentheses.

Table 10: continued.

3.2.2 Discussion of Table 10: Distribution of Comestor material

As the table shows, the distribution of material from the *Historia scholastica* in Rudolf's *Weltchronik* is very uneven. Whereas in Rudolf's coverage of Genesis direct parallels are restricted to a few details, in his narration of the events of Exodus he draws heavily on Comestor, so that almost no chapter in the Bible remains 'uncontaminated', though the Vulgate is still the main source here. The section corresponding to the book of Leviticus is less than 300 lines long, but details from the *Historia scholastica* are included. Rudolf takes much from Comestor's account of Numbers, and for his treatment of Deuteronomy Comestor is the main source. For the events of the book of Joshua the Vulgate is again the main source with extra material from Comestor; the same applies to the book of Judges, though use of Comestor is more consistent here. The books of Samuel contain evidence of some use of Comestor, and in the many cases where Rudolf refers to Josephus at this point in his narration, the direct source is frequently the *Historia scholastica*. The same is true of Rudolf's account of the events of the books of Kings: there is little non-biblical substance, but Rudolf's combination of material from Kings and Chronicles makes it likely that Comestor, who also follows this procedure, is the direct source.

It is assumed that Rudolf's authorship ceased at line 33321, though his death is not referred to until line 33479 ff. This 'first continuation' from line 33321 shows more dependence on the *Historia scholastica* and continues the practice of combining the accounts of the Bible books of Kings and Chronicles. The second continuation (corresponding to IV Rg 5), appended in Ehrismann's edition, and not contained in his main manuscript, also shows strong similarities with Comestor.

3.3 The *Historia scholastica* and the Sources of the *Weltchronik*

3.3.1 Analysis of a Section from the Account of Exodus in Rudolf's *Weltchronik*

The following section examines Rudolf's narration of the events surrounding the birth and early life of Moses with regard to the position of, and approach to, the *Historia scholastica*.[15] The beginning of this passage is discussed above as an introduction to the problems encountered in the analysis of the sources of the *Weltchronik*, but whereas there the emphasis lay on the extent of

[15] For the commentary tradition on Exodus, see the discussion of Comestor's sources, section 1.2.1.

Rudolf's use of Comestor, here it is the way in which the material is processed by the later author which is at the forefront of the investigation.

The first forty lines of Rudolf's treatment of Exodus[16] have been discussed in detail in section 3.2.1. Rudolf interweaves material from the Vulgate and the *Historia scholastica*, though the function of the Comestor material seems at this point to be merely to corroborate the Vulgate version. The following analysis will focus on the *Weltchronik*'s account of the birth and early life of Moses (*Wchr* 8877–9271; Ex 2:1–10) as here the *Historia scholastica* fulfils a different function as a source also of narrative material. As in the earlier passage, though, Rudolf fits his source material to his conception of his work, expanding and contracting the account at will.

His first adaptation is to make Moses' father the highest of the Israelites, and he omits the fact, mentioned in both Exodus and the *Historia scholastica*, that Moses' parents are of the same tribe. In the Vulgate they are first named in Exodus 6:20, but Rudolf follows Comestor in giving this information before the birth of Moses. He mentions only one of the two versions of the father's name suggested by Comestor. There appears to have been some variation also in the mother's name, and Ehrismann here favours the reading in his second manuscript (p) in calling her Jacobet.[17] His main manuscript (Z) gives 'Jocabet', which corresponds with Migne; however, 'Jacobeth' is the more common reading in the printed tradition of the *Historia scholastica* (see section 1.4).

Exodus 2	*Weltchronik*	*Historia scholastica*
[1]egressus est post haec de domo Levi accepta uxore stirpis suae	do was bi dén Leviten in dem geslehte von Levi der hohste under in der in was bi. der selbe was Amram genant und Jacobet sin wip: [...]	Cap. V. *De ortu, et educatione Moysi.* 'Egressus est post haec vir levita (*Exod.* II)', nomine Aram, vel Amram, qui accepit uxorem contribulem nomine Jocabeth, [...] (col. 1143)

Rudolf then adds a description of Jacobet's character, where she is praised for the same virtues as the Hebrew midwives, for which she too is rewarded:

[16] Exodus in the *Weltchronik* covers lines 8406–12,910.

[17] Universitätsbibliothek Heidelberg, Cod. pal. germ. 146 [p]. See Ehrismann's introduction 'Das Verhältnis der Handschriften', p. XXXV: 'Der Hauptzug von p ist eine große Treue gegen die Überlieferung. An vielen Stellen hat p das Ursprüngliche bewahrt, wo Z [then Wernigerode, now München Cgm 8345] und noch mehr P [UB Heidelberg, Cod. pal. germ. 327], oder ZP, ändern. In solchen, oft gerade textkritisch schwierigen Fällen steht also p an Zuverlässigkeit sogar vor Z' and p. XXXVI: 'Für die Herstellung des Textes war also Z zu Grunde zu legen und p notwendig als Korrektiv beizuziehen. P konnte seinerseits wieder in Zweifelsfällen zwischen Z und p den Ausschlag geben'.

'die vant / man îe mit demuͤte / gein Gote und in wibis guͤte, / des si empfie vil werden lon (ll. 8881–8884). Moses' siblings are also introduced into the account now: 'der beider sun hiez Aaron / und ein tohter hiez Maria' (ll. 8885–8886). In the Bible and the *Historia scholastica* they are not mentioned until later.

The subsequent section of the *Weltchronik* has no equivalent in the Bible:

Weltchronik

do Amram die not alda,
den kumber und das ungemah
an sinim liebin kúnne sach,
er meit sin wip, lag bi ir niht
von der vorhte zůversiht,
ob in wrde ein sun geborn,
das er den muͤste han virlorn
durh der lantlúte gebot.
do irschein im in dem slafe Got
und hiez in das er pflege
sins wibis und bi ir lege:
wand im wurde ein sun geborn,
der ze vorhte wurde irchorn
Egipte dem lande da.

Historia scholastica

[...] qui nolebat accedere ad uxorem post edictum, malens carere liberis quam in necem procreare. Cui Deus per somnium astitit, ut ait Josephus, dicens, ne timeret uxorem cognoscere, quia puer, quem timebant Aegyptii, nasciturus esset ex ea: etiam de sacerdotio Aaron significavit. (col. 1143)

Here one can see how Rudolf treats Comestor's account as the skeleton which he then pads out with flesh in a process of rhetorical elaboration. The German text appeals to the emotions: it stresses the horror of the times and Amram's difficult decision, and the story comes alive. A transition has taken place between factual history and true life story. Rudolf is as concerned as Comestor about the truth of his account, but is also aware of his lay audience and their demands. The human aspect of Moses' conception is also more apparent in the German text's 'bi sinem wibe lag er sa, / dú wart eins suns swanger do' (ll. 8901–2) than in the Vulgate's 'quae concepit' and Comestor's 'Tandem concepit mulier'.

Rudolf omits the *Historia scholastica*'s prophecy of the priest Aaron at this point (the incident, though not the name, has already been mentioned in ll. 8535–8546), and instead anticipates the joy of the Israelites in subsequent generations: 'des wart sit al das kúnne vro / das in dén selben jaren / Israhelis kint gebaren, / an dén der zwelf geslehte stam / urhap und anegenge nam' (ll. 8903–8907). Here, as above (ll. 8886–8889), Rudolf is interested not only in the individual characters and events, but in their place in the whole of Sacred History.

Then Moses is born; the German text omits Comestor's extra details about the silence and the ease of the birth:

Exodus 2	*Weltchronik*	*Historia scholastica*
2(cont.) et peperit filium et videns eum elegantem abscondit tribus mensibus	Do das kint geborn wart, ez was nach menschlichir art so minnenclich, so wol getan das ih des niht gelesen han das îe ouge davor ê schoner kint gesehe me. des wurdin si do beide von liebe und ouh von leide beidú trurig unde vro vater unde mûter do: ir vroide was das er geborn in was, und mûster sin virlorn das were ir hohstes herzeleit. mit listeclichir kúndekeit dú mûter do des kindis wielt: drie manode sis behielt und barch ez, swie im kindis site in kindis sitin wontin mite, so heinlike und virborgen gar das ez niman wart gewar, [...]	'[...] et peperit filium' sub silentio, eo quod non multum ei dolores partus institerint. 'Et videns puerum elegantem, abscondit eum tribus mensibus. [...]' (col. 1143)

The child's extraordinary beauty is commented on later in the *Historia scholastica*,[18] but the hyperbolic statement that he was so lovely that 'ih niht gelesen han / das îe ouge davor ê / schoner kint gesehe me' (an exclusively literary viewpoint) is Rudolf's own, and can be compared with the subsequent statement that 'kint nie bas irzogen wart' (l. 9003), as a feature of his narrative style. The idea of mingled joy and sorrow at the birth of the endangered son is also an addition, as is the emphasis on the difficulties of keeping such a young child hidden from the world.

The passage about the making of the basket again shows parallels with the *Historia scholastica*:

Exodus 2	*Weltchronik*	*Historia scholastica*
3 cumque iam celare non posset sumpsit fiscellam scirpeam et linivit eam bitumine ac pice posuitque intus infantulum	bis das si fúrhten des began das si virratin wurde dran und man ez wrde innen. do hiez si ir gewinnin ein wol gezúnit kôrbelin, das man sach gevlohten sin, gedrungen nahe alsam ein krebe. mit zehim letten unde klebe hiez si vil wol bestrichen das fúr wazzer und hiez in das vaz	'[...] Cumque celare non posset, sumpsit fiscellam scirpeam' in modum fisci, id est sacci rotundi, vimine complexam, 'et linivit eam bitumine ac pice, et ponens intus infantulum [...]' (col. 1143)

[18] *PL* 198, col. 1144: 'Tantae vero pulchritudinis fuit, ut ait Josephus, ut nullus adeo severus esset, qui ejus aspectui non haereret, multique, dum cernerent eum per plateas ferri, occupationes in quibus studebant, desererent'.

mit vesteklichen sachen
das kindelin virmachen.
Des kindis swester Maria
half das kint virmachin sa
in das vaz.

Comestor's addition to the material in the Vulgate is echoed in the German 'gevlohten..., gedrungen nahe alsam ein krebe'. Rudolf characteristically adds a human touch with the picture of the child's sister helping to put him in the basket, a detail which is not in the source works.[19]

In the subsequent section, Rudolf omits the Bible's statement that the basket was placed in the shelter of the bank, and Comestor's reason for this, and instead implies that the basket was safe by saying that they chose a place where the river was wide and slow-moving:

Exodus 2	*Weltchronik*	*Historia scholastica*
3 (cont.) et exposuit eum in carecto ripae fluminis	[...] als das geschah, si leiten ez an einin bach, der was in gůter maze groz, in senftem vluze er lise vloz. daran gelegen nahe was Pharaonis palas.	[...] in carecto ripae eum exposuit, ne impetu fluminis raperetur, [...] (col. 1143)

The proximity of the chosen spot to the Pharaoh's palace is a detail added by Rudolf.

Moses's sister keeps watch nearby and waits to see what will happen:

Exodus 2	*Weltchronik*	*Historia scholastica*
4 stante procul sorore eius et considerante eventum rei	niht verre nidewendig in da hate sih gefúrdirt hin des kindes swester.	[...] et stante procul sorore parvuli Maria, exspectante rei exitum, ex matris praecepto. (col. 1143)

Here the German text is more similar to the Vulgate than the *Historia scholastica*; Comestor gives slightly more detail, and states that the girl was carrying out her mother's instructions, whereas in the Bible and the *Weltchronik* she appears to act on her own initiative.

In the following passage Comestor quotes the beginning of the Vulgate verse more-or-less verbatim, but adds the name of the Pharaoh's daughter from Josephus. When one turns to the German text one notes that all three of Ehrismann's manuscripts concur in giving 'Termůt' as the girl's name, where Migne has Terimith. The *Historia scholastica* manuscript tradition knew

[19] See Herkommer, *St. Galler Kodex*, p. 240 for further examples of Rudolf's attempts to enliven his material for the entertainment of his readers.

both versions of the name, but 'Termuth' seems to have been more common.[20]

The princess goes down to the river:

Exodus 2	*Weltchronik*	*Historia scholastica*
5 ecce autem descendebat filia Pharaonis ut lavaretur in flumine et puellae eius gradiebantur per crepidinem alvei	[...] ouh was dar von Gotis ordenunge gar Termůt des kúnegis tohter komen: dú wolte, als ih han virnomin, sih han irkůlet inden bah.	'Ecce autem descendit Terimith filia Pharaonis, ut lavaretur in flumine, [...] (col. 1143)

The Pharaoh's daughter's companions are not mentioned explicitly by Comestor or Rudolf. Comestor does not change the reason for the royal trip to the river, but in Rudolf's society princesses do not wash in rivers and he gives an explanation which is more plausible for the readers he has in mind.

The wording of the following passage is closer to the Vulgate than to Comestor, who summarizes extensively:

Exodus 2	*Weltchronik*	*Historia scholastica*
5(cont.) quae cum vidisset fiscellam in papyrione misit unam e famulis suis et adlatam 6 aperiens cernensque in ea parvulum vagientem miserta eius ait de infantibus Hebraeorum est	do si das ko̊rbelin zůvliezen sah mit dem seligen kinde, si hiez ir balde und geswinde das korblin gwinnin. das geschah. do man das korblin uf gebrah, das schonste kint man drinne vant das in davor îe wart bekant.	'[...] quae videns alveolum, et afferre sibi jubens, vidit parvulum vagientem, et miserta est ejus dicens: De infantibus Hebraeorum est hic. Sic enim Deus eum venustaverat ut etiam ab hostibus dignus alimento haberetur. (col. 1143)

The motif of the child's unusual and compelling beauty is not in the Bible, but comes rather through Comestor from Josephus. However, Rudolf merely mentions it as a fact, integrated into the narrative, whereas for Comestor it is part of God's plan (explained in an interpolated comment), and a motivating factor in Moses' adoption by the Pharaoh's daughter. The account of her recognition of his Hebrew descent, quoted from the Vulgate by Comestor, is omitted in the German text.

The princess's decision to adopt the child precedes her search for a wetnurse in Rudolf's account; in the Bible and the *Historia scholastica* it comes after the child is weaned and returned to her:

[20] If the selection of manuscripts I have consulted is representative, 'Termuth' may have been the more common form: *termuth* ABGM; *terimith* F; for manuscript and early printed tradition, see sections 1.3 and 1.4 above.

Weltchronik	*Historia scholastica*
das irkos dú kúnegin ir selbir fúr ein kindelin in der liebe als ob ez were ir kint und sis gebere oder hette geborn. do ez wart von ir irkorn ze kinde und si sihs underwant, si besante sa zehant dar ein lantwip, dú solte ez sorgin. als si wolte im die brust bieten dar, ez nam ir dekeine war und kerte sih hin widir dan: ir brust woltez niht recken an.	Et cum Aegyptiae plures ei admovissent ubera ad lactandum, faciem advertebat. (col. 1143)

The initial attempt to find an Egyptian wet-nurse, which fails when the child rejects the breast, is an addition of Comestor's from Josephus and does not occur in the account in the Bible. Rudolf modifies the account slightly in having just one Egyptian where Comestor has several.

Miriam offers to find a Hebrew wet-nurse:

Exodus 2	*Weltchronik*	*Historia scholastica*
7cui soror pueri vis inquit ut vadam et vocem tibi hebraeam mulierem quae nutrire possit infantulum	Als das des kindis swester sah, si stůnt da bi unde sprah zer kúnegin, ob si wo̊lte das si ir gewinnen so̊lte zammin ein ebreische wip, dú ir zuge des kindis lip.	Et ait Maria: Vis, inquit, Hebræam adducam, forte ubera gentis suae sequetur. (col. 1143)

Rudolf's wording is closer to the Vulgate than the *Historia scholastica*, though the information is the same in both sources; he refers to 'des kindis swester' rather than 'Maria', and the phrase 'ein ebreische wip, dú ir zuge des kindis lip' is almost an exact translation of the Vulgate.

The child's mother is fetched and is charged by the unsuspecting princess with the office of foster-mother:

Exodus 2	*Weltchronik*	*Historia scholastica*
8respondit vade perrexit puella et vocavit matrem eius 9ad quam locuta filia Pharaonis accipe ait puerum istum et nutri mihi ego tibi dabo mercedem tuam suscepit mulier et nutrivit puerum adultumque tradidit filiae Pharaonis 10quem illa adoptavit in locum filii	das lopte si. do ilte dan des kindis swester und gewan sin můter ime zammen dar. von Gotis ordenunge gar si sih des kindes undirwant	Et praecepto ergo Terimith abiens, matrem parvuli, tanquam alienam, adduxit, et accessit ad ejus ubera puer. (col. 1143)

Here the exact source is again not clear. The adoption of the child, which has already taken place in the German account, occurs at this point in the Bible's order of events. The explicit mention of God's guiding hand in the proceedings is slightly reminiscent of the passage in the *Historia scholastica* relating to the function of the child's beauty (discussed above), though Rudolf's statement is more general, whereas for Comestor God plays a direct and specific role.

In the discussion of Moses' name, Rudolf combines the wording of the *Historia scholastica* and the Vulgate:

Exodus 2	*Weltchronik*	*Historia scholastica*
10(cont.) vocavitque nomen eius	das kint wart Moyses genant:	et dictus est Moyses. Aegyptii
Mosi dicens	wan dú juncfrŏwe den knaben	enim *Moys*, aquam, *is* salvatum
quia de aqua tuli eum	uz dem wazer hat irhaben	dicunt. (cols 1143 – 1144)
	ubir Egipte das lant.	
	das wazir ist Moys genant:	
	da von wart er alda zehant	
	nah Moys Moyses genant,	
	den Got der israhelschen diet	
	ze einim hûter uz beschiet,	
	das er ir lerere	
	Gotis ê und gerihtes were,	
	als úns dú scrift urkúnde git.	

Rudolf first paraphrases 'quia de aqua tuli eum', and then goes on to explain this, though unlike Comestor he only gives the meaning of the first syllable 'Moys'. Rudolf characteristically places the event within its broader context and emphasizes Moses' role in the whole of Salvation History. The rhetorical formula 'als úns dú scrift urkúnde git' occurs frequently throughout the work and stresses the truth and authenticity of the account.[21]

The order of Rudolf's account again differs from the Bible in the following passage, which has its equivalent in the Vulgate before the naming of the child:

Exodus 2	*Weltchronik*
9 ad quam locuta filia Pharaonis	nah der selben tage zit,
accipe ait puerum istum et nutri mihi	da Moyses fúr ungelogen
ego tibi dabo mercedem tuam	von sinir mûter wart irzogen,
suscepit mulier et nutrivit puerum	das nah mûterlichir art
adultumque tradidit filiae Pharaonis	kint nie bas irzogen wart,
	si brahte ez Termûte.
	dú londe ir wol mit gûte
	der mûterlichir erbeit
	die si hate an das kint geleit.

[21] See von Tippelskirch, *Geschichtsauffassung*, pp. 61–72.

The *Historia scholastica* has no reference to Jacobet being paid for her services as wet-nurse.

The Midrashic story of the infant Moses throwing the Pharaoh's crown on the floor (ll. 9008–9070) is narrated by Comestor, partly from Josephus, partly from other, possibly oral, sources.[22] Rudolf expands the material considerably, imagining what happens in more detail. The first scene describes the presentation of the child to the Pharaoh:

Weltchronik

Nu brahte ouh das kindelin
Termût dú junge kúnegin
ir vater Pharaone
einis tagis, da er mit krone
saz mit hohir werdekeit,
und was mit richeit geleit
groz vliz an sine krone.
nah ir abgot Hamone
was ein bilde irhaben vor,
das stûnt uf der krone embor,
als ez dort stûnt da wip und man
in ir bethûs ez betten an:
das was algemeine
von edelem gesteine
uf golde wol durhvieret.
dú krone was gezieret
mit richeit kúnigliche.
Pharao der riche
empfie das kint mit vroiden groz
und saztes fúr sih uf sin schoz.
er sach ez minnenchlichen an:
vil sere in wundirn began
wie ez nah wunsche were so gar,
so schone gar, so wol gevar
und also wunschliche gestalt.
sin zarten was vil manigvalt,
das er tet dem kinde alda.
uf des houbit sazter sa
die krone.

Historia scholastica

Quem dum quadam die Terimith obtulisset Pharaoni, ut et ipse eum adoptaret, admirans rex pueri venustatem, coronam, quam tunc forte gestabat, capiti illius imposuit. Erat autem in ea Ammonis imago fabrefacta. (col. 1144)

Rudolf omits the question of the Pharaoh adopting Moses, and concentrates instead on depicting the scene, elaborating on the data which Comestor provides. We are presented with a picture of the Pharaoh seated in state on his throne; Comestor's simple statement that the crown contained a statue of Ammon serves as a cue for Rudolf to explain who Ammon is, where the statuette came from, and how it is set into the crown with surrounding gold and jewels; he expands Comestor's phrase 'admirans rex pueri venustatem'

22 See section 1.2 on Comestor's sources.

into a hyperbolic statement about the child's perfect beauty and a description of the delighted and affectionate Pharaoh dandling him on his knee.

Comestor's main source here is Josephus. However, the reference to Ammon is not known in any version of this story before the *Historia scholastica*, so that here one can see how at each step the author combines material inherited from the source and his own additions, according to his own interpretation and agenda. Comestor, the lecturer in biblical history, is concerned particularly with the motivations of biblical characters; Rudolf, who wishes not only to instruct, but also to entertain, presents a more visual account.[23]

The moment is ruined when the child snatches the crown and throws it on the ground, where it smashes into fragments:

Weltchronik

do greif dar der knabe
und zuhte si vil balde drabe
und warf si mit unwerde
nidir uf die erde,
das si ze stucken gar zerbrah.

Historia scholastica

Puer autem coronam projecit in terram, et fregit. (col. 1144)

Here each action which makes up the account is broken down into its constituent parts and qualified: 'projecit' becomes 'greif', 'zuhte vil balde' and 'warf mit unwerde'; 'fregit' becomes 'zerbrah ze stucken'; and the whole is characterized by the adverbial phrase 'mit unwerde'.

In the subsequent passage Comestor has more detail than Rudolf, who chooses to omit the name of the priest and his action in jumping up from his place by the Pharaoh's side:

Weltchronik

da stůnt ein ewart unde sprah:
'diz ist das kint, des wenich wol,
das noh Egipte stŏren sol.
sit úns das Got iroiget hat,
so tŏden ez, das ist min rat,
das wir beliben sorgin vri!'

Historia scholastica

Sacerdos autem Heliopoleos a latere regis surgens, exclamavit: Hic est puer, quem nobis occidendum Deus monstravit, ut de caetero timore careamus, et voluit irruere in eum, sed auxilio regis liberatus est, [...] (col. 1144)

The priest's words, however, are a close translation of the Latin, with the addition of the phrases 'des wenich wol' and 'das ist min rat', his assessment of the situation and advice. This is another example of Rudolf's slight adjustments of the individual roles at the Pharaoh's court (as in the case of the advisors discussed above). Rudolf omits the priest's attempt to seize Moses.

One of the Pharaoh's advisors argues that the child meant no harm and should be given the benefit of the doubt:

[23] Herkommer, *St. Galler Kodex* (pp. 238–240) discusses Rudolf's dual aspirations (as expressed, for example, in *Wchr* ll. 21712–21715), and points to parallels in his other works.

Weltchronik

nu stůnt ein wisir man dabi,
der began mit warheit jehin
ez were von kintheit geschehen:
das wolter machin in bechant.

Historia scholastica

et persuasione cujusdam sapientis qui per ignorantiam hoc factum esse a puero asseruit. (col. 1144)

Rudolf's own evaluation intrudes with the words 'mit warheit', and a certain amount of suspense is created by the way in which the story is narrated, but the content of the German text is at this point very similar to the Latin.

The subsequent account of the trial by ordeal is again much more elaborate in Rudolf's version than Comestor's. In the German account the incident is divided into two stages: an advice-scene precedes the actual realization of the plan.

The wise-man explains his plan to the Pharaoh:

Weltchronik

er hiez dem kúnege ein glůjenden brant
gen in die hant: grifes den an
da er niht glůte noh embran,
so můster des im helfen jehen,
ez were mit kúndekeit geschehen
und niht von kintlichen siten.

Historia scholastica

In cujus rei argumentum cum prunas allatas puero obtulisset, puer eas ori suo opposuit, [...] (col. 1144)

The difference of approach of the two authors is apparent in the manner of their narration: Comestor conveys the facts; Rudolf describes the scene.

The plan is put swiftly into action:

Weltchronik

do wart langir niht virmitten
ê das man im bot in die hant
einin brenden brant:
den greif ez kintlichen an
vor an dem fúre da er bran,
und stiez in an der selben stunt
also brennenden an den munt
und brand sinir zungen ort,
das er iê darnah sinú wort
mit lispindir zungin sprah.
swer die kintliche site sah,
der half des mit warheit jehen
das ez von kintheit were geschehen.
und hulfen im das er genas.

Historia scholastica

[...] puer eas ori suo opposuit, et linguae suae summitatem igne corrupit. Unde et Hebraei impeditioris linguae eum fuisse autumant. (col. 1144)

Rudolf emphasizes the idea of burning through constant repetition, and draws our attention to the childlike eagerness of the action with the words 'greif' and 'kintlichen'. Speed is conveyed by the phrases 'do wart langir niht virmitten' and 'an der selben stunt'. Rudolf also introduces onlookers who bear witness to the events.

Lines 9074–9167 in Ehrismann's edition relate the anger and sorrow of Termut at this treatment of her adopted son. These lines, which have no parallel in the Bible or the *Historia scholastica*, occur only in a few manuscripts and are assumed, on the basis of their different style and limited occurrence, to be a later addition and not by Rudolf. This fact is noted by Ehrismann in his apparatus.[24] Rudolf's authorship is accepted again from line 9168, and with it the strong correlation with the *Historia scholastica* also resumes:

Weltchronik

Termůt dú junge vrŏwe klůg
das kint do von ir vater truog
an ir heinlihe hin
und leite grozen vliz an in,
das nie mit liebe sunder haz
kint ê wart irzogen baz,
liepliche untz an sinú jar.
nu was so nah wunsche clar
das ez enkein so herter man
an sah das er von im dan
dú ougin môhte bringen.
sin schône konde twingen
der lúte mere danne gnůg.
swa man ez an die straze trůg,
da liezens ir unmůze gar
und namen da niht andirs war
wan das wip unde man
das kint gar můsten sehin an.

Historia scholastica

Tantae vero pulchritudinis fuit, ut ait Josephus, ut nullus adeo severus esset, qui ejus aspectui non haereret, multique, dum cernerent eum per plateas ferri, occupationes in quibus studebant, desererent. (col. 1144)

Here Rudolf's wording corresponds closely with that of the *Historia scholastica*, though he omits the reference to Josephus. There are also strong similarities with the *Antiquitates Judaicae* itself:[25]

Antiquitates

nam quantum ad speciem nullus erat ita severus ut Moysen videns eius pulchritudinem non haereret multisque contingebat dum eum cernerent per plateas ferri, ut converterentur quidem ad aspectum puerum et ea in quibus videbantur studium habere desererent, delectati eius potius visione.

Weltchronik

nu was so nah wunsche clar
das ez enkein so herter man
an sah das er von im dan
dú ougin môhte bringen.
sin schône konde twingen
der lúte mere danne gnůg.
swa man ez an die straze trůg,
da liezens ir unmůze gar
und namen da niht andirs war
wan das wip unde man
das kint gar můsten sehin an.

Historia scholastica

Tantae vero pulchritudinis fuit, ut ait Josephus, ut nullus adeo severus esset, qui ejus aspectui non haereret, multique, dum cernerent eum per plateas ferri, occupationes in quibus studebant, desererent. (col. 1144)

[24] For Ehrismann's principles of edition, see above, n. 17. This passage occurs in his main manuscript, but not in his two subsidiary ones.

[25] Franz Blatt, *Latin Josephus*, p. 200; *PL* 198, col. 1144.

In light of the fact that in both the *Historia scholastica* and Rudolf's *Weltchronik* this passage directly follows the account of the trial of the child (which is not in the *Antiquitates*), it would seem extremely unlikely that Josephus was the direct source for this. However, it cannot be denied that the wording of the German text is slightly more similar to the original than to Comestor's version: 'twingen der lúte mere danne gnůg' is closer to 'multisque contingebat', and 'und namen da niht andirs war wan das wip unde man das kint gar muͤsten sehin an' is closer to 'delectati eius potius visione' than the more concise text in the *Historia scholastica.* It is possible that such similarities indicate some knowledge of the *Antiquitates Judaicae.*[26]

That is the end of the account of Moses' childhood in both the *Weltchronik* and the *Historia scholastica.* Chapter six of Comestor's 'Historia Libri Exodi', and Rudolf's lines 9186–9271 narrate the story of the defeat of the Egyptians, under Moses' leadership, over the Ethiopians, and how Moses takes an Ethiopian wife. The only reference to this incident in the Bible is in Numbers 12,1: 'locutaque est Maria et Aaron contra Mosen propter uxorem eius aethiopissam'; Comestor obtains his information from Josephus and an unknown source (see section 1.2 above).

Weltchronik

Do Moyses irzogen wart
so wol nah lieplicher art
das er, als ich han virnomen,
was ze sinen tagen komen,
die Moͤre von Etiopia
bestůnden mit urlúge sa
die von Egipte mit kraft
und rittens an herhaft
untz Menphin die stat.
das lant lút do dé goͤte bat
das si in helfe tetin kunt.
do seiten si in sa ze stunt
das si in an disin dingin
muͤste misselingen
sin hettin ein ebreischen man, [...]

Historia scholastica

Cap. VI *De uxore Moysi Aethiopissa*
Factum est autem cum adultus fuisset Moyses, Aethiopes vastaverunt Aegyptum, usque ad Memphim et mare, quo circa conversi ad divinationes Aegyptii, acceperunt responsum, ut auxiliatore uterentur Hebraeo; [...] (col. 1144)

With the expression 'als ich han virnomen' Rudolf places himself within a tradition without mentioning a specific source or authority. He refers to the Ethiopians as 'Moͤre' and 'vastaverunt' becomes the much more organized 'bestůnden mit urlúge' and 'rittens an herhaft'. He does not translate 'divinationes' exactly, but instead paraphrases and says that the Egyptians asked their gods for help.

[26] The question of whether Rudolf von Ems used the *Antiquitates* is discussed in section 3.3.2 below.

They will fail without a Hebrew leader:

Weltchronik

der sih ir woͤlte nemen an
und ir houbit herre sin.
do baten si die kúnegin
das si den jungen wisen man
lieze mit in varen dan,
wan er was mit mannis kraft
vreh, kuͤne, wise und ellinthaft,
das er ir pflege uf der vart.
vil kume si des irbeten wart
also das si ir swͤrin,
swa si mit im hin fuͤren,
das er fuͤre mit in uf der vart
vor allem ubil wol bewart:
in dem gedinge hiez si in varn.

Historia scholastica

et vix obtinuerunt a Terimith, ut exercitui, quem paraverant, Moysen praeficeret ducem, prius praestitis sacramentis, ne ei nocerent. Erat autem Moyses vir bellicosus, et peritissimus, [...] (col. 1144)

Here Rudolf takes the most important elements of Comestor's account and narrates them in a slightly different order and combination. The idea of Moses' leadership of the expedition is now linked with the prophecy of the gods; Comestor links the question of leadership with Terimith's permission, which in the German text is more closely linked with the precondition of their promise to take care of him. Moses' bold and fearless nature is now given as a further reason for the Egyptians' choice of him as leader, whereas in the *Historia scholastica* it comes at the beginning of the account of their adventures on the march to Ethiopia, which is omitted by Rudolf.[27]

The virtues ascribed to Moses in line 9207 are again an elaboration of those in the Latin text, and are the same as those ascribed to the Israelites earlier in the account of Exodus, and thus begin to seem like a multipurpose formula.[28] Otherwise the paraphrase is quite close to the *Historia scholastica*, despite the different order. Rudolf includes both the request and the response, where the more succinct Latin gives only the reply, but the princess's reluctance ('vix') and the precondition in the ablative absolute construction are retained in the German phrases 'vil kume' and 'in dem

[27] *PL* 198, col. 1144: 'Erat autem Moyses vir bellicosus, et peritissimus, qui fluminis iter tanquam longius praetermittens, per terram duxit exercitum itinere breviori, ut improvisos Aethiopes praeveniret. Sed per loca plena serpentibus iter faciens, tulit in arcis papireis super plaustra ibices ciconias, id est Aegyptiacas, naturaliter infestas serpentibus, quae rostro per posteriora immisso alvum purgant, castraque metaturus praeferebat eas, ut serpentes fugarent, et devorarent, et ita tutus per noctem transibat exercitus'.

[28] *Wchr* ll. 8493–8497, where the Latin virtues to which they correspond are less war-like and more intellectual. See discussion in section 3.2.1.

gedinge...'. Whereas Comestor's account shows her concern that they themselves might harm the young Israelite, in the German text her worries appear more general.

The parallels with the *Historia scholastica* are less close in the following passage:

Weltchronik

mit dén egiptischen scharn
fůr er inder Mo̊re lant
mit so werlichir hant
das si im entwichen da.
Ein stat hiez Sabbareia,
das was ein stat also genant: [...]

Historia scholastica

Tandem praeventos Aethiopes expugnans inclusit eos fugientes, in civitatem Sabba regiam, quam post Cambyses a nomine sororis suae Meroem denominavit. (col. 1144)

Rudolf again refers to the Ethiopians as Moors. 'Sabbareia' would appear to be a distortion of Comestor's 'Sabba regiam', and occurs in two of Ehrismann's manuscripts, the other (p) has 'Sabaregia'.[29] Comestor's reference to the renaming of Sabba is omitted altogether in the German text.

Rudolf omits the technical details about military tactics here and throughout the account:

Weltchronik

da besaz der wise wigant
Moyses der ellens riche
die Mo̊re gewaltecliche.
nu was in Sabareia
der Moere kúnegis tohter da
besezzen, dú hiez Tarbis.
dú gesach den degin wis
Moysesin den werden man.
als in gesach mit ougin an,
si begunde insinin minnin
so hitzzen unde brinnen
das si mit dem wisin man
getrůg das mit ir botschaft an:
wolter si ze wibe han,
si wolte im machin undirtan
beidú die stat unde das lant.
das wart gelopt.

Historia scholastica

Quam cum, quia inexpugnabilis erat, diutius obsedisset, oculos suos injecit in eum Tarbis filia regis Aethiopum, et ex condicto tradidit ei civitatem, si duceret eam uxorem, et ita factum est. (col. 1144)

Rudolf does not give a reason for the siege. He refers to Moses by the epithets 'der wise wigant' and 'der ellens riche', again stressing wisdom and

[29] For Ehrismann's principles of edition see n. 17 above. Josephus reads 'in Saba civitate regia Aethiopiae quam postea Cambysis Meroin denominavit a sororis suae nomine' (Blatt, *Latin Josephus*, p. 202).

bravery as his two attributes. Characteristically, Rudolf elaborates on Tarbis's feelings for Moses, and where Comestor's 'oculos suos injecit in eum' makes no mentions of love, the German text, written within an established German literary tradition and with a courtly audience in mind, shows her smitten with the traditional symptoms of 'minne'.[30] It is also in keeping with the different aims of the two authors that Comestor, the lecturer on biblical history, links this event with the corresponding reference in the Vulgate, where Rudolf, the historical novelist, does not find this information relevant.[31]

The economical mention of the pact and marriage in the *Historia scholastica* ('ita facta est') forms the basis for a much more detailed account in the *Weltchronik*:

Weltchronik

do wart zehant
des nahtes im gegeben dú stat
und sie mit dén si was besat,
damitte der wise wigant
des landes not gar ubirwant
und wart im das edil wip.
dú mintin fúrbaz danne ir lip
und trůg im also holden můt
das si den wisin degin gůt
nie wolte lazen von ir hein:
swie dicke er des wart inein
das er ze lande wolte
keren und da solte
billiche unde gerne sehen
sin frúnt, des lie si niht geschehen
und wante das. das můte in.

Historia scholastica

Dum autem redire voluisset, non acquievit uxor. (col. 1144)

Rudolf gives the motivations of the two protagonists, and in so doing creates characters for them. Tarbis, in Comestor's account merely a hindrance to be overcome, in Rudolf's emerges as a sympathetic character whose only fault is that of being too possessive of the man she loves. Moses is drawn back

[30] In this Rudolf again draws closer to the older source, Josephus, though the correspondences are occasional and only on the level of the nature of the account, so that direct consultation remains highly improbable: 'Tharbis filia regis Aethiopum fuit. dum haec Moysen circa muros exercitum applicantem fortiterque pugnantem videret eius efficaciam experientiamque mirata et desperantibus iam pridem Aegyptiis libertatis auctorem eum extitisse bono suae felicitatis existimans. Aethiopibus scilicet exultantibus in his quae contra eos gesserant, eum tunc periculis inhaerere conspiciens, in amorem eius est lapsa crudeliter, et cum passio praevaleret, misit ad eum fidelissimos servulorum, ut ei de nuptiis loquerentur', Blatt, *Latin Josephus*, p. 203; see Mark Balfour, 'Moses and the Princess: Josephus' *Antiquitates Judaicae* and the *Chansons de Geste*', *Medium Aevum* 64 (1995), pp. 1–16.

[31] 'Inde est quod Maria et Aaron jurgati sunt adversus Moysen pro uxore ejus Aethiopissa (*Num.* XII)', *PL* 198, col. 1144.

to Egypt by a feeling of duty and a desire to see his friends again. This is more than mere rhetorical elaboration: it shows the story-teller at work, making his dry historical fact more palatable for his readers.

Comestor too enjoys a good story:

Weltchronik

nu hater alse wisen sin
das er wol mit dén listen sin
meistern kunde ein vingerlin
mit solichir meisterschaft
das ein wip mit sinir kraft
vergezzen můste, als ih ez las,
swas ir allir liebeste was,
das si das uz ir můte lie,
so si das vingerlin gevie,
und ez virgaz alse gar
das sis nam niemer mere war
und ez ir uz dén sinnen kam.
als si das vingerlin genam,
si virgaz sin sa zehant.
do fůr der junge wigant
Moyses der wise man
von ir ze lande widir dan,
da er nah selichlichir art
lieplih und wol empfangen wart.

Historia scholastica

Proinde Moyses tanquam vir peritus astrorum duas imagines sculpsit in gemmis hujus efficaciae, ut altera memoriam, altera oblivionem conferret. Cumque paribus annulis eas inseruisset, alterum, scilicet oblivionis annulum, uxori praebuit; alterum ipse tulit, ut sic pari amore, sic paribus annulis insignirentur. Coepit ergo mulier amoris viri oblivisci, et tandem libere in Aegyptum regressus est. (col. 1144)

Here there are more differences than similarities: in Comestor's account there are two rings and it is the inset figures sculpted from precious stones which have the opposite effects of conferring memory and oblivion; in Rudolf's account Moses fashions one ring, which has the more specific effect of making a woman forget what is dearest to her. This raises the question of whether the *Historia scholastica* is the source here at all, or whether other intermediary or earlier sources may have been consulted by Rudolf. Comestor's own source for this has not been traced (see section 1.2.1 above); possibly it might also prove to be the basis of Rudolf's account. With the familiar phrase 'als ih ez las' Rudolf attests the authority of a written tradition without giving a specific source.

Moses' joyful home-coming and welcome (ll. 9269–9271) are also not mentioned by Comestor.

The remaining 3400 lines of Rudolf's coverage of the events of Exodus follow much the same pattern of alternating between and combining elements from the Vulgate and the *Historia scholastica*. This is substantially the same pattern as was observed in the case of the *Schwarzwälder Predigten* discussed above, and raises similar questions about the actual method of composition and the role played by the source works in this. The unusual manuscript tradition of the sermon collection allows an insight into the probable method of its authors: it appears that there material from different sources was added in several stages. This may also have been the approach of Rudolf von Ems. However, if this was his method, it seems likely that the task of compiling the material from the different source works occurred at an early stage in the composition: the finely crafted verse of the final version mingles elements of varying provenance in a seamless whole. It is impossible to assess the role of memory in this process; sometimes the wording of the German is so close to the Latin that it seems that it must be a direct and immediate translation, but the presence of elements from different sources would then have to imply a complicated, and frequently apparently non-functional, synoptic approach.

If one tries to characterize the type of material Rudolf draws from the *Historia scholastica* in the section of the account of Exodus discussed above, the following picture emerges. The most substantial sections based on the *Historia scholastica* are the apocryphal legends which derive from midrashic commentary and which Comestor includes from Josephus and other unknown sources. Rudolf also frequently includes those sections which give the motivations of the protagonists, such as the reasons for the Egyptians' hatred of the Jews, for the Pharaoh's decision to spare female babies, or for Amram's reversing his decision to refrain from sexual relations with his wife. Extra details such as the name of the Pharaoh's daughter are also added from the *Historia scholastica*, but Comestor's onomastic and etymological explanations are generally omitted. Where Comestor outlines a theological debate or suggests various interpretations for a difficult passage of the Bible, Rudolf tends to omit all element of discussion and incorporate one or more of the suggestions into the narrative (as is the case with the interpretation of the 'civitates tabernaculorum' built by the oppressed Israelites).[32]

These are the general tendencies observed in the analysis of the above section. However, Rudolf's approach defies any attempt to oversystematize: there is no apparent reason, for example, for his decision not to include the

[32] Herkommer, 'Die Beziehung zur Bibelexegese', in: *St. Galler Kodex*, pp. 203–218, gives three examples where Rudolf does include elaborate theological discussions from the *Historia scholastica*, the *Glossa ordinaria* and other sources; these are the exceptions in a work which concentrates firmly on the historical narrative. Rudolf's occasional allegorical interpretation of objects and incidents from the Old Testament can be seen as part of his emphasis on history as a process, on the links between the figures and of events of those times and his own.

information about Moses' daring strategy to overtake the Ethiopian plunderers by leading his Egyptian army along a more direct but dangerous route.

The most striking point in common of the material which is characteristically included by Rudolf from the *Historia scholastica* in the above section is its provenance from Jewish sources, either Josephus or the Midrash. The more discursive interpretation from the Christian commentary tradition tends to be omitted, which is perhaps what one would expect, given the different nature of Rudolf's project: to produce an entertaining narrative. This is a particular aspect of the role of the *Historia scholastica* as a mediator between different traditions: material from different sources and traditions is collected by Comestor and is passed on in this synthesis to the vernacular author. The recurrent problem, as has been discussed above, is determining whether Rudolf has consulted Comestor's own sources directly. This question has occupied scholars throughout the past hundred-and-fifty years of investigation into Rudolf's sources. It has been discussed in the above section with relation to the Vulgate; the following section will concern the question of whether Josephus' *Antiquitates Judaicae* are a direct source for the *Weltchronik*.

3.3.2 The *Historia scholastica* and the *Antiquitates Judaicae* as Sources of the *Weltchronik*

This section will discuss the relationship between the *Historia scholastica* and one of its own main sources, the *Antiquitates Judaicae* of Josephus Flavius, as possible direct sources for the *Weltchronik*. One of the functions of the *Historia scholastica* for Rudolf von Ems is to provide him with citations of earlier authorities, such as Pseudo-Methodius or Pseudo-Philo.[33] However, in other cases, particularly the *incidentia* which refer to contemporary events in secular history, Comestor provides the cue for Rudolf to consult other works which give more detail. The question of whether Comestor is the direct source of the eighteen citations of Josephus in the *Weltchronik* has been addressed, but left open, by Tippelskirch, and perhaps a more systematic approach, with detailed textual analysis of the parallel passages, can lend closer definition to the picture she outlines.[34]

Tippelskirch compares Migne's *Historia scholastica* with the German translation of the original Greek version of Josephus' *Antiquitates Judaicae*,

[33] Tippelskirch, *Geschichtsauffassung*, pp. 27–33.
[34] Tippelskirch, *Geschichtsauffassung*, pp. 38–48.

whilst realizing the limitations of this approach. She is dubious about the representativeness of Migne (see section 1.4 above) and of this version of the *Antiquitates*, which was known, in the Middle Ages, not in Greek, but in a sixth-century Latin translation.[35] The present study is based on the Latin text of the *Antiquitates* and checks Migne against the earlier transmission of the *Historia scholastica* in cases of doubt.[36] Tippelskirch's further reservation, that one cannot assess the extent to which Rudolf's copy of the *Historia scholastica* contained marginal notes which referred more frequently to Josephus, cannot be countered, but is a commonplace for all studies of reception.[37]

That Comestor is not the direct source of all of the citations is demonstrated by the occurrence in the *Weltchronik* of material which is derived, directly or indirectly, from the *Antiquitates*, but which has no equivalent in the *Historia scholastica.* The one clear-cut example of this is Rudolf's praise of the witch of Endor, who recalls Samuel from the dead at Saul's request. As Tippelskirch states, this material, which is correctly attributed to Josephus, cannot be found in the *Historia scholastica.*[38] Comestor is familiar with Josephus' version of this event and alludes to it, but is preoccupied with the difficult matter of whether a witch can have the power to resuscitate a dead prophet, and does not present the Pytonisse as a positive figure. Rudolf's account corresponds closely to that of Josephus:

Antiquitates

Iustum est autem laudare mulieris largitatem. quia licet eius ars a rege fuisset exerceri prohibita. tamen dum venissent in domum eius quos nunquam viderat prius. non habuit mali memoriam vituperando eum qui eius prohibuerat disciplinam. nec auisata est peregrinum. et cuius consuetudinem nequaquam habuerat. sed condoluit et consolata est. dum eum cognouisset regem. et circa quem potuerat animo ingrata consistere. eum pocius ut

Weltchronik

Nu lobit lobeliche
Josephus der künste riche
an dem heidinischim wibe
die tugint an ir libe
das si groze gůte
begie mit demůte
das so dem half das er genas,
der davor ir vient was,
und sin so lobeliche gar

[35] See section 1.2. Tippelskirch, *Geschichtsauffassung*, p. 38, note 25, wrongly attributes the translation to Rufinus, who translated Josephus' other major work, the Jewish War, in the fourth century.

[36] Blatt, *Latin Josephus*, provides a critical edition of the first five books of the *Antiquitates*; for the remaining books I have used the incunable printed by J. Schüssler in Augsburg in 1470 (which has no page-numbering). For the transmission of the work, see Blatt's introduction.

[37] Tippelskirch, *Geschichtsauffassung*, p. 46.

[38] Josephus, *Ant*, VI, xiv, col. 2; (compare *PL* 198, cols 1320–1321); Tippelskirch, *Geschichtsauffassung*, p. 42.

comederet inuitabat. et quod ei solummodo in paupertate fuerat. hoc libenter largiterque conferebat. non aliquam retribucionem eius expectans. non munus aliquid aucupans. quippe quem proxime moriturum agnouerat cum plerumque natura sit hominum. boni aliquid aut repensaturis beneficium exhibere. aut a quibus aliquid se credunt accipere. his mutuare. Bonum est ergo illam imitari mulierem. et benefacere cunctis egentibus. et nichil arbitrari melius esse. nec amplius aliquid generi humano conpetere. potius quam hoc. ut deum propitium et boni largitorem semper habeamus. Igitur de illa muliere dixisse sufficiat.

nam mit so richir spise war,
doch ir das rechte were irchant
das si darnah von sinir hant
empfienge niemir lop noh dang,
wan das ir hohe tugint si twang
dass imz so minnencliche bot
und si douh wúste sinin tot
kúnftig an dem andern tage.
dén tuginde richin zeinir hage,
dén kargen ze itewizze
lopter mit solhem vlize
des selbin wibis gůtlich gůt,
das îegelich mensche den můt,
das tugint irchennen wolte,
dabi wol bezzern solte
und in vroelichir wise
teilen sine spise
dem der zůzim kerte,
darnah dú state lerte,
durh Gotis lon, durh ere,
nah gotlichir lere,
alse Got und rehter tuginde rat
geboten und geleret hat.

Rudolf paraphrases fairly exactly, though some changes have occurred: Rudolf prefers the more general 'tugint' to Josephus' 'largitas', which corresponds to 'guͤte' in line 25883 and 'guͤtlich gůt' in line 25899. He also praises the woman's 'demuͤte'. He omits Josephus cynical comment about human nature and instead stresses the moral purpose of this eulogy: to strengthen the virtuous in their good intentions and show up the mean. Rudolf paraphrases 'benefacere' as 'teilen sine spise', in this case more specific than Josephus. 'deum propitium' is translated exactly as 'Gotis lon', but Rudolf adds 'ere' to the benefits one will receive from following the example of the Pytonisse's generosity. In this case the correspondences are so close that one can state with a high degree of certainty that Rudolf followed Josephus' text, and that his citation refers to direct consultation.

Sometimes Rudolf combines material from the *Antiquitates* with material from the *Historia scholastica.* One example of this is information about the reasons for Saul's death, again attributed to Josephus:[39]

Antiquitates	*Weltchronik*	*Historia scholastica*
Hunc itaque finem saul prophetante samuel habuit. quia obediens deo non fuit. propter man-	Nu sprichit Josephus also, das Got bi dén ziten do ubir Saulen die erbeit	'Historia libri I Regum', Cap. XXVIII. *De morte Saul et filiorum ejus.* [...]

[39] Josephus, *Ant*, VI, xiv, col. 7; *PL* 198, cols 1323–1324; Tippelskirch, *Geschichtsauffassung*, p. 43.

data que contra amalechitas acceperat et quod abimelech sacerdotis generacionem. et ipsum abimilech. et sacerdotum vna peremit vrbem, [...]

sante und ouh das herzeleit
und das klagelich ungemah
das im inder zit geschah
an libe, an kindin, dú das lebin
so jemirliche mûsten gebin,
durh drú ding dú er begie:
das er das kúnne lebin lie
von Amalech, das Gotis gebot
in toedin hiez, damit er got
mit zornne irzurnde sere;
ouh rach Got an im mere
das er der ewarten schar
hiez ane schulde slahin gar,
do si trûgen redelichú kleit;
ouh rah Got die tumpheit
das er mit zoubir hiez besehen
was im solte geschehin,
die Phitonisse und das sin eit
so dicke mit unwarheit
ubirgie und zerbrah
mit wanche dú wort dú er sprach,
[...]

Nota quod in Paralipomenon legitur: 'Mortuus est Saul propter iniquitates suas (*I Paral. X*),' et additur, quasi in cumulum peccati, sed insuper consuluit pythonissam, propter quod interfecit eum Dominus.

Rudolf gives three reasons, of which two can be found in the *Antiquitates* and the third in the *Historia scholastica* and the Vulgate.[40] He combines the material from various sources. This is another passage which can be used to argue for the theory that Josephus was a direct source for the *Weltchronik*.

Direct consultation of the *Antiquitates* is also a possibility in Rudolf's account of the evil spirits which torment King Saul:[41]

Antiquitates

Samuel quidem dum hec monuisset abscessit. diuinitas autem ad dauid saul relicto migrauit Et ille quidem prophetare cepit. scito super se spiritus veniente. saul vero quedam passiones et demonia repente comprehenderunt suffocaciones ei et angustias inferentes.

Weltchronik

Dú schrift dú dirre warheit giht,
hat úns bescheiden rehte niht
was geistis Saule were gesant.
nu tût úns Josephus irchant:
do Saule der gûte geist benomen
was und us sinin sinin komen,
ein valschir geist troug in die naht,
der in stetecliche an vaht
mit túvillichin bilden gar,
dú der tievil fúr in dar
brachte unde in irschrachte mite:

Historia scholastica

'Historia libri I Regum', Cap. XVI. *De unctione David in domo patris.*

Et recessit Spiritus Domini a Saul, et exagitabat eum spiritus nequam missus 'a Domino.' Dicit Josephus David tunc accepisse spiritum propheticum, sicut ille quidem prophetare coepit, sancto super se Spiritu veniente. Sed quia dictum est spiritum recessisse a Saul, et directum in David, videtur

[40] I Par 10,13–14: 'mortuus est ergo Saul propter iniquitates suas / eo quod prevaricatus sit mandatum Domini quod praeceperat et non custodierit illud sed insuper etiam pythonissam consuluerit / nec speravit in Domino / propter quod et interfecit eum et transtulit regnum eius ad David filium Isai'

[41] Josephus, *Ant*, VI, viii, col. 2; *PL* 198, col. 1310; Tippelskirch, *Geschichtsauffassung*, p. 42.

so twungin in sin tobesite
das er uf fůr und sih zewer
sazte gein des tievils her,
der in ze trieginne pflag.

quod de eodem spiritu dicatur, id est, de gratia Spiritus, qua hucusque Saul victor hostium exstiterat.

Here the situation is more complicated. Comestor is familiar with the passage from the *Antiquitates*: he builds on Josephus' reference to prophecy. Rudolf is concerned not so much with David's new powers as with the evil spirits tormenting Saul, but he too refers to Josephus as the source of these extra details. It is difficult to tell at this point whether he consulted Josephus directly: the torments he describes are not in the *Antiquitates*, but Josephus does give more detail on the effects of these devils than the Vulgate or Comestor, so that the attribution would not seem to be completely coincidental. Whether Josephus is consulted directly or not, his name is added here, as in the *Historia scholastica*, to lend the weight of authority to Rudolf's discussion. In this passage, then, the use of Josephus is possible, but not proven.

A substantial part of the material in the *Weltchronik* which derives from the *Antiquitates* is quoted via an intermediate source, the *Historia scholastica* or the *Glossa ordinaria*. Dependency on the *Historia scholastica* can be demonstrated, for example, in Rudolf's description of the plague of frogs, when he cites Josephus as his source:[42]

Antiquitates

ranarum namque infinita multitudo eorum terras late depasta est, plenusque his erat etiam fluvius et polluebatur eorum potus et animalibus ebi putrescentibus foetor cunctis noxius exhalabat ex aqua. eratque cuncta regio huiusmodi malo plena ebullientibus ranis et morientibus quae domestica eorum habitacula valde vexabant, dum in cibis saepius invenirentur et poculis et cubilibus eorum inambulantes foetorque crudelis erat et abhominabilis, morientibus ranis ac putrescentibus.

Weltchronik

der werde wise Josephus
scribit und seit ùns alsus:
so si werin lebende irkant,
das si sturbin sa zehant
und fulten sa, so wart der smack
so groz der in dem wazzer lag,
das ouh niemanne tôhte
ders iht geniezen môhte,
davon das als unreinir smag
mit fúle indem wazer lag.
uz dén lant wazzern ouh
der kroten vil unde mere krouh
in dú hus zallin stunden,
das si ligende funden
an ir slaf steten bi in.
si liten manegen ungewin
von in in maneger wise:
si fundins inir spise,
ze beten und ze tischen [...]

Historia scholastica

'Historia libri Exodi', Cap. XVI. *De ranis.*

[...] 'Et ascenderunt ranae et operuerunt terram Aegypti.' Quae ut dicit Josephus, ortae, in brevi moriebantur, et putrescentibus cadaveribus fetor nimis noxius exhalabat ex aqua, imo quaedam quasi domesticae domos intrantes saepe in cibis, et potibus, et lectis inveniebantur.

[42] Blatt, *Latin Josephus*, p. 209; *PL* 198, col. 1150; Tippelskirch, *Geschichtsauffassung*, pp. 38–39.

It is clear that Josephus was consulted directly by Comestor at this point; Rudolf's wording, however, is more similar to Comestor's than to the original, and it seems likely that the mention of Josephus was taken from the *Historia scholastica* along with the information derived from this source. Rudolf's 'so si werin lebende irkant, das si sturbin sa zehant' is a close paraphrase of Comestor's 'Ortae, in brevi moriebantur'; Josephus does not state that they died immediately. The expression 'si fundins inir spise, ze beten und ze tischen' is also more similar to Comestor's 'in cibis, et potibus, et lectis inveniebantur' than to Josephus' more detailed description.

Another example in which the *Historia scholastica* can be demonstrated to be the direct source of material attributed to Josephus is the account of the wives and children of King David. Rudolf's account is introduced with the general formula 'seit dú scrift fúr war'; the Vulgate, the *Historia scholastica* and the *Antiquitates* concur in their naming of the six wives and sons. But Rudolf takes the number six to refer specifically to David's wives in Ebron, and adds a seventh wife and son to the list, attributing this information to Josephus:[43]

Antiquitates

Quo tempore nati sunt davidi filii. numero sex. ex totidem mulieribus. Quorum senior quidem qui de achinoe matre progenitus. appellatus eum ammon. secundus autem de uxore abigail nomine eliab. tercius absolon. qui natus est de maacha. filia tholmai regis gessur. quartum vero habuit de muliere agit. quem vocauit adoniam. quintum habuit de saphatia filium habital. sextum ietraam de egla natum denominauit.

Weltchronik

[...]
der fúnfte hiez Saphatia,
den im ze sune gwan alda
ein sin wip hiez Abital.
der selbin tage und jare mal
ein sun von sinim libe kam,
der was geheizen Getraam,
Egla des mûter was genant.
nú tût úns Josephus irchant
das sin sun ouh were Nathan,
als ih von im gelesin han,
bi Saulis tohter, dú sin wip
eliche was: do der lip
an einis sunis geburt irstarp,
sit nah der zit si sus virdarp.

Historia scholastica

'Historia libri II Regum', Cap. IV. *De filiis David*

[...] sextus Jetthraam*, quem Josephus vocat Nathan de Egla uxore sua, quam Hebraei aiunt fuisse Michol; quae sola dicitur uxor ejus, quia in adolescentia sua primam sortitus est uxorem. Quod non videtur posse stare cum in sequentibus legatur Michol in Jerusalem subsannasse David, et dicitur, quod non est natus ei filius de David, usque in diem mortis suae, quia in ipso partu occubuit. Sed potuit fieri, ut vicina partui de Jerusalem descenderet in Hebron, ut ibi pareret, tanquam in primitivo loco regni.

**Additio.* 1. Quod Jettrhaam natus sit David in Hebron, non videtur verum, audi causam et solutionem.

The situation is a complex one. Both Rudolf and Comestor cite Josephus as their source for the name 'Nathan'; for Comestor this is an alternative name

[43] Josephus, *Ant*, VII, i, col. 4; *PL* 198, col. 1326; Tippelskirch, *Geschichtsauffassung*, p. 43.

for Jethram, Rudolf takes it to refer to a seventh son. But the name does not occur at all in the account in the *Antiquitates*, nor does Josephus mention Saul's daughter. The name 'Nathan' seems to result from a misreading, by Comestor or an earlier scribe, of the phrase 'sextum jetraam de egla natum denominauit' as 'Nathan denominauit'. Comestor discusses the Hebrews' assertion that Egla is to be identified with (Saul's daughter) Michal, who was his first wife in his youth, but died bearing his child. It seems probable that this account lies at the base of Rudolf's confusion: he has taken over the reference to Josephus and the detail that the marriage with Saul's daughter, as the first, was David's only true marriage.[44] Comestor's own preoccupation with the place of birth also contributes to the confusion.

Rudolf next refers to Josephus in line 27146, in giving an alternative outcome of the combat between the chosen warriors of Joab and Abner. In the Bible the heroes are equally matched and slay each other;[45] in the alternative version, attributed to Josephus, Joab's twelve heroes are victorious:[46]

Antiquitates

Dicente vero abner ad eum. velle se probare. quis eorum robustiorem haberet exercitum. convenit inter vtrosque. ut duodecim viros pugnaturos mitterent. et procedentes inter medias acies qui ex utraque parte ducum fuerant ad certamen electi. eductisque gladiis viri dauid. et tenentes capita hos-

Weltchronik

nu kamen an ein andir sa
die scharn und hûben da den strit
so stritecliche bi der zit
dass alle ein ander slûgen do.
iedoh seit Josephus also
das alda Joabis schar,
die er ze kempfen schichte dar,
slûgin Abneris man:
swelhin ie der man kam an

Historia scholastica

'Historia libri II Regum', Cap. III. *De regno Isboseth*

[...] Eo tempore ortum est intestinum bellum inter Hebraeos. Porro egressus est Abner et pueri ejus de castris in Gabaon. Joab autem et pueri David occurrerunt eis ad piscinam Gabaon, et convenit inter eos, quod duodecim

[44] The whole question of Michal's children appears to be very confused. The cause of the confusion is that there are different readings in the main manuscript versions of the Vulgate: in II Reg. 6:23 it is stated that as a punishment for mocking David's dancing before the ark, 'igitur Michol filiae Saul non est natus filius usque ad diem mortis suae'; yet in II Reg. 21:8, in some versions, one reads of the five children she bore to Adriel, son of Barzillai. The *Glossa ordinaria* which provides Comestor with the Hebrew view for his discussion (from the *Quaestiones*), reads: 'De egla. R. Hec est michol. quae sola vxor dicitur. quia eam dauid in adolescentia sua primam sortitus est vxorem. hec in partu dicitur occubuisse vnde in sequentibus scriptum est. Igitur michol filie saul non est natus filius: vsque ad diem mortis sue: quia in ipso partu occubuit.' (*Glossa ordinaria*, II, p. 52).

[45] II Reg. 2: [14]dixitque Abner ad Ioab / surgantque pueri et ludant coram nobis / et respondit Ioab surgant / [15]surrexerunt ergo et transierunt numero duodecim de Beniamin ex parte Hisboseth filii Saul / et duodecim de pueris David / [16]adprehensque unusquisque capite conparis sui / defixit gladium in latus contrarii et ceciderunt simul / vocatumque est nomen loci illius ager Robustorum in Gabaon.

[46] Josephus, *Ant*, VII, i, col. 3; *PL* 198, cols 1325–1326; Tippelskirch, *Geschichtsauffassung*, p. 40.

tium eorum lumbos et latera suis gladiis perforarunt. donec omnes quasi ex uno constitu perimerent. His autem cadentibus. etiam reliquus direptus est exercitus	der im ze kempfin was gesant, an dem gesigte er zehant so gar das er im abe slůg das houbit und das dannen trůg widir zů den sinin hin, das si sigehaft sehin in.	tantum ex utraque parte pugnarent in medio exercituum, et apprehenso unusquisque capite comparis sui defixit gladium in latus contrarii, et ceciderunt simul. Ob hoc dictus est locus ille ager Robustorum. Josephus tamen videtur velle, quod pueri David superstites occiderunt compares suos.

The wording of the Latin translation of the *Antiquitates*, which at this point appears to differ substantially from the Greek,[47] is ambiguous, and has been understood by Comestor to mean that David's (Joab's) men survived. Whether Rudolf consulted the *Antiquitates* directly or borrowed the information and the reference to Josephus from the *Historia scholastica* is impossible to determine. Neither Latin text refers to decapitation. The case for the *Historia scholastica* is more one of context: it was seen above that the chapter directly following this one in Comestor's account provided Rudolf with the Josephus material for the previous passage about David's wives and children.

Rudolf cites Josephus as the authority for the information that the Queen of Sheba introduced balsam to Solomon:[48]

Antiquitates	*Weltchronik*	*Historia scholastica*
Dicunt autem quia et radicem balsami quam hactenus fert nostra prouintia. ipsa dederit regi.	Ein meister heisset Josephus, der seit ouh da von alsus: si brechte wrzen balsami, von den gemachet in Engadi ein edil balsam garte wart, dem kúnige liep unde zart.	Cap. XXVI. *De regina Saba.* [...] Dicit etiam Josephus, eam dedisse regi radicem balsami, unde propagatae sunt in Engaddi vineae balsamitae.

Here again it appears more than likely that the direct source was the *Historia scholastica* as Josephus does not give a specific location for the balsam plantation.

It is thought that Rudolf's authorship of the *Weltchronik* ends with line 33320,[49] but there is one more reference to Josephus in the first continuation, in line 33463:[50]

[47] The English translation of the Greek text reads: 'Accordingly there advanced to the space between the opposing lines the men who had been chosen by either of the commanders. They threw their spears and then drew their swords and each, taking hold of his opponent's head and holding him fast, pierced the other's ribs and flanks with his sword until all were killed as though by agreement.' (*Josephus*, trans. by H. St. J. Thackeray and Ralph Marcus, V, p. 365, Loeb Classical Library). Clementz' German translation of the Greek original confirms that the Latin text is a variation (*Jüdische Altertümer*, I, p. 393).

[48] Josephus, *Ant* VIII, iii, col. 14; *PL* 198, cols 1369–1370; not mentioned by Tippelskirch.

[49] Ehrismann, note to line 33479, p. 469.

[50] Josephus, *Ant* VIII, iii, col. 18; *PL* 198 col. 1371; not mentioned by Tippelskirch.

Antiquitates	*Weltchronik*	*Historia scholastica*
Mortuus est itaque salomon valde longeuus. qui regnauit quidem annis quadraginta. vixit autem quatuor et nonaginta. et sepultus est in in hierosolimis	do er gerihte fúr war alles Israhel vierzig jar, do fůr er die gemeine vart. ze David er begraben wart. Josephus der seit fúr war er rihte die riche ahzig jar, und wrden alle gezalt, er was vier und núnzig jar alt.	Cap. XXVII. *De feminis adversariis Salomonis, et morte ejus.* [...] dicit Josephus ita. Mortuus est Salomon valde longaevus, qui regnavit annis octoginta. Vixit autem nonaginta quatuor annis, [...]

It is impossible to say here which is the direct source of the German text, as Josephus is quoted exactly by Comestor. However it is more probably the *Historia scholastica* since the subsequent lines in the *Weltchronik* correspond closely to it:

Weltchronik	*Historia scholastica*
uf dise missehellunge zal so sprechent die meister úber al das verswigen si von schulden der jar die er wider Gotes hulden lebte und sin súntlich leben der heiligen schrift nit wrde geben.	sed divina Scriptura eos tantum annos exprimit, quibus regnavit antequam praevaricaretur. (col. 1371)

In the examples discussed above, Rudolf takes over both the material and the source-reference from Comestor, who cites Josephus by name. However, there are several instances where Comestor does not name his source, but where Rudolf appears to recognize it, and correctly attributes the material to Josephus. One such example is the discussion of God's prophecy to Eli about the total eradication of his line of descent:[51]

Antiquitates	*Weltchronik*	*Historia scholastica*
Hec siquidem contigerunt. sicut deus sacerdoti helii prophetauit. propter iniquitates duorum filiorum eius dicens prolem eius radicitus euellandam.	Josephus der wise giht das mit der selben geschicht wurde irfúllet das wort das dem ewarten dort, Ely, hate vor geseit Samuel in sinir kintheit: das al sin kúnne irsturbe einis tagis und virdurbe, [...]	'Historia libri I Regum', Cap. XXII. *De morte Abimelech, et octaginta quinque sacerdotum.* [...] Percussit quoque Saul Nobe viculum sacerdotum, et mulieres, et viros, et jumenta secundum quod Deus Heli sacerdoti prophetaverat, prolem ejus radicitus evellendam.

Comestor quotes Josephus almost verbatim here, but does not acknowledge his source, so that the fact that Rudolf is correct in his attribution might indicate direct consultation of the *Antiquitates*. However, the possibility cannot be ruled out that the copy of the *Historia scholastica* used by Rudolf contained

[51] *PL* 198, col. 1316; Josephus, *Ant*, VI, xiii, col. 3; Tippelskirch, *Geschichtsauffassung*, pp. 39–40.

a marginal reference to Josephus, or that this was an enlightened guess on Rudolf's part. Because of the close verbal parallels between Comestor and Josephus, it is not possible to determine Rudolf's direct source on this basis, but the phrase 'wurde irfúllet das wort' does echo Josephus' 'Hec [...] contigerunt', which is not quoted directly in the *Historia scholastica*.

Another passage where it is difficult to tell whether Rudolf consults the *Historia scholastica* or its own unnamed source, the *Antiquitates*, is the discussion of the origin of Solomon's wealth. Rudolf cites Josephus as his source for this information:[52]

Antiquitates

Fecit autem rex etiam. multas naves in sinu egipciaco maris rubri. in quodam loco qui asyongaber apellatur. non procul a ciuitate hellena. que nunc beronica vocatur. Hec enim regio fuit primitus iudeorum. Habuit vero ad edificandos naues beneficia regis yram. Ipse namque multos viros gubernatores et in marinis rebus edoctos misit. quos iussit nauigare cum dispensatoribus suis ad locum qui olim ophyra. nunc terra aurea nuncupatur. est autem inindia. ut aurum deferrent. et colligentes quadraginta talenta. ad regem denuo sunt reuersi,

Weltchronik

Wa der degin hogemůt,
Salomon, das groze gůt
und die richeit neme
und wannen ez im keme,
das hat bescheidin úns alsus
der kúnste riche Josephus:
zẘ iseln ligint in India,
in dén selbin isiln da
me goldiz und silbirs wirt,
das der isiln lant gebirt,
danne iender uf der erde
goldiz und silbirz werde.
das irfůr sin wisheit,
und als ez im wart geseit
ane widir rede wer,
er sante zů dem roten mer
in Asiongaber die stat do sa
und hiez im do gewinnin da
die besten schiflúte zehant
die man in dem lande vant,
und hiez nah dem willen sin
vil wol bereiten gelin
und sante si in India.
dú ein isil hiez Argira,
Ophir dú andir was genant:
von danne wart im do gesant
der groste hort, als ih ê sprah,
den ieman ê davor gesah,
und was der hort im komen dar
ê des ieman wrde gwar.

Historia scholastica

Cap. XXV. *De operibus Salomonis.*
[...]
Classem quoque fecit rex Salomon in insula quadam Aegyptiaca Rubri maris, quae dicitur Asiongaber, et navigabant cum servis Salomonis viri nautici de Tyro, quae tunc insula erat, et deferebant de Ophir aurum multum,
[...]

The source situation here is again a complex one. Either Rudolf or an intermediary source has misunderstood the geographical details in this passage in the *Antiquitates* and/or the *Historia scholastica*, in which Comestor

[52] Josephus, *Ant* VIII, iii, col. 13; *PL* 198, col. 1369; Tippelskirch, *Geschichtsauffassung*, pp. 40–42.

himself makes certain geographical mistakes. Rudolf refers to two islands in India, Ophir and Argira; his source for the latter is unknown, and Ophir is not otherwise described as an island. However, this could have occurred through contamination with the references in the *Historia scholastica* to the islands of Tyre and Asiongaber.[53] Comestor does not mention Josephus by name, and does not locate Ophir in India. This might indicate that Rudolf here consulted Josephus directly, but both these details can be also be found in (some versions of) the *Glossa ordinaria*.[54]

That Comestor was the main source for the above passage, with the addition of details from either the *Antiquitates* or the *Gloss*, is made still more probable by the fact that the continuation, in which the sailors return with their treasures, is very close to Comestor's account, which also follows directly in the *Historia scholastica*:

Weltchronik

swenne die boten kamen hin
ze werbenne um den gwin,
si kamin widir ubir drú jar
und brahten danne, das ist war,
bi dem horde an dem selbin zil
dem kúnege kleinődis vil,
dú dannoh bi dén jaren
dem lande vromde waren:
affin und helfande,
die nieman da bechande;
pfawin und edil helfinbein,
das schőne wiz und edil schein;
und edil holz, túre und wert,
des darzů wart von im gegert
das man der vazze machte vil
dú hőren suln ze seite spil,
herphin, gigin, lirin.

Historia scholastica

et circumeuntes Indiam et Siciliam, post elapsum triennium, referebant Salomoni aurum quadringentorum viginti talentorum, et argentum, et dentes elephantorum, et simias, et pavos, et gemmas, et ligna thina multa nimis, quae erant similia ligna setim, et odorifera; de quibus fecit rex Salomon fulcra, et sedilia domus Domini, et domus regiae, et citharas, et lyras cantoribus, nam cynara, et nabla ex electro constituit. (col. 1369)

[53] These observations are also made by Tippelskirch, pp. 40–41; however, her statement (p. 40) that the forms of the place names used by Rudolf are more similar to those used by Comestor than Josephus does not hold if the Latin version of the *Antiquitates* is considered.

[54] There is some variation here in the textual tradition of the *Gloss*. The edition printed by Rusch in 1480 (*Glossa ordinaria*, II, p. 119) does not mention Josephus, although he would appear to be the source, and reads: 'In ophir. Rab. Ophir nomen est provincie in india. ab uno ophir de posteris heber nominata. que et terra aurea appellatur. eo quod montes aureos habeat qui a leonibus et seuissimis bestijs incoluntur. Ad quos nullus aliter accedere audet nisi qui in naui stantes iuxta litus terram quam vnguibus leonem effossam inuenerint: in suam nauem recipiunt: vt si bestie eos senserint facile in mari recipiantur'. The edition printed in Venice in 1588 (no page-numbering), in its comment on III Reg. 9, reads: 'In Ophir: Nomen provinciae Ophir, ab uno posteriorum heber vocata, ex cujus stirpe venientes, a fluvio Cophene usque ad regionem Indiae quae vocatur Geria habitasse Josephus refert'.

Rudolf does not mention that Solomon also made furniture from the wood they brought back, and adds live elephants to list of exotic animals (which could have been suggested by the reference to ivory), but his account is otherwise a direct paraphrase of Comestor's.[55]

Josephus is cited in line 31195, when Rudolf explains the thinking of King David when he is forced to confront the prospect of divine punishment for his presumption in numbering the Israelites (IIRg 24:14). In the Bible, David, when offered the choice between seven years of famine, three months of defeat at the hands of his enemies, or three days of pestilence, leaves the decision to God, who inflicts the latter punishment. Josephus, however, makes us party to David's deliberations, and states that David himself chooses pestilence as it is the only option that will affect him and his family as much as his subjects. This passage from the *Antiquitates* is quoted in both the *Glossa ordinaria* and the *Historia scholastica*,[56] so that it is again difficult to determine the direct source. All the necessary information for Rudolf's account can be found in the *Historia scholastica* except, in Migne, at any rate, the reference to Josephus.[57] The *Glossa ordinaria*, on the other hand, does give Josephus as its source. Rudolf's wording is here on the whole different from all the Latin works; however, there are more verbal parallels with the more extensive original version (which is quoted by the *Gloss*) than with Comestor's brief summary. It is impossible to say whether Rudolf at this point consulted the *Antiquitates* as such, or merely the excerpt in the *Glossa ordinaria*, but it seems probable that one of the two, and not the *Historia scholastica*, was his direct source.[58]

Comestor is, however, the direct source of Rudolf's description of the burial of King David in Jerusalem and the treasure buried with him, which is discovered later by Johannes Hircanus. The material for this account is again derived from Josephus, who is named twice by Rudolf, but not by Comestor at this point:[59]

[55] Comestor here combines Josephus's account of the return of the sailors (Josephus, *Ant* VIII, iii, cols 14–15) with the account in the Bible (III Reg. 10,22).

[56] Josephus, *Ant*, VII, xiii, col. 2; *PL* 198, cols 1345–1346; *Glossa ordinaria*, II, p. 87; Tippelskirch, *Geschichtsauffassung*, pp. 44–45.

[57] Though this possibility can never be ruled out, spot-checks in several manuscripts (MSS ABCDE) shows no evidence of this information; see section 1.3 for sigla.

[58] For more detailed discussion of this example, see Sherwood-Smith, 'Reception', pp. 183–185.

[59] Josephus, *Ant*, VII, xvi, cols 2–3; *PL* 198, cols 1349 and 1525.

Antiquitates

Sepeliuit autem eum filius salomon in hierosimis decenter nimis. et aliis rebus que solent circa exequia regias ministrari. et multas diuitias cum eo recondidit. Quarum magnitudinem ex his que dicturus sum poterit quilibet agnoscere. Post tempus enim annorum mille trecentorum. hircanus pontifex dum ciuitas obsideretur ab antiocho rege qui pius cognominatus est filio demetrii. volens ei dare pecu-

Weltchronik

er wart so riliche
begrabin, das úns Josephus
mit rehter warheit scribit sus,
das ahte hórde richeit
zůzim wurdin geleit
in ahte vesten sarchen,
vesten unde starchen,
mit zoubirlichir meistirschaft
und mit virborgenir liste kraft,
das sie nieman funde
und nieman vinden kunde.
doh vant ir einin darnah sit
ubir maneger jare zit
Johannes Ircanus,
als úns scribit Josephus,
und ubirwant mit al die not
die im mit urlúge bot
und mit vientlichir kraft
dú virworhtú heidinschaft,
als si waren ie gewon,
unde stifte doh davon
ze Jerusalem den spital,
da manig notdúrftig mal
durh Got almůsens vil geschiht,
als man teglih mit warheit siht
und iemermere sehin mag
werliche untz an den
jungesten tag,
biz daz dú welt mag gestan.

Historia scholastica

'Historia Libri III Regum', Cap. III. *De morte David.* [...]
Circa tumulum ejus fecit Salomon octo loculos thesaurorum, quorum unum post mille trecentos annos aperuit Hircanus pontifex, et alium Herodes, sicut infra dicemus. Alii vero nondum manifestati* sunt, mechanicae artis modo reconditi.
* *Additio 1.* Quaedam Scripturae videntur dicere quod non manifestabuntur, usque ad tempora Antichristi (col. 1349 – 1350)

'Historia Libri II Machabæorum', Cap. III. *De institutione Xenodochiorum, et de morte Joannis.* Post hoc Antiochus Ponticus rex Syriae obsedit Jerusalem. Quamobrem aperuit Hircanus duos de octo loculis circumstantibus sepulcrum David, et sustulit ex eis plusquam tria millia talentorum deditque trecenta talenta Antiocho, ut ab obsidione recederet. Et ut placaret murmur populi de apertione sepulcri, de reliqua pecunia primus instituit xenodochia pauperum in Jerusalem. (col. 1525)

Here again the reference to Josephus is problematic, as Comestor does not cite him as his source for this material. However, he is mentioned in connection with John Hircanus in the chapter of Comestor's account of II Maccabees directly preceding the passage quoted above. That the *Historia scholastica* and not the *Antiquitates* is the direct source, is demonstrated by the reference to eight treasure-chests, where the number is not specified by Josephus, and to the founding of a hospice in Jerusalem.[60]

In these examples one can conclude that the mentioning of Josephus' name may indicate that Rudolf is aware that an account of this matter is to be found in Josephus, even though he himself uses Comestor. This familiarity

[60] Tippelskirch appears unaware of the later account in the *Historia scholastica*, which leads her to the false observation that 'nur die "Weltchronik" kennt den Vornamen Johannes und schreibt ihm die Stiftung des Jerusalemer (Johanniter-?) Spitals zu', *Geschichtsauffassung*, p. 42.

might remain from an earlier reading of the *Antiquitates*. In light of this possibility, further correspondences with Josephus, which could be fortuitous, could also be explained in terms of memory.[61]

Despite the indications that Rudolf von Ems is familiar with the *Antiquitates*, not all citations of Josephus in the *Weltchronik* should be taken at face value; there are several instances where Rudolf adduces Josephus as an authority for non-scriptural details which he has derived from another source. In lines 25727–25236, in introducing the Pytonisse of Endor, Rudolf identifies Phiton with Apollo, and cites Josephus as his authority. Though the figure of the Pytonisse was well-known in the Middle Ages, and was associated with Apollon Pythios and the oracle in Delphi, Josephus does not in fact mention any link.[62] Thus here the citation of Josephus is a fabrication.[63]

The above analysis of the position of the *Antiquitates* as a possible source for the *Weltchronik* of Rudolf von Ems allows the following conclusions. Rudolf frequently cites Josephus as an authority for non-scriptural historical material. Much of the Josephus material in the *Weltchronik* can be demonstrated to have entered the work via an intermediate source, the *Historia scholastica* or the *Glossa ordinaria*. In one case, however, Rudolf includes material which derives, directly or indirectly, from Josephus, but which has no parallel in the other two works. In view of this, a number of further correspondences with Josephus, that might be fortuitous, could indeed equally derive from the same source. Although there are six instances when Rudolf's citations of Josephus must be considered fabrications, in the majority of cases he is correct about the ultimate source of the material, even when Josephus is not named by the intermediate source. This could indicate that the attribution may have been made because Rudolf was aware that this information could be found in the *Antiquitates*, which raises the possibility that the passage about the witch of Endor, and perhaps a few others, shows direct consultation of Josephus. There is, however, insufficient evidence to prove the point.

[61] There are 7 instances in which Rudolf's text shows parallels with Josephus which could result from his earlier reading of the *Antiquitates*. These are discussed in Sherwood-Smith, 'Reception', pp. 186–191.

[62] Herkommer, *St. Galler Kodex*, p. 205, note 380; Tippelskirch, *Geschichtsauffassung*, p. 43. The information can be found in the *Glossa ordinaria*, (II, p. 45): 'Phytius dicitur apollo'.

[63] There are 5 further occasions on which Rudolf falsely cites Josephus as the authority for non-scriptural details he has derived from another source. For detailed discussion of these passages, see Sherwood-Smith, 'Reception', pp. 192–196.

3.3.3 Conclusion: the Function of the *Historia scholastica* as a Source for the *Weltchronik* of Rudolf von Ems

Table 10 shows that correspondences with the *Historia scholastica* occur throughout Rudolf von Ems' *Weltchronik*. These vary in distribution and in closeness, so that there are passages where the similarities are incidental and can best be attributed to 'common knowledge' or a common source, and others where the extent and detail of the parallels make it virtually certain that Comestor's work was consulted directly.

The main difficulty in assessing the function of the *Historia scholastica* for Rudolf is that the nature of his use of it is too varied to be characterized neatly. In the case of Honorius Augustodunensis' *De imagine mundi*, for example, it is possible to define a relatively specific context in which it is consulted, and thus to state that its function for Rudolf was to furnish geographical and ethnological material for his account. The *Historia scholastica* is itself so diverse that it is problematic to determine when and why it is consulted. However, some general conclusions can be drawn about the position of the work with regard to the other main sources consulted by Rudolf von Ems for his *Weltchronik*.

The main function of the *Historia scholastica* in the *Weltchronik* is to provide extra details and background information to corroborate the main account according to the Vulgate. Rudolf adds names, locations and descriptions from Comestor to make his account more historical; he adds entertaining incidents, generally derived by Comestor from the Jewish traditions of the Midrash, to make it more vivid. This is the function of the *Historia scholastica* for Rudolf's account of the events of Genesis and Leviticus, and is particularly evident in the account of Exodus.

Another function of the *Historia scholastica* for Rudolf which one can isolate is to provide 'digested' material. This can be seen in the account of Deuteronomy, where Comestor's summary of the laws of Moses is used as a guide-line to extract the points about ancient Jewish customs which are most relevant to contemporary Christians. A similar use of the *Historia scholastica* can be seen later, where Comestor's combined account of the books of Kings and Chronicles serves a basis for Rudolf.

Comestor also provides references to authorities, which Rudolf occasionally cites. This has been discussed in detail in the case of the citations of Josephus, for which the *Historia scholastica* is frequently the direct source. In these cases the *Historia scholastica* is a mediator, not only of information, but also of authority.

Herkommer refers to another function of Comestor's work, that of an 'Orientierungsrahmen'.[64] The overall concept of the *Weltchronik*, in which events from sacred and secular history are juxtaposed, is clearly influenced by the *Historia scholastica*, and Comestor provides the cue for Rudolf to insert additional material from other sources, such as Honorius Augustodunensis or the unknown sources of the more detailed accounts of Greek myths.[65]

The structural influence of the *Historia scholastica* is where Rudolf's approach to the Vulgate differs most from that of the authors of the *Schwarzwälder Predigten*. This is as one would expect, given that, as was discussed above, in the sermons, the stories from the *Historia scholastica* do not occur within a chronological framework. The anonymity of the source remarked on in the context of the sermons remains a feature of Rudolf's approach: he never refers to Comestor or the *Historia scholastica* by name or by any specific formula, and does not distinguish between it and the Vulgate as a source of biblical material. As has been seen in the analysis above, apocryphal material is either assimilated silently into the main account (section 3.3.1), or attributed to Comestor's own source (section 3.3.2). Commentary material tends to be introduced under the heading 'glose', which may refer to the *Historia scholastica*, the *Glossa ordinaria*, or another source.

In this one can begin to establish a certain pattern in the approach to the *Historia scholastica*, which here again seems to be preferred in its capacity to provide extra narrative detail and clarity, rather than for its commentary on the Scriptures. The following chapter will investigate the *Scolastica* of Jacob van Maerlant, another narrative work written about 20 years after the *Weltchronik* but not dependent on it, and will assess to what extent it can be seen to conform to the same pattern.

[64] Herkommer, *St. Galler Kodex*, p. 221.

[65] The direct source of the extra details with which Rudolf supplements the information found in Comestor's *incidentia* remains the matter of speculation. Herkommer discusses the possible provenance of individual details (*St. Galler Kodex*, pp. 184–187, 196–200), but cannot suggest a direct source. My own analysis of the *incidentia* relating to the book of Judges suggests that there is no reason to see Godfrey of Viterbo's *Pantheon* as a source; the closest parallels in this section are to be found in Ovid's *Metamorphoses*.

4 THE *SCOLASTICA* OF JACOB VAN MAERLANT

4.1 Introduction: The *Scolastica* of Jacob van Maerlant

Jacob van Maerlant's *Scolastica*, also known as his *Rijmbijbel*, is a reworking of the *Historia scholastica* in Middle Dutch verse, commissioned by an unknown patron and completed in 1271.[1] It is the only vernacular reworking to cover the whole of Comestor's text from Genesis to the end of the Gospel harmony.[2] The *Scolastica* is the first work to offer an overview of the Bible to those in the Dutch-speaking area who could not read Latin; it stands at the beginning of the tradition of vernacular translations of biblical material in the Low Countries. The work is preserved in fifteen (more-or-less) complete manuscripts and in a further fifty fragments.[3]

In the other works investigated in this study, the *Historia scholastica* is a secondary source, consulted in conjunction with the Vulgate and/or other works. The detailed analysis of their use of the *Historia scholastica* frequently involves identifying the material from this source and considering possible reasons for its inclusion. In Jacob van Maerlant's *Scolastica* the situation is very different: Comestor is the main source, and Maerlant explicitly sets out to make the Latin work available in the vernacular. He states his intention in the prologue: 'Scolastica willic ontbinden / Jn dietsche word vten latine' (ll. 21–22). In this case the emphasis in the analysis of the relationship between the *Scolastica* and the *Historia scholastica* will be on the selections made by the later author: his omissions from, and additions to, the material from his main source, and in what way he understood the process of 'ontbinden' in practical terms.

1 See Jaap van Moolenbroek and Maaike Mulder, 'Maerlants *Rijmbijbel* of *Scolastica*. Een inleiding', in: *Scolastica willic ontbinden*, pp. 7–12; Frits van Oostrom, *Maerlants Wereld* (Amsterdam, 1996). Editions: *Rijmbijbel*, ed. Jean David, 4 vols (Brussels,1858–1859); *Rijmbijbel*, ed. Maurits Gysseling, 2 vols, *CMNT* II,3–4 (Leiden, 1983).

2 Jaap van Moolenbroek, 'Maerlants *Scolastica*: een Waagstuk?', in: *Scolastica willic ontbinden*, pp. 13–34, here p. 19; the *Historia scholastica* was also translated into Portuguese and Czech in the fourteenth century (see Vollmer, Materialien 2,1, pp. XX–XXI) and into German in the early fifteenth century (edition in Vollmer, Materialien 2, 1–2).

3 Maaike Mulder, 'De handschriftentraditie van de *Rijmbijbel*', in: *Scolastica willic ontbinden*, pp. 71–82; 145.

4.2 Jacob van Maerlant's Approach to his Source

The relationship between Maerlant's *Scolastica* and its source has already been investigated in detail for the Genesis section by Goudriaan, and in a general survey by Berendrecht.[4] Their research has identified the main tendencies of Maerlant's adaptation of Comestor's work, which reflect the different purpose of the vernacular author. Although there is continuing debate over Maerlant's patron and intended primary audience for this work, suggestions ranging from rich bourgeoisie to nobility to Franciscan lay-brothers, the fact remains that Maerlant's *Scolastica* is not an academic text-book.[5] Many of the changes in the work are what one would expect from this:[6] Maerlant omits most of the more technical notes and source-references which are spread throughout the text, generally omits Comestor's polemics, and, when confronted with various alternative interpretations, chooses one. However, he does retain and transpose Comestor's etymologies wherever possible. Comestor himself already reduces the accounts of Jewish laws, rites and sacrifices from the Bible; these are scarcely mentioned at all by Maerlant (who explains this policy in terms of his sensibilities and the unsuitability of such material for lay people).[7] He tends to omit Comestor's prologues about the authorship of each book of the Bible and often concentrates on different aspects of non-sacred history, particularly where this coincides with his own earlier works, to which he sometimes refers the reader for more detail. He also adds details from the Vulgate. His interest in the invention and transmission of human skills exceeds even Comestor's own.

Maerlant's main addition to the text, and that which changes its character the most, is a series of typological interpretations of events or realia, which emphasize the whole aspect of Salvation History. This is a fundamental change,

4 Koen Goudriaan, 'Maerlants bronnen in de *Scolastica*: Comestor en de anderen', in: *Scolastica willic ontbinden*, pp. 35–51; Petra Berendrecht, *Proeven van bekwaamheid. Jacob van Maerlant en de omgang met zijn Latijnse bronnen* (Amsterdam, 1996), pp. 87–116 (a slightly revised version of her article: 'Maerlants "Scolastica" (c.q. "Rijmbijbel") in relatie tot zijn directe bron. Een verkenning', *TNTL* 108 (1992), pp. 2–31).

5 Ada Postma, 'Voor wie schreef Jacob van Maerlant zijn *Rijmbijbel*', in: *Scolastica willic ontbinden*, pp. 53–70; Frits van Oostrom, 'Slotbeschouwing: de *Rijmbijbel*, balans en perspectief', in: *Scolastica willic ontbinden*, pp. 127–143; van Oostrom, *Maerlants Wereld*, esp. pp. 299–302; 442–446.

6 The following brief discussion of the main tendencies of Maerlant's approach to his source is a summary of Goudriaan's 'De verhalende stof' in: 'Maerlants bronnen', pp. 38–42.

7 'Maer weet wel dat mine roec / De sacrificien te bescriuene; / Het ware mi pijnlijc te bedriuene / Ende leec volc soud qualic verstaen', ll. 5213–5218.

introducing the other senses of the Bible which Comestor felt belonged to a later stage of exegesis. The direct source for the typology is disputed, but it seems likely that some interpretations are taken from the *Glossa ordinaria*, while the mariological interpretations frequently coincide with Maerlant's poem, *Die Clausule vander Bible*, and probably derive from the same unknown source.[8]

Maerlant's specific purpose in writing the *Scolastica* is difficult to determine, and is obviously linked with the question of the intended readership. The didactic function of the text is borne out by the tone of the whole work, and by Maerlant's frequent exhortations to the reader such as 'nu merct dat', 'weetmen wale', 'weet ouer waer', 'ghelovet das' (ll. 1422–1434), 'verstaet aldus', 'sijt seker das'. The importance of truth and the authority of the written tradition are frequently attested by such phrases as 'alsict las', 'al sonder lieghen', 'als ict vernam'. However, this respect for authority does not prevent Maerlant from giving his own explanations at times, such as in lines 5221–5228, where he pronounces that the eating of blood was forbidden not because it was a sin in its own right, but to distinguish the Jews from their gentile neighbours. He also feels free to include social criticism, particularly of the modern clergy.

The following study of a selected section of Maerlant's adaptation of Comestor's 'Historia Libri Exodi' presents a close analysis of these passages in the *Scolastica* and their relation to their source. It considers them against the backdrop of Goudriaan's and Berendrecht's observations, but concentrates more specifically on the context of the reception of the *Historia scholastica* and the tradition of the Bible book in question, bearing in mind the debate about the intended readership and the question of Maerlant's purpose in writing the *Scolastica*. The section from Exodus was chosen to show the similarities and differences of Maerlant's approach and that of Rudolf von Ems (section 3.3.1 above) and the author of the *Historiebijbel van 1360* (section 5.2 below).

4.3 Analysis of a section from the Account of Exodus in Maerlant's *Scolastica*: lines 3443 – 3589.

The birth and early life of Moses are covered in *Scolastica* in lines 3443 to 3639. This corresponds with chapters 5 to 8 of the *Historia scholastica*.[9]

8 Goudriaan, 'Maerlants bronnen', pp. 45–49.

9 *PL* 198, cols 1143–1145. In quoting from Gysseling's diplomatic edition of *Scolastica* I do not mark abbreviations, column-endings and reconstructions, and I incorporate the corrections suggested by Gysseling into the text, distinguishing them by shading. The punctuation is my own.

The story begins with the marriage of Moses' parents:

Scolastica

Jn dien tiden was Amram,
Een man geboren van Leui,
Ende nam een wijf – gheloues mi –
Van sinen gheslachte, hiet Iocabet.

Historia scholastica

Cap. V. *De ortu, et educatione Moysi.*
'Egressus est post haec vir levita (Exod. II)', nomine Aram, vel Amram, qui accepit uxorem contribulem nomine Jocabeth, [...] (col. 1143)

Here the Dutch is a generally close translation of the Latin text, but there are some alterations. Characteristically, Maerlant chooses one of the alternative names offered by Comestor, and will use it consistently. 'Post haec' is paraphrased as 'Jn dien tiden', and echoes of the wording of the Vulgate, universally familiar to the school-educated strata of medieval society to which Maerlant belonged, can be seen in the phrases 'geboren van leui' and 'van sinen gheslachte'. The only addition at this point is the narrator's call to the audience: 'gheloues mi'. Such expressions attesting the truth and credibility of the story or the source occur frequently throughout the work, although in this case the function would seem to be mainly rhetorical, for the rhyme.

Jacob van Maerlant manipulates the material he finds in his source to give even stronger emphasis to God's direct role in guiding events in the world according to a pre-ordained plan. The story of the Egyptian prophet's vision, told in chapter 3 of the *Historia scholastica*'s account of Exodus in partial explanation of the fact that the Egyptians massacred only the male infants, is postponed until this point in the Dutch version, and is linked with the motif of Amram's decision not to have another child. The prophecy fulfils a different function in this new context as an explicit reference to Moses' destiny.

Scolastica

Nochtanne scuede hi hare let:
Hi wilde eer sonder kinder bliuen,
Dan hise also saghe ontliuen.
Doe was oec een Egyptien,
Die dat seide hi hadde vorsien,
Dat in Ysrahel soude sijn gheboren
Een kind, ende soude Egypten storen.
Tien tiden onse here hiet
Amram, dat hi ne scuede niet
Sijn wijf; hi sal winnen den sone
Daer of – dat seide die gone –
Die Egypten souden breken.

Historia scholastica

[...] qui nolebat accedere ad uxorem post edictum, malens carere liberis quam in necem procreare. Cui Deus per somnium astitit, ut ait Josephus, dicens, ne timeret uxorem cognoscere, quia puer, quem timebant Aegyptii, nasciturus esset ex ea: etiam de sacerdotio Aaron ei significavit. (col. 1143)

Although the basic outline remains the same, the wording of the Dutch version is very different, and many details are omitted by the later author.

It is no longer specified that God appeared to Amram in a dream, and the matter-of-fact tone of 'onse here hiet Amram...' contributes to the impression that God is a protagonist in world history. Comestor's 'puer, quem timebant Egyptii', referring back to his earlier story, serves as a cue for Maerlant's telling of it. Aaron's role is generally diminished in *Scolastica*, and the prophecy of his priesthood is accordingly omitted altogether. Comestor's source-reference is also omitted here, although others are incorporated into the Dutch text.

Jocabet gives birth to Moses in secret:

Scolastica	*Historia scholastica*
Jocabet – dus hore wi spreken – Ghenas ens kints met stilre ale; Ende helt, hemelike ende wale, Drie maende sonder ghelud.	Tandem 'concepit mulier, et peperit filium' sub silentio, eo quod non multum ei dolores partus institerint. 'Et videns puerum elegantem, abscondit eum tribus mensibus. (col. 1143)

Jacob van Maerlant retains the motif of the silent birth but omits Comestor's explanation, as well as the factor of the child's beauty. He places extra emphasis on the hiding of the child quietly and secretly ('hemelike'). The phrase 'dus hore wi spreken' loosely situates the work in a tradition and occurs frequently in *Scolastica*.

The Dutch author does not include any details about the making of the basket, the materials or the construction:

Scolastica	*Historia scholastica*
Doch sachse, het moeste comen hud Ende deet in een vaetkin sciere, Dat vast was, ende leit in die riuiere Een deel buten den grote strome. Tkints suster hiet soe, dat soe gome Wat dat dar of sal ghescien.	Cumque celare non posset, sumpsit fiscellam scirpeam' in modum fisci, id est sacci rotundi, vimine complexam, 'et linivit eam bitumine ac pice, et ponens intus infantulum in carecto ripae eum exposuit', ne impetu fluminis raperetur, et stante procul sorore parvuli Maria, exspectante rei exitum, ex matris praecepto. (col. 1143)

He does not mention the rushes or the river-bank, but instead concentrates on the implications of Comestor's reason for the choice of this location, stating that the child's mother placed the basket out of reach of the current. Moses' sister is not named by Maerlant at this point.

The Pharaoh's daughter, Terimith, finds Moses:

Scolastica	*Historia scholastica*
Ter riuieren cam mettien Pharaons dochter Termit; Soe wilde hare koelen ende maken wijt. Dat vaetkin heuet soe bekint Ende dar in screien dat kint.	Ecce autem descendit Terimith filia Pharaonis, ut lavaretur in flumine, quae videns alveolum, et afferre sibi jubens, vidit parvulum vagientem, [...] (col. 1143)

In the *Historia scholastica* Terimith wishes to wash in the river; here the element of cooling down is added.[10] *Scolastica*'s order of narration differs from the Bible and the *Historia scholastica* in telling about the discovery of child in the basket. In Maerlant's version the Pharaoh's daughter sees the crying child from the first, rather than finding the baby with surprise on opening the basket.

The simultaneous presentation of both baby and basket facilitates the introduction at this point of one of the typological comparisons which are an important feature of *Scolastica*, and the main addition to the material from the *Historia scholastica*.[11] These typological parallels are part of the body of medieval general knowledge, and speculations on Maerlant's direct source for them here and in his similar poem, 'Die Clausule vander Bible', have not yielded any concrete suggestions.[12] Whatever their source, these typologies introduce the spiritual sense of the Bible, which Comestor felt belonged to a later stage of exegesis.[13]

Scolastica

Tfat – dat buten was belijmt
Ende bepect ende begrijmt,
Datter gheen water in ne mochte,
Ende Moysesse te lande brochte –
Betekent den lechame Marien,
Dien soe also wilde castien,
Met penitentien die soe nam,
Datter nie sonde in ne cam.
So droech onsen Moyses,
– Jhesus – die beweende des,
Dat wi laghen in dien sonden.

[10] This has a parallel in Rudolf von Ems' *Weltchronik*, where the idea of washing in the river is omitted altogether (see section 3.3.1 above).

[11] This innovation of van Maerlant's influences the Dutch reception of Comestor, and is copied in the *Noordnederlandse Historiebijbel* (see Sherwood-Smith, 'Reception', pp. 269–286).

[12] J.R. Smeets argues convincingly on the basis of one example that the *Aurora* of Peter Riga (itself a versification of the *Historia scholastica*) might be van Maerlant's direct source for the typological passages, but this is not borne out by the more thorough investigation by Goudriaan, 'Maerlants bronnen', in: *Scolastica willic ontbinden*, pp. 45–49.

[13] See Comestor's preface to the *Historia scholastica*, *PL* 198, cols 1053–1056; Van Oostrom, *Slotbeschouwing*, in: *Scolastica willic ontbinden*, p. 131, suggests that Maerlant's inclusion of the spiritual level of exegesis is part of a striving to combine as much as possible in one book, whereas Comestor, writing as he was in the specific context of the schools, could rest assured that further study of the spiritual sense of the Bible would follow in its proper place.

Hi halp ons, met sinen wonden,
Huten Egypten; dat lud mede
'Sonden ende deimsterhede'.
Gheliker wijs dat dat gheuel,
Dat dat tfolc van Ysrahel
Van Moysesse was verlost
Ende van den beduanghe vertrost,
Also heueti ons gheleet
– Vp dat ons die sonden sijn leet –
Van den Helschen Pharao,
Die ons gheuaen hadde also.

Though the allegorical interpretation of the sealed Moses basket as a reference to the immaculate conception is a common one in the Middle Ages, the detailed elements of the interpretation are unusual, and are not shared by the corresponding strophe of 'Die Clausule van der Bible'.[14] Maerlant relates the materials used to make the little coracle watertight to the acts of penitence undertaken by Mary to guard against sin. Sin, mentioned four times in these 22 lines, is given a particular emphasis: it occurs here in two images related to the story of Moses, both as the hostile water which surrounds the coracle (with the associated image of sinners wallowing in it), and in the parallel between Egypt and Hell. Christ is prefigured both by the child Moses in the coracle (His birth to a sinless mother) and the adult Moses liberating the Israelites from the tyranny of the Egyptians (the Harrowing of Hell).

Then Maerlant returns to Comestor and the narrative, describing Terimith's reaction on opening the basket:

Scolastica

Soe hiet hare bringhen van dart lach,
Ende teersten dat soe tkint sach:
"Dit kint" seit so, "dat wetic wel,
Dits van den volke van Ysrahel".
Hare ontfarmets, want so scone
Hadden ghemaect God van den Trone,
Dat sine viande sijns ontfarmede
Ende therte dar omme carmende.

Historia scholastica

[quae videns alveolum,] et afferre sibi jubens, [vidit parvulum vagientem,] et miserta est ejus dicens: De infantibus Hebraeorum est hic'. Sic enim Deus eum venustaverat ut etiam ab hostibus dignus alimento haberetur. (col. 1143)

The motif of Moses' beauty, ordained by God so that his enemies would not be able to resist him, is retained by the Dutch author but slightly modified: it is no longer applied specifically to the child's physical survival, but rather to his general capacity to attract affection.

[14] The lyric poem contains only the simplest interpretation: 'Ghi sijt tfaetken, Vrouwe scone, / Daer dor die vrese van Faraone / Moyses in wilen screide', 'Die Clausule van der Bible', in: *Jacob van Maerlant's Strophische Gedichten*, ed. J. Franck and J. Verdam (Groningen, 1898), pp. 120–135, here p. 124.

Egyptian wet-nurses are found but are rejected by the strong-minded infant, who in Maerlant's version would rather die than suckle any of them:

Scolastica

Die Egypse wiue boden hem de borste;
Maer al sout steruen van dorste,
Hen wilder altoes zughen ne ghene.
Maria, die suster diet wachte allene
Seide: "ghebenedide ioncvrouwe,
Ghebiet dijt, ic hale eene ebreusce vrouwe;
Het sal, wanic, bi auenturen
Zughen bi rechter naturen
Eeneghe van sinen gheslachte.
"So doet", sprac soe, "ic sta ende wachte".
De moeder haelt so met desen,
Alse of soe vremde hadde ghewesen;
Dat kint soech die moeder saen.

Historia scholastica

Et cum Aegyptiae plures ei admovissent ubera ad lactandum, faciem advertebat. Et ait Maria: Vis, inquit, Hebræam adducam, forte ubera gentis suae sequetur. Et praecepto ergo Terimith abiens, matrem parvuli, tanquam alienam, adduxit, et accessit ad ejus ubera puer. (col. 1143)

Here the process of 'ontbinden' works in the opposite direction: the compact Latin account is loosed, expanded into a more dramatic account. In the same vein, 'praecepto ergo Terimith' is changed to direct speech and the imperative 'So doet'.

The influence of the Vulgate can be seen again in the following section:

Scolastica

Ende soe heuet dar ontfaen
Van Termit, diet hare lonen woude,
Onthier dat ment spanen soude.
Ende doe soe tkint hadde ghespant,
Heuet soe te houe ghesent.
Die ioncvrouwe maecter of mede
– Na die wet ende na der zede
Van den lande – haren sone.
'Moyses' hiet soene, dor dat gone
Dat soene vten watre hief.
So scone waest, elc man had lief.

Historia scholastica

Suscepit ergo Terimith alendum puerum, et ablactatum reddidit filiae Pharaonis, quae adoptavit eum in filium, et dictus est Moyses. Aegyptii enim *Moys*, aquam, *is* salvatum dicunt. (cols 1143–1144)

Comestor does not mention the fact that Moses' mother was paid for her services as wet-nurse, but this detail from the Bible is included in *Scolastica*. Comestor's detailed Egyptian etymology of Moses' name is also replaced by the simpler version from the Vulgate.[15] In this one can see that Maerlant

15 Exodus 2: [9]ad quam locuta filia Pharaonis accipe ait puerum istum et nutri mihi / ego tibi dabo mercedem tuam / suscepit mulier et nutrivit puerum adultumque tradidit filiae Pharaonis / [10]quem illa adoptavit in locum filii / vocavitque nomen eius Mosi dicens / quia de aqua tuli eum

does not follow the *Historia scholastica* blindly or slavishly; he is aware of slight variations from the Bible.

Maerlant adds his own gloss on 'adoptavit', that it was in accordance with the laws and customs of the country. This emphasis on the historical nature of the account permeates the *Scolastica* and is another area where the influence of the source can be observed. The additional mention of Moses' beauty would appear to be motivated mainly by the demands of the rhyme-scheme.

Terimith presents Moses to her father in the hope that he will approve her decision:

Scolastica

TEnen tiden heuet so brocht
Haren vader ende besocht,
Of hiet wilde horen,
Dat soet te kinde hadde vercoren.
Sere wonderde Pharaone
Sine vulmaecteit so scone
Ende sette hem sine crone vpt houet,
Dar anghesmeet was – des ghelouet –
Eene ymaedse van Iupiterre.
Tkint nam die crone ende was erre,
ende waerpse ontve ieghen den vloer.
Mettien een vroet man dar vp voer
Ende seide: "dit tkint slawi doed!
So sijn wi quite van alre noed".
Mar Pharao behilt hem tleuen.
Ende andre vroede was dar beneven
Ende seide, dat hem kinscheit dede;
Dat proeuedi dar ter stede:
Hi brochte hete colen vorem dart stond;
Dar warpt eene in sinen mond,
Dat hi nemmer scone ne sprac;
Hi hadder of sulc onghemac.

Historia scholastica

Quem dum quadam die Terimith obtulisset Pharaoni, ut et ipse eum adoptaret, admirans rex pueri venustatem, coronam, quam tunc forte gestabat, capiti illius imposuit. Erat autem in ea Ammonis imago fabrefacta. Puer autem coronam projecit in terram, et fregit. Sacerdos autem Heliopoleos a latere regis surgens, exclamavit: Hic est puer, quem nobis occidendum Deus monstravit, ut de caetero timore careamus, et voluit irruere in eum, sed auxilio regis liberatus est, et persuasione cujusdam sapientis qui per ignorantiam hoc factum esse a puero asseruit. In cujus rei argumentum cum prunas allatas puero obtulisset, puer eas ori suo opposuit, et linguae suae summitatem igne corrupit. Unde et Hebraei impeditioris linguae eum fuisse autumant. (col. 1144)

Here too Maerlant circumvents the question of adoption: in the *Historia scholastica* Terimith's aim is that her father should himself adopt the child also. Comestor's suggestion that the Pharaoh might have been wearing his crown at the time is omitted. The image on the crown is that of the Roman God Jupiter rather than the Egyptian Ammon.[16] The account of the reaction of the Pharaoh's advisors and their opposing suggestions is reduced, particularly the role of the priest, Heliopoleos, who is no longer even named. His reference to the earlier prophecy is also omitted. The details of what part

[16] This is also the case in the *Noordnederlandse Historiebijbel*, which drew on the *Scolastica* (see Sherwood-Smith, 'Reception', pp. 269–286).

of his tongue Moses burned with the hot coals are also not included in the Dutch account.

The passage about how Moses' beauty affects people is also abridged:

Scolastica

So scoene waest: hi ne was so fel,
Sach hijt, hi ne word ghezeet wel;
Om hem te siene was menich droemen
In straten, dar menne sach comen.

Historia scholastica

Tantae vero pulchritudinis fuit, ut ait Josephus, ut nullus adeo severus esset, qui ejus aspectui non haereret, multique, dum cernerent eum per plateas ferri, occupationes in quibus studebant, desererent. (col. 1144)

The adult Moses is chosen to lead an Egyptian military expedition against the Ethiopians:

Scolastica

Doe Moyses ghewassen was,
So ghesciede – als ict las –
Dat dat volc van Ethyopen
Bede roueden ende dor cropen
Tland van Egypten al wel naer.
Do seide hare afgode ouer waer,
Dat sijt wreken souden dan
Bi eenen ebreuschen man;
Doch dat cume alle die gone
Thermid ghebaden, haren sone
Moysesse teenen leedsman;
Ende bi diere redenen nochtan,
Hem ghene mesquame te doene.

Historia scholastica

Cap. VI *De uxore Moysi Aethiopissa*

Factum est autem cum adultus fuisset Moyses, Aethiopes vastaverunt Aegyptum, usque ad Memphim et mare, quo circa conversi ad divinationes Aegyptii, acceperunt responsum, ut auxiliatore uterentur Hebraeo; et vix obtinuerunt a Terimith, ut exercitui, quem paraverant, Moysen praeficeret ducem, prius praestitis sacramentis, ne ei nocerent. (col. 1144)

Here the geographical detail about the exact area of Egypt that was plundered is omitted, and a reference to the written tradition added.[17] Otherwise this is an example of Maerlant's skill in combining all the elements from the earlier account and reworking them so that all the details are included.

Moses is a good leader and prepares the expedition well:

Scolastica

Moyses was sterc ende coene
Ende van horloghen wijs ende vroed.
Therre ledde he, tors ende te voed,
Mids in wostinen sonder sparen,
Die al wl serpente waren.
Met hem voerde hi odevaren,
Jn husekine die biesin waren;
Die sine voghele aten
Worme ende serpente vtermaten,
Ende daer si laghen, liet hise gaen;
Si verdreuen die worme saen.

Historia scholastica

Erat autem Moyses vir bellicosus, et peritissimus, qui fluminis iter tanquam longius praetermittens, per terram duxit exercitum itinere breviori, ut improvisos Aethiopes praeveniret. Sed per loca plena serpentibus iter faciens, tulit in arcis papireis super plaustra ibices ciconias, id est Aegyptiacas, naturaliter infestas serpentibus, quae rostro per posteriora immisso alvum purgant, castraque metaturus, praeferebat eas, ut serpentes fugarent, et devorarent, et ita tutus per noctem transibat exercitus. (col. 1144)

17 The omission of geographical material is relatively unusual in Maerlant's *Scolastica*; Goudriaan, 'Maerlants bronnen', p. 41.

Jacob van Maerlant adapts the material from Comestor, omitting all mention of an alternative route and adding that they went through the desert, and that the army was made up of both infantry and cavalry. The detail about the rushwork baskets for the storks is retained, but other details, such as the exact sub-species of stork and the way in which they attack their prey, are omitted.

As in the *Weltchronik* of Rudolf von Ems, Tarbis' love for Moses is presented as courtly 'minne':

Scolastica

[Si verdreuen die worme saen.]
Ende waren in Ethyopen comen,
Eermens tvint hadde vernomen,
Ende eer dandre waren ghekert,
Die Egypten hadden ontert;
So dat alt folc, verre ende na,
Vlo in die houet stad Sabba.
Die stede was also vast,
Dat sire langhe waren gast.
So dat des coninx dochter versach
– Tharabis – Moysesse dar hi lach
Ende word beuaen met sire minne;
So belouedene te latene inne,
Met sinen here, sonder waen,
Wilde hise te wiue ontfaen:
Dus wan he die stad met heren.

Historia scholastica

Tandem praeventos Aethiopes expugnans inclusit eos fugientes, in civitatem Sabba regiam, quam post Cambyses a nomine sororis suae Meroem denominavit. Quam cum, quia inexpugnabilis erat, diutius obsedisset, oculos suos injecit in eum Tarbis filia regis Aethiopum, et ex condicto tradidit ei civitatem, si duceret eam uxorem, et ita factum est. Inde est quod Maria et Aaron jurgati sunt adversus Moysen pro uxore ejus Aethiopissa (*Num.* XII). (col. 1144)

The onomastic material about the later name of the town of Sabba is omitted, but the story of the siege is told in detail.[18] The full meaning of the Latin phrase 'oculos suos injecit in eum' is brought out in Maerlant's skillful translation of the two aspects 'versach' and 'word beuaen met sire minne'. The reference to Aaron and Miriam's later reproaches to Moses is not included in the Dutch account.

After a time, Moses wishes to return to Egypt, but his wife is reluctant to let him go:

Scolastica

Mar doe wilde hi te lande keren,
Ne wilds Tharabis niet ghedinghen.
Hi, die vroed was van vele dinghen,
Grauerde in tve diere stene
Tve beeldekine harde clene;
Teen dede ghedinken, tander vergheten.

Historia scholastica

Dum autem redire voluisset, non acquievit uxor. Proinde Moyses tanquam vir peritus astrorum duas imagines sculpsit in gemmis hujus efficaciae, ut altera memoriam, altera oblivionem conferret. Cumque paribus annulis eas inseruisset, alterum, scilicet oblivionis annulum, uxori praebuit; alterum

[18] This has an exact parallel in Rudolf's treatment (see section 3.3.1 above).

Teen gaf hi Tharabis, wil dijt weten, So dat soe der minne vergat, Ende hi kerde weder te sire stat.	ipse tulit, ut sic pari amore, sic paribus annulis insignirentur. Coepit ergo mulier amoris viri oblivisci, et tandem libere in Aegyptum regressus est. (col. 1144)

The story of the two gems is simplified in the *Scolastica*: Moses' exact area of knowledge is not specified, and the various levels of production are combined in a more general account. As in the account in the *Weltchronik* of Rudolf von Ems (see section 3.3.1), the heightened element of deception of the ostensible symbolism of the rings is also omitted.

Thus although *Scolastica*'s relationship to the *Historia scholastica* is very different from any of the other texts included in this study, similarities can be observed in the treatment of this part of Exodus, particularly in the omission or simplification of geographical and etymological material from Comestor's work. Rudolf von Ems and Jacob van Maerlant place a common emphasis on the place of the figures and events they describe in the greater context of Salvation History, and the immediacy of God's guiding hand in the affairs of the world. They also share a tendency to heighten the element of human interaction within the account (the discovery of the baby Moses, the love-affair of Moses and Tarbis etc.) and to focus on the narrative aspect of Comestor's text. This emphasis on the narrative, which is possibly not what a modern reader would associate with the *Historia scholastica*, emerges in all three studies thus far as an extremely important aspect of the vernacular reception of the work.

4.4 Conclusion: The *Historia scholastica* as Source in Maerlant's *Scolastica*

Where the conclusions to the above chapters about the *Schwarzwälder Predigten* and the *Weltchronik* of Rudolf von Ems examined the position of the *Historia scholastica* among the various sources of these works, and its specific function within the network of sources consulted by the vernacular authors, the different nature of the relationship between Jacob van Maerlant's *Scolastica* and Comestor's work gives rise to different questions. In studying the reception of the *Historia scholastica* in this work one must ask why the vernacular author set out to make this academic text book available in his own language. This question is obviously closely connected with that of the intended readership of the work.

Analysis of Jacob van Maerlant's reworking of Comestor's account of the books of Exodus and Tobias corroborates the view that the primary public for this work should be assumed to be a courtly one.[19] Van Oostrom suggests convincingly that the *Scolastica* was commissioned by the circles of the young count of Holland, Florens V (1266–1296) for the primary purpose of educating this young leader, who was less than two years old when he succeeded his father.[20] In this context the project to provide access to the *Historia scholastica* can be seen, with Maerlant's other translations of academic texts, such as his *Der naturen bloeme* (1266, after Thomas of Cantimpré's *Liber de natura rerum*) and *Spiegel historiael* (1284–1288, after Vincent of Beauvais' *Speculum historiale*) as part of a specific didactic programme.[21]

The reason for the choice of the *Historia scholastica* for the biblical component of this education remains the matter of speculation, and this is where the context of the reception of Comestor can be illuminating. Jacob van Maerlant shares the interest in the narrative with the authors of the *Schwarzwälder Predigten* and Rudolf von Ems, and also this latter's preoccupation with the truth of his account. The question of the orthodoxy of the *Historia scholastica* (see section 1.1) is another possible factor in this choice. This will be discussed further in chapter five in the context of the Dutch *Historiebijbels*.

[19] For the medieval tradition of the book of Tobias, and detailed analysis of van Maerlant's use of the *Historia scholastica* in his treatment of Tobias, see Sherwood-Smith, 'Reception', pp. 219–257.

[20] Van Oostrom, *Maerlants Wereld*, pp. 441–446.

[21] Van Moolenbroek and Mulder, 'Maerlants *Rijmbijbel*', in: *Scolastica willic ontbinden*, pp. 11–12; Van Oostrom, *Maerlants Wereld*, pp. 151–303; For analysis of Maerlant's approach to his source in the *Spiegel historiael*, see Berendrecht, *Proeven van bekwaamheid*, pp. 139–205.

5 THE *HISTORIEBIJBEL VAN 1360*

5.1 The Dutch 'Historiebijbels' in their European Context

There are two 'Historiebijbels' in Dutch, the *Noordnederlandse Historiebijbel* (*NNHB*) and the *Historiebijbel van 1360* (*1360HB*).[1] The word 'Historiebijbel' refers to the genre; these works are entirely independent, but both form part of a broader European tradition of such biblical paraphrases, which flourished in the fourteenth and fifteenth century.[2] Hans Vollmer's definition of the genre in German literature is still current today, and is equally applicable to the Dutch texts. He defines 'Historienbibeln' as 'Prosatexte, die in freier Bearbeitung den biblischen Erzählungsstoff, möglichst vollständig, erweitert durch apokryphe und profangeschichtliche Zutaten und unter Ausschluß oder doch Zurückdrängung der erbaulichen Glosse darbieten, ganz gleichgültig, ob dabei gereimte Quellen oder die Vulgata, Historia scholastica, das Speculum historiale oder sonstige die heilige in Verbindung mit profaner Geschichte behandelnde Texte als Vorlage dienten'.[3]

The *Noordnederlandse Historiebijbel* survives in full in seven manuscripts, of

1 These titles have been chosen in accordance with the suggestions of Marianus K.A. van den Berg, 'Tekstgeleding in de "Noordnederlandse Historiebijbel"', in: *Boeken voor de Eeuwigheid*, ed. Thom Mertens (Amsterdam, 1993), pp. 266–281, to avoid the confusion in the earlier critical literature, particularly Jan Deschamps, *Middelnederlandse handschriften uit Europese en Amerikaanse bibliotheken*, Handelingen van der Koninklijke Zuidnederlandse maatschappij voor taal- en letterkunde en geschiedenis 24 (Brussels, 1970), pp. 152–159.

2 Brief overview in Astrid Stedje, *Die Nürnberger 'Historienbibel'* (Hamburg, 1968), pp. 18–20; for the German tradition, see Christoph Gerhardt, 'Historienbibeln', *VL*², IV, cols 67–75; for the French tradition, see Clive R. Sneddon, 'The "Bible du XIIIe siècle": its medieval public in the light of its manuscript tradition', in: The Bible and Medieval Culture, ed. W. Lourdaux and D. Verhelst (Leuven, 1979), pp. 127–140, and Rosemarie Potts McGerr, 'Guyart Desmoulins, the Vernacular Master of Histories, and his Bible Historiale', *Viator* 14 (1983), pp. 211–244; for the English tradition, see Morey, 'Peter Comestor'.

3 Hans Vollmer, *Bibel und deutsche Kultur. Veröffentlichungen des deutschen Bibelarchivs in Hamburg*, Materialien 1,1 (Berlin, 1921), p. 5.

which six were copied by a single scribe; two fragments of a Low German version also survive.[4] The *Historiebijbel van 1360* appears to have been more popular than its Northern counterpart; it survives in 32 manuscripts.[5] The author of the *Historiebijbel van 1360* remains anonymous, but on the basis of dialectal features and various comments he makes in this and other works ascribed to him, Coun has formulated the hypothesis that he was a Flemish Carthusian working at the monastery of Herne, near Edingen, on the border between Hainault and Brabant.[6] This hypothesis has become generally accepted.[7]

The 'Bible-translator of 1360', as he is commonly known, was active between about 1357 and about 1390 and was extremely prolific. He translated thirteen biblical, patristic and related works from Latin into Dutch, including most of the Old and New Testament, the *Legenda Aurea*, the Benedictine Rule, homilies of St. Bernard and St. Gregory, Bonaventure's *Lignum vitae* and the pseudo-Bonaventuran *Stimulus amoris*.[8]

The *Historiebijbel van 1360* forms the basis of the Old Testament in the series *Corpus Sacrae Scripturae Neerlandicae Medii Aevi* (CSSN), edited by C.C. de Bruin, but the passages for which the *Historia scholastica* is the main source have been omitted in this edition.[9] A future project will be to edit the missing sections of the work, which De Bruin estimates to take up approximately a third of the total body of text in the manuscripts.[10] Preliminary stages of this planned edition will be included in the textual analysis in this chapter.[11]

[4] Marianus K.A. van den Berg (ed.), *De Noordnederlandse Historiebijbel: een kritische editie met inleiding en aantekeningen van Hs. Ltk 231 uit de Leidse Universiteitsbibliotheek* (Hilversum, 1998). His introduction (pp. 17–41) discusses the genre of the 'Historiebijbel', the place of the Dutch 'Historiebijbels' in the European tradition and the history of research into these works. He discusses parallels with the *Historia scholastica* in the notes to the edition, and provides a list of such correspondences in Appendix 5, pp. 193–199. A summary in German is provided on pp. 835–845. For analysis of the use of the *Historia scholastica* in the book of Exodus in *NNHB*, see Sherwood-Smith, 'Reception', pp. 269–286.

[5] Deschamps, *Middelnederlandse handschriften*, pp. 152–156.

[6] Theo Coun, *De oudste Middelnederlandse vertaling van de Regula S. Benedicti* (Hildesheim, 1980), pp. 214–220.

[7] Cornelis Cebus de Bruin, (ed.) *Het Oude Testament*, CSSN, Series Maior, 3 vols (Leiden, 1977–1978), I, p. XI.

[8] C.C. de Bruin, 'Bespiegelingen over de >bijbelvertaler van 1360<. Zijn milieu, werk en persoon' *Nederlands Archief voor Kerkgeschiedenis* 50 (1969–1970), pp. 11–27, here pp. 14–16; Coun, *Regula*, pp. 194–213.

[9] De Bruin, *Oude Testament*, I, 'Woord vooraf', here p. XV.

[10] De Bruin, *Oude Testament* I, p. XV.

[11] I follow the same manuscript as De Bruin: London, British Library, MSS Add. 15310–15311; he confirmed the reliability of his choice by comparison with other manuscripts

The main model for the Dutch 'Historiebijbels' is undoubtedly the *Bible historiale* of Guyart Desmoulins, written in the last decade of the thirteenth century, which was itself modelled on the *Historia scholastica.* In his preface, Guyart states that his policy has been to translate the text of the Bible first, in large letters, and then to follow this with the relevant section from the *Historia scholastica*, distinguished by smaller lettering.[12] 'Si ai escript le tiexte de la bible premierement de grosse lettre. Et puis apres en ordre les hystoires du plus deliee lettre *id est* poi'.[13] The idea of Bible sections interspersed with sections from Comestor is taken up in both Dutch 'Historiebijbels', and the importance of distinguishing between the two source elements becomes a major issue in the *Historiebijbel van 1360.*

The *Historia scholastica* is far more than a source of commentary and non-biblical material; it is fundamental to the concept and structure of such works. In the case of both Guyart and the 'Bible-translator of 1360' , the original project included only the historical books of the Old and New Testament, precisely the books which Comestor had selected for his own work.[14] Thus in many ways the 'History-Bibles' can be seen as attempts to adapt the *Historia scholastica* for a new readership by supplying the relevant text from the Bible, rather than translations of the Bible with inserted commentary from Comestor.[15] Unlike the clerics for whom Comestor's work was originally intended, the vernacular readers did not have ready access to the text of the Bible, and the vernacular author must compensate for much of the knowledge and familiarity which Comestor assumes.[16]

That with time the demand for translations of the actual text of the Scripture increased more and more, is shown by the development of Guyart's

---

from the area in which the work was composed: 'De verschillen zijn zo miniem dat de tekstcodex aangemerkt mag worden als een betrouwbare basis voor de uitgaaf', De Bruin, *Oude Testament*, I, pp. XVI–XVII, here p. XVII.

12 Potts McGerr, 'Guyart Desmoulins', p. 219; Oxford, Bodleian Library, MS Douce 211, f. 2v.

13 Quoted from Potts McGerr, 'Guyart Desmoulins', p. 219.

14 De Bruin, *Oude Testament*, I, p. XIII.

15 'In the French *Bible Historiale Complétée* and its European offspring each Bible passage is interrupted at the appropriate point for the accompanying commentary on that passage, thereby producing not only a complete Bible text but also a virtually complete text of the *Historia scholastica*', Sarah Hindmann, 'Fifteenth century Dutch Bible Illustration and the *Historia scholastica*', *Journal of the Warburg and Courtauld Institutes* 38 (1974), pp. 131–143, here p. 132.

16 Potts McGerr, 'Guyart Desmoulins', p. 215.

work and the subsequent tradition. From approximately 1314, the 'text' sections of his French *Bible historiale* were expanded by the addition of parts of an extant, near-contemporary translation of the Vulgate. The popularity of this extended version is attested by the fact that this combination, known as the *Bible historiale complétée*, is preserved in seventy-eight manuscripts, whereas no manuscript of the fundamental version of the text of the *Bible historiale* survives.[17] However, the transmission also demonstrates that this interest in the Scriptures did not bring with it any waning in the popularity of the accompanying sections from the *Historia scholastica*: the *Bible du XIIIe siècle* survives in its 'pure' form in only three manuscripts.[18]

For the Dutch tradition, Hindmann's analysis of the thirteen illustrated manuscripts of the *Historiebijbel van 1360* also highlights the importance of both strands of text to early readers: 'That the contents of the *Historia scholastica* was carefully digested in the *Eerste Historiebijbel* [= *1360HB*] is certainly indicated by the miniatures in the Dutch vernacular Bibles. The process of assimilation of the text involved a thorough reading of its two principal components in close conjunction with each other. Examination of the miniatures has demonstrated that this close perusal influenced the illustration of details, entire episodes, and occasionally the choice of the subject itself, based often on the accompanying *Historia scholastica*. For the most part, this was done to create a more lucid and, at the same time, continuous narrative'.[19]

It is clear that for the author of the *Historiebijbel van 1360* and his readers, as for the readers of the *Bible historiale*, both the Bible and the *Historia scholastica* sections are important, and are designed to be read in combination. De Bruin's assertion that 'Noch de vertalers noch hun lezers namen genoegen met het schoolboek voor theologisch hoger onderricht, waarop de *Rijmbijbel* gebaseerd was; wat zij wensten, was de 'naakte' tekst van de komplete bijbelboeken, wel nog toegelicht met gedeelten uit de *Scholastica*, maar deze werden zo geplaatst dat de goede lezer ze als van bijkomstig belang zou herkennen' is based on an anachronistic premise which supposes that respect for the word of the Scriptures and for the *Historia scholastica* must be mutually exclusive.[20] The above observations about the transmission and reception of

[17] Sneddon, 'Bible du XIIIe siècle', p. 129.

[18] Sneddon, 'Bible du XIIIe siècle', pp. 129–131; Morey, 'Peter Comestor', p. 22; Potts Mc Gerr, 'Guyart Desmoulins', pp. 216–218.

[19] Hindmann, 'Illustration', p. 141.

[20] De Bruin, 'De Prologen van de Eerste Historiebijbel geplaatst in het raam van hun tijd', in: *Bible and Medieval Culture*, pp. 190–219, here p. 216.

the French and Dutch works show that far from being 'van bijkomstig belang', the *Historia scholastica* was seen as an essential, and popular, ingredient for a vernacular translation of the Bible.

This goes hand in hand with an awareness of the integrity of the scriptural text and the importance of differentiating it from commentary material. The main concern of these early translators, which reflects that of the clerical hierarchy, seems to have been the danger of heresy if unauthorised interpretations of the Scripture got into the wrong hands. And in this precarious field of translation, which makes the Bible accessible to untrained lay people, the accuracy of the translation and the orthodoxy of the interpretation are of equal importance. The latter is ensured by the inclusion of Comestor's *Historia scholastica*, 'a basic, orthodox training book of biblical interpretation used to educate those who would eventually minister to the Church's flock'.[21]

In his prologue to Genesis, the author of the *Historiebijbel van 1360* himself states his reasons for including material from Comestor, and outlines his policy, similar to that of Guyart, of distinguishing clearly between it and the text of the Bible itself:

> 'Echter soe sal men weten ende verstaen, om dat die bibele in menigher stat es soe doncker van verstandenissen, soe sal ic tallen steden daert profijt ende orbere wesen sal, nemen uut Scolastica Historia ende settent biden texte, mer dat salic wel tallen steden onderscheiden, waert beghint ende eynde neemt, met roden encke'.[22]

The author emphasizes the importance he lays on this distinction still further by continuing with a warning to future scribes to be especially careful:

> 'Ende soe wie hier namaels uut desen boeke enen anderen scryven wilt, hi moet naerstelijc merken ende hem wachten dat hine scryve alsoe dese gheordineert es, of hi soude dwerc seer blameren ende sijn pine verliesen'.

This warning is repeated almost word for word in the prologue to the book of Joshua.[23]

One cannot dispute that this concern to note the origin of the different elements exceeds even that shown by Guyart. However, I would argue that,

[21] Potts McGerr, 'Guyart Desmoulins', p. 216; see also Morey, 'Peter Comestor', pp. 6–7, 23.

[22] De Bruin, *Oude Testament*, I, p. 4; also quoted in Claudius Henricus Ebbinge Wubben, *Over Middelnederlandsche vertalingen van het Oude Testament* (Den Haag, 1903), pp. 110–111.

[23] De Bruin, *Oude Testament*, I, p. 273.

far from implying that the *Historia scholastica* is included grudgingly as a concession to the disapproving authorities, this awareness of the composition of the text and the citation of Comestor's work are part and parcel of the same desire to safeguard the integrity of the Scripture. This is confirmed by a comment by the author of the *Historiebijbel van 1360* in his prologue to the books of Esdras and Nehemiah:

> 'Nu salmen weten dat Esdras ende Neemyas... zeer doncker ende zwair sijn te verstaen ende tonthoudene. Dairom sullen wij dairaf die historie scriven also als hystoria scolastica hout, ende settent int duytsche'.[24]

The *Historia scholastica* presents difficult, and potentially dangerous, material in so straightforward a form that not even lay people could misinterpret it.

In many of his prologues he speaks of his fears of official opposition to his undertaking to make some books of the Bible accessible to lay people, and he is at pains to cover himself against all charges of heresy or unorthodoxy.[25] This appears to be almost a topos associated with the translation of biblical material into the vernacular, and opinions vary about the extent and nature of the Church's resistance and whether it posed a serious threat to the translator.[26] This debate need not concern us here; all that is important is the fact that the Bible-translator of 1360 is an advocate of such translations.

The question of the church's attitude to such translations of the Bible into the vernaculars is closely connected with the question of the intended readership of the work. The patrons, where they are mentioned, belong to the ruling classes of Brussels; many of the manuscripts were commissioned for, or owned by, communities of nuns. But in his prologues to various Bible books or series of books, the translator himself speaks of his purpose

[24] Quoted from Ebbinge Wubben, *Middelnederlandsche vertalingen*, p. 113.

[25] Ebbinge Wubben, *Middelnederlandsche vertalingen*, pp. 127–139.

[26] Ebbinge Wubben and Potts McGerr argue that there was concern, rather than prohibition; the argument that there was a very real danger (Margaret Deanesly, *The Lollard Bible and other medieval biblical versions* (Cambridge, 1920) and C.C. de Bruin, 'Prologen') draws heavily on the case of the supposed official objection to Jacob van Maerlant's *Scolastica*, which is refuted convincingly by Jaap van Moolenbroek, 'Maerlants *Scolastica*: een waagstuk?', in: *Scolastica willic ontbinden*, pp. 13–34, esp. pp. 24–34; see also Freimut Löser and Christine Stöllinger-Löser, 'Verteidigung der Laienbibel. Zwei programmatische Vorreden des österreichischen Bibelübersetzers der ersten Hälfte des 14. Jahrhunderts', in: *Überlieferungsgeschichtliche Editionen und Studien zur deutschen Literatur des Mittelalters: Kurt Ruh zum 75. Geburtstag*, ed. Konrad Kunze, Johannes G. Mayer and Bernhard Schnell, pp. 245–313, esp. pp. 251–259.

and his target audience in different terms. He wishes to translate the 'fundament vander Scriftueren', by which, as he has already explained, he means 'die historie', in the hope that the 'ghemeyne lude' may pass their free time profitably in reading it, rather than 'datmen ydelheiden [in] tavernen ende andere idele spele bedrijft als dansen, reyen, springhen, datmen al doet om den onreynen lichaem te oncuyscheiden te biedene, ic late staen menighe oncuysche sonde die men op dusdane daghe doet'.[27] From this it would appear that he has in mind a readership of urban lay people.

The aim of the following analysis of a section from the book of Exodus in the *Historiebijbel van 1360* will be to examine the author's approach to the *Historia scholastica*, and the way in which material from Comestor is used to complement material from the main source, the Vulgate.

5.2 Analysis of Exodus 2 in the *Historiebijbel van 1360*

Chapter two of Exodus in the *Historiebijbel van 1360* begins with a direct translation of the account of the birth and concealment of the baby Moses in the Vulgate (Ex 2:1–2):[28]

Exodus 2	**Text ij**
1egressus est post haec vir de domo Levi accepta uxore stirpis suae 2quae concepit et peperit filium et videns eum elegantem abscondit tribus mensibus	Hier na soe ghinc een man uute van Levi huse ende nam een wijf van sinen gheslechte, ende si ontfinc (57v) ende ghebaerde enen sone. Ende om dat sine vrome sach, soe verbarch sine iii maende.

The section is given the designation 'Text' to distinguish it from passages based on the *Historia scholastica*, and comparison with the Vulgate reveals it to be an accurate translation: the alterations, the replacement of the relative pronoun 'quae' by the nominative pronoun 'si', and of the present participle 'videns' by the causal construction 'om dat sine ... sach', do not change the meaning. The change from 'elegantem' to 'vrome' is also minor.[29]

The child can no longer be hidden and is exposed by being set out in a basket:

27 De Bruin, *Oude Testament*, I, p. 2.

28 De Bruin, *Oude Testament*, I, pp. 76–78.

29 The word *vrome* is generally used to translate *robustus* (*MNW*, IX, cols 1397–1404, with the meaning 'worthy'); there is some variation in the manuscripts here: Vienna, Österreichische Nationalbibliothek, MS 2771 (W) reads 'schoen', which could be taken to be a direct rendering of 'elegantem'.

Exodus 2

3 cumque iam celare non posset sumpsit fiscellam scirpeam et linivit eam bitumine ac pice
posuitque intus infantulum
et exposuit eum in carecto ripae fluminis
4 stante procul sorore eius et considerante eventum rei

1360HB: Exodus 2

Ende doement te hant niet helen en mochte, soe nam si een biesen corfelken ende si bestreect met lyme ende met pecke, ende si leider tkindekijn in, ende si settet uut in bies aent oever vander ryvieren, daer des kints suster van verren bi stont, ende mercte, hoe die dinc vergaen solde.

Here too there are no significant changes: the subject of the first phrase is changed to the impersonal pronoun 'men', and the ablative absolute construction is replaced with an active phrase.

The child is found by the Pharaoh's daughter:

Exodus 2

5 ecce autem descendebat filia Pharaonis ut lavaretur in flumine
et puellae eius gradiebantur per crepidinem alvei
quae cum vidisset fiscellam in papyrione
misit unam e famulis suis et adlatam
6 aperiens cernensque in ea parvulum vagientem
miserta eius ait
de infantibus Hebraeorum est

1360HB: Exodus 2

Ende siet, Pharaons dochter quam neder, om datte mense dwaen soude inder rivieren, ende die joncfrouwen ghingen aenden cant vanden oevere, ende doe si dat corfelken ghesien hadde inden biese, soe sant si een van haren joncfrouwen, ende doe si haer tcorfelken bracht hadde, soe ontdede sijt. Ende doe sier in sach dat cleyn kint weenende, soe ontfermde haer sijns ende si seide: Dits een vanden hebreuschen kinderen.

The pattern of syntactical changes which do not alter the meaning of the passage continues. The rank of the princess's maids is reflected in the translation of 'puella' by 'joncfrouwe'.

The child's sister fetches her mother as a wet-nurse:

Exodus 2

7 cui soror pueri vis inquit ut vadam et vocem tibi hebraeam mulierem quae nutrire possit infantulum
8 respondit vade
perrexit puella et vocavit matrem eius
9 ad quam locuta filia Pharaonis accipe ait puerum istum et nutri mihi
ego tibi dabo mercedem tuam
suscepit mulier et nutrivit puerum adultumque tradidit filiae Pharaonis
10 quem illa adoptavit in locum filii
vocavitque nomen eius Mosi dicens
quia de aqua tuli eum

1360HB: Exodus 2

Ende des kints suster seide haer: Wilstu dat ic gae ende roepe een hebreusch wijf die tkint voeden mach? Si seide: Ganc. Ende dmeisken ghinc ende riep skints moder. Ende Pharaons dochter sprack haer aen ende seide: Neemt dit kint ende voedet my, ic sal di dinen loen gheven. Dwijf ontfinct ende voedet kint. Ende doet op ghevoedt was, so leverde sijt Pharaons dochter, ende si begherden te haren behoef te houdene in die stat eens soens, ende si hiet sinen name Moyses, ende seide: Want ic namene uuten watere.

Here again the changes to the Vulgate text are not significant. The Dutch author makes it explicit whom the girl is addressing by adding 'haer', and further clarifies by repeating 'skints moder', where the Vulgate has 'matrem eius'.

This translation of Exodus 2:1–10 from the Vulgate is followed by the corresponding passage from the *Historia scholastica*. The author recapitulates, now giving Comestor's version of the story. In this one can see his very careful distinction between scriptural text and *Historia scholastica* in practice. This contrasts with the technique in the *Noordnederlandse Historiebijbel*, where the author frequently incorporates extra details from Comestor's biblical paraphrase into the main body of his text.

If one notes the differences between the Dutch and Latin for the passage from the *Historia scholastica* it is immediately clear that the translator approaches his ancillary source in a different way from the Vulgate, and that here he is not aiming to produce a verbatim translation:[30]

1360HB: Exodus 2

Scolastica hystoria

Doe Pharao, alsoe voerseit es, gheboden hadde <datsi> alle die cnapelkine verdrincken solden, soe was een man van Leuijs gheslechte hiet Amram; ende hi nam een wijf wt sinen gheslechte hiet Iocabech. Ende doe hi aen haer ghewonnen hadde Aaron ende Mariam sijnre suster, soe en woude hi nvmmeer met haer sijn; want hi hadde lieuer zonder kinder te bliuene dan dat hi kinder wynnen soude ende dat hise dan soude moten verdrincken. Ende onse here openbaerde hem inden slape ende hiet hem dat hi mit sinen wyue wesen soude, want si soude ghebaren dat kint dat die van Egipten ontsaghen. Ende oec seide hi hem van Aarons paepscap. (f. 57v)

Historia scholastica

Cap. V. *De ortu, et educatione Moysi.*

'Egressus est post haec vir levita (Exod. II)', nomine Aram, vel Amram, qui accepit uxorem contribulem nomine Jocabeth, qui nolebat accedere ad uxorem post edictum, malens carere liberis quam in necem procreare. Cui Deus per somnium astitit, ut ait Josephus, dicens, ne timeret uxorem cognoscere, quia puer, quem timebant Aegyptii, nasciturus esset ex ea: etiam de sacerdotio Aaron ei significavit. (col. 1143)

The Dutch author starts by giving the context, which might not be apparent in this non-consecutive account, expanding Comestor's 'post edictum' to make it clearer. He opts for just one of Comestor's alternative versions of the name of Moses' father, and adds that the couple already have two children, Aaron and Maria. He paraphrases 'malens... procreare', and is more specific about the type of death threatened for the children, repeating the reference to drowning. The reference to Josephus is omitted in *1360HB*.

The same selective approach to Comestor can be observed in the following passage, where the author of *1360HB* omits several details from Comestor's account, and, by mingling motifs, subtly changes the reason for the mother's actions:

30 The 'Scolastica historia' sections, which de Bruin omits from his edition (see section 5.1), are quoted from London, British Library, MS Add. 15310, with my own punctuation.

1360HB: Exodus 2

Hier na waert tkint gheboren ende die moder verbercht iij maent; want doe sijt ghebaerde en hadde si gheen groete pine. Ende do sijt niet ghebergen en mochte, soe sette sijt in een corfelken int bies vander ryuieren, om dat die stroem vander ryuieren tkint niet licht wech dryuen en solde. Ende Maria, skints suster, stont daer bi ende wachte hoe die dinc vergaen soude. (f. 57ᵛ)

Historia scholastica

Tandem 'concepit mulier, et peperit filium' sub silentio, eo quod non multum ei dolores partus institerint. 'Et videns puerum elegantem, abscondit eum tribus mensibus. Cumque celare non posset, sumpsit fiscellam scirpeam' in modum fisci, id est sacci rotundi, vimine complexam, 'et linivit eam bitumine ac pice, et ponens intus infantulum in carecto ripae eum exposuit', ne impetu fluminis raperetur, et stante procul sorore parvuli Maria, exspectante rei exitum, ex matris praecepto. (col. 1143)

In Comestor's account the motif of the silence and ease of the birth is used to explain why it remained secret from the Egyptians, and possibly to emphasize that Moses is a special child. The Dutch author changes the function of the motif, which now replaces the child's beauty as the reason for the mother's decision to hide him. The making of the basket and its composition are omitted entirely in *1360HB* and the motivation of the sister in watching over the basket is changed slightly by the omission of 'ex matris praecepto'.

The Egyptian princess is named Termuch:[31]

1360HB: Exodus 2

Daer na quam Termuch, Pharaons dochter, om datmense daer dwaen soude inder ryuieren. Ende doe sij tcorfelken hadde ghesien, soe dede sijt haelen, ende ondeet. Ende doe si daer dat vrome scoene kint daer in sach weenende, soe ontfermdes haer, ende seide dat een vande ioden kindere ware. Ende si dede vele vrouwen van Egipten halen om tkint te voesterne. Ende tkint en woude negheenre borst sughen, mer het keerde sijn aensichte daer af. Doe seide Maria, skints suster, tot Termuch: Willic di halen een hebreeusch wijf die tkint voesteren mach? Ende si seide: Gaet. Ende doe haelde si skints moder; ende tehant soe ghinc tkint haer borst sughen. Ende si voedde tkint op ende dan leuerde sijt Termuch. Ende si begheret te haren behoef te houdene in eens soens stat. Ende si hietene Moises om dat sine wten water verloest hadde: want in Egipten tale bediet 'mos', 'water', ende 'is', 'verloesten'. (f. 57ᵛ)

Historia scholastica

'Ecce autem descendit Terimith filia Pharaonis, ut lavaretur in flumine, quae videns alveolum, et afferre sibi jubens, vidit parvulum vagientem, et miserta est ejus dicens: De infantibus Hebraeorum est hic'. Sic enim Deus eum venustaverat ut etiam ab hostibus dignus alimento haberetur. Et cum Aegyptiae plures ei admovissent ubera ad lactandum, faciem advertebat. Et ait Maria: Vis, inquit, Hebræam adducam, forte ubera gentis suae sequetur. Et praecepto ergo Terimith abiens, matrem parvuli, tanquam alienam, adduxit, et accessit ad ejus ubera puer. Suscepit ergo Terimith alendum puerum, et ablactatum reddidit filiae Pharaonis, quae adoptavit eum in filium, et dictus est Moyses. Aegyptii enim *Moys*, aquam, *is* salvatum dicunt. (cols 1143–1144)

Here the omissions are of a less incisive nature than those in the previous section, and again there are few additions: the reason for Moses' name is

[31] See section 1.4.1 for variations in the printed transmission of the *Historia scholastica*. Variant spellings in manuscripts of the *Historia scholastica* are: *termuth* ABGM, *terimith* F (see section 1.3 and Table 1).

clarified still further and the child's beauty is remarked on when Termuth finds the basket. The Dutch author omits Comestor's comment on the specific function of Moses' beauty within the Divine plan, and the motif of the race of the wet-nurse is toned down with the omission of Miriam's suggestion that 'forte ubera gentis suae sequetur'. The pretence that the child's mother is a stranger is not referred to explicitly in the Dutch text.

The presentation of Moses to the Pharaoh follows:[32]

1360HB: Exodus 2	*Historia scholastica*
Op enen dach daer na gheuielt dat Termuch Pharao haren vader Moisen brachte om dat hyne oec begheren soude te hebben tot enen sone. Ende den coninc verwonderde van des kints scoenheit, ende nam sijn croen van sinen hoefde ende settese den kinde opt hoeft. Ende aen die crone was ghewracht Hamons, dier van Egipten gods, beelde. Ende tkint begreep die crone ende werpse onder sijn voete op der erden soe dat si brac. Ende die pape van Heliopoleos, die neuen den coninc sat, stont op ende riep dat dit tkint waer dat hem God vertoent hadde dat sijt doeden souden, ende datsi hon voertmeer niet en dorsten ontsien van dien kinde. Ende hi woude doe tkint doeden. Mer met sconincs hulpen ende bi eens vroets mans rade, soe waert tkint verloest: want (58r) si seiden dat dit tkint dede van onnoselheiden. Ende dit te proeuene daden si den kinde gheuen bernende colen; ende tkint stac enen cole in sinen mont ende daer mede verbernde hi sijn tonghe. Ende hier bi seggen die Ioden dat hi te qualiker sprac. (ff. 57v–58r)	Quem dum quadam die Terimith obtulisset Pharaoni, ut et ipse eum adoptaret, admirans rex pueri venustatem, coronam, quam tunc forte gestabat, capiti illius imposuit. Erat autem in ea Ammonis imago fabrefacta. Puer autem coronam projecit in terram, et fregit. Sacerdos autem Heliopoleos a latere regis surgens, exclamavit: Hic est puer, quem nobis occidendum Deus monstravit, ut de caetero timore careamus, et voluit irruere in eum, sed auxilio regis liberatus est, et persuasione cujusdam sapientis qui per ignorantiam hoc factum esse a puero asseruit. In cujus rei argumentum cum prunas allatas puero obtulisset, puer eas ori suo opposuit, et linguae suae summitatem igne corrupit. Unde et Hebraei impeditioris linguae eum fuisse autumant. (col. 1144)

There are many minor alterations to the source here. Comestor suggests that the king might have been wearing his crown, but in the Dutch text this is a certainty. The author explains who Ammon is.[33] The child throws the crown underfoot, which emphasizes the symbolic significance of the event as a reference to the defeat of the Egyptians. The words of the priest are reported rather than direct speech as in the *Historia scholastica*. The assertion that the action was merely one of childish caprice is attributed to both the Pharaoh and his advisor rather than just the latter. Other details, such as

[32] See section 1.2.1 above for Comestor's sources for the non-scriptural stories about Moses' childhood and youth.

[33] Most of the early printed versions of the text (bdfhjlmoqrst) read *hamonis* (see section 1.4 above).

which part of his tongue Moses burns, and the exact nature of the role of the wise-man, are omitted in the later work.

The citation of Josephus, and his comments on the effects of the child's extraordinary beauty are also passed on to *1360HB*:

1360HB: Exodus 2	*Historia scholastica*
Iosephus seit dat Moyses soe scone was dat niemant soe fel en was, hi en hadde ghenuechte in, hem te siene. Ende vele lude, doe sine saghen liden doer die straten, si lieten haer werc om hem te siene.	Tantae vero pulchritudinis fuit, ut ait Josephus, ut nullus adeo severus esset, qui ejus aspectui non haereret, multique, dum cernerent eum per plateas ferri, occupationes in quibus studebant, desererent. (col. 1144)

Although the wording of the Dutch passage does not correspond exactly to Comestor's (in the phrase 'ejus aspectui non haereret', for example) all the elements of the account are present in this very close paraphrase.

Moses is chosen to lead an expedition against the Ethiopians:

1360HB: Exodus 2	*Historia scholastica*
Hoe Moises die van Ethiopien verwan Het ghesciede doe Moyses volwassen was dat die van Ethiopien Egipten destrueerde totter Roeder Zee ende Nimphie. Ende hier om ghinghen die van Egipten haren afgoden te rade, ende die antwoerden hon dat si nemen souden teenen maerscalc enen Hebreuschen man. Ende met groter pinen mochten si cume van Termuch ghewinnen dat si maerscalc maken wolde Moysen van haren here dat si vergadert hadden. Ende eer sijt doen woude, soe swoeren haer alle die voerbarichste van Egipten, dat si Moysen negheen quaet doen en souden.	Cap. VI *De uxore Moysi Aethiopissa* Factum est autem cum adultus fuisset Moyses, Aethiopes vastaverunt Aegyptum, usque ad Memphim et mare, quo circa conversi ad divinationes Aegyptii, acceperunt responsum, ut auxiliatore uterentur Hebraeo; et vix obtinuerunt a Terimith, ut exercitui, quem paraverant, Moysen praeficeret ducem, prius praestitis sacramentis, ne ei nocerent. (col. 1144)

Here the Dutch author frequently interprets Comestor's information rather than translating or giving a close paraphrase. He specifies that the sea in question is the Red Sea, and the other geographical name has become distorted.[34] The practice of divination is referred to as 'asking advice from idols' and the form which the help of a Hebrew will take is specified from the outset. The Dutch text is also more specific about who swore the oath to Termuth not to harm Moses.

Moses chooses the shortest route to Ethiopia:

[34] MS W also shows variation from Comestor here: *mphin*; the transmission of the *Historia scholastica* itself is remarkably uniform (see section 1.4 above). Memphis is mentioned elsewhere in the Bible (e.g. IV Rg 25–26), but not in Exodus.

1360HB: Exodus 2

Want Moyses was alte wel gheleert van oerlogen, ende oec van alre sciencien van Egipten. Ende hi en woude te Ethiopien waert niet varen doer die ryuiere, om dat die wech te lanc was. Maer hi leidde sijn heer te lande den cortsten wech, om dat hi comen soude op die van Ethiopien eer sijt weten solden. Maer om dat die wech daer hi liden soude al vol serpenten was, soe voerde hi met hem op waghene im kisten van papier ghemaect eenrehande odeuaren die in Egipten waren, die di serpenten pleghen tetene. Ende alsi tenten gheslaghen hadden, soe liet hi die odeuaren wt gaen al omtrent die tenten, om dat si die serpente verdreyuen solden ende eten. Ende aldus so waert theer snachts versekert van desen serpenten, ende hi ledense ouer. (f. 58r)

Historia scholastica

Erat autem Moyses vir bellicosus, et peritissimus, qui fluminis iter tanquam longius praetermittens, per terram duxit exercitum itinere breviori, ut improvisos Aethiopes praeveniret. Sed per loca plena serpentibus iter faciens, tulit in arcis papireis super plaustra ibices ciconias, id est Aegyptiacas, naturaliter infestas serpentibus, quae rostro per posteriora immisso alvum purgant, castraque metaturus, praeferebat eas, ut serpentes fugarent, et devorarent, et ita tutus per noctem transibat exercitus. (col. 1144)

At this point the Dutch text follows the *Historia scholastica* very closely, although it gives less detail about the storks and the way in which they attack their prey. It is possible, considering how accurate the paraphrase is here, that this information was missing from the author's exemplar of the Latin work.[35] Comestor's 'bellicosus' is interpreted as skilled at war rather than war-like. Other changes are merely on a syntactic level, and do not significantly alter the meaning of the passage.

The following passage, which relates Moses' arrival in Ethiopia and the circumstances of his marriage to Tarbis, is unusual in containing an extra comment over and above the information given by Comestor:

1360HB: Exodus 2

Ende daer na quam hi op die van Ethiopien. Ende hi verwanse ende beleidse in die coninclike stat die Saba hiet, die welke Cambises, die coninc van Persen, hier namaels na sijn suster name hiet Merorem. Ende om dat dese stat soe vaste was datmense niet wynnen en mocht so, ende daer Moyses langhe voer gheleghen hadde, soe warten Tharbis, sconincx dochter van Ethiopien, mynnende om dat hi soe scoen was. Ende si gheloefde hem die stede op te gheuen woude hise te wyue nemen. Ende het gheuiel also. Ende van deser Morinne verweten Aaron ende Maria, sijn

Historia scholastica

Tandem praeventos Aethiopes expugnans inclusit eos fugientes, in civitatem Sabba regiam, quam post Cambyses a nomine sororis suae Meroem denominavit. Quam cum, quia inexpugnabilis erat, diutius obsedisset, oculos suos injecit in eum Tarbis filia regis Aethiopum, et ex condicto tradidit ei civitatem, si duceret eam uxorem, et ita factum est. Inde est quod Maria et Aaron jurgati sunt adversus Moysen pro uxore ejus Aethiopissa (*Num.* XII). (col. 1144)

[35] The same information is omitted from *NNHB*, though there the general approach to the source is so much freer that it is not so striking. However, study of the printed editions of the *Historia scholastica* shows minimal variation at this point (see section 1.4 above), which suggests that the account of the storks can be regarded as a fixed component of the Latin tradition.

suster, Moisenne, doe si ieghen hem scouden inden boke vanden Ghetale. Enighe andere segghen dat die van Madian heeten More, ende die Morinne daer Aaron ende Maria Moysenne af verweten was Sephora, Iechro dochter, spapen van Madian, die Moises hier na te wyue nam. (f. 58ʳ)

It is not clear whether the alternative interpretation of the reference in Numbers 12:1 to Moses' Ethiopian wife is an addition by the Dutch author, or whether the manuscript he used contained information, either integrated into the text or in an annotation, which does not occur in Migne.[36] In any case Comestor's version is presented as the standard truth, whereas the alternative, which derives from Augustine's commentary on the book of Numbers, is merely the opinion of 'a few'.[37] Perhaps the information that Cambyses was 'coninc van Persen' could also be linked to Augustine's discussion of 'Saracens', or is part of the same confusion about non-Europeans.[38] The reference to the book of Numbers (Nm 12:1) is incorporated into the text. In the Dutch text the future name of the town of Sabba is given as 'Merorem'; this version of the name is attested in the printed tradition of the *Historia scholastica*.[39] The phrase 'oculos suos injecit in eum' implies that it is Moses' appearance that attracts Tarbis, but this is explicitly stated by the Dutch author.

When Moses later wishes to return to Egypt he encounters resistance from his wife:

1360HB: Exodus 2	*Historia scholastica*
Doe Moises wter voerseider stat weder keren woude te lande, soe en woude sijn wijf niet	Dum autem redire voluisset, non acquievit uxor. Proinde Moyses tanquam vir peritus astrorum duas

[36] However, as with similar additions in the book of Judges in *1360HB* (see Sherwood-Smith, 'Reception', p. 363), the fact that this information does not occur in any of the manuscripts of the *Historia scholastica* checked (ABCDE), or in the printed editions (see section 1.4), makes it more likely that the Dutch author is responsible for this comment.

[37] 'De uxore Moysi Aethiopissa quaeri solet utrum ipsa sit filia Iothor an alteram duxerit uel superduxerit. sed ipsam fuisse credibile est; de Madianitis quippe erat, qui reperiuntur in Paralipomenon Aethiopes dicti, [...]. Nam in his locis dicitur eos persecutus populus Israhel, ubi Madianitae habitant, qui nunc Saraceni appellantur. Sed nunc eos Aethiopes nemo fere appellat, sicut solent locorum et gentium nomina plerumque uetustate mutari', Augustine, *Quaestiones in Heptateuchum*, CCSL 33, p. 247; see also Balfour, 'Princess', n. 46, p. 15.

[38] 'In the Middle Ages, the specific and different identities of peoples in the East were often hopelessly muddled by Western writers', Balfour, 'Princess', p. 7.

[39] This reading occurs only in one printed edition of the *Historia scholastica*, h (see section 1.4 above); MS W of the *Historiebijbel* reads *nemoren.*

ghedoeghen. Ende want Moyses was een vroet astronomijn – dats vroet vanden sterren – soe nam hi ij preciose stene, die beide alleens schenen; mer die een hadde die cracht dat hi dede vergheten, ende die ander dede onthouden. Ende daer in groveerde hi twee bielden, die al eens waren, ende maecter .ij. vingherline af, beide ghelijc. Ende hi gaf tvingherlijn daer die steen der verghetelheit in was sinen wyve, ende dander hilt hi selue, als oft hi woude dat si beide ghelijc vingherline draghen souden, die beide deen dander seer mynden. Ende aldus beghonste dwijf der groter mynnen te verghetene. Ende daer na so keerde hi weder in Egipten. (f. 58^r)

imagines sculpsit in gemmis hujus efficaciae, ut altera memoriam, altera oblivionem conferret. Cumque paribus annulis eas inseruisset, alterum, scilicet oblivionis annulum, uxori praebuit; alterum ipse tulit, ut sic pari amore, sic paribus annulis insignirentur. Coepit ergo mulier amoris viri oblivisci, et tandem libere in Aegyptum regressus est. (col. 1144)

Here the Dutch author again proceeds more freely with the source, and although all the elements of Comestor's account do reoccur, the order of narration is altered. The similarity of the rings is emphasized in *1360HB*; the author points out repeatedly that they look identical in every way.

The author of the *Historiebijbel van 1360* now reverts to the Vulgate as his main source but occasionally inserts commentary from the *Historia scholastica* in glosses.[40] True to his policy of distinguishing clearly between scriptural and non-scriptural sources, he separates the extra material from Comestor from the main body of the text. Comestor mitigates the severity of Moses' crime of murder by specifying that his victim was one of the Egyptian foremen who persecuted the Israelites; this information is considered relevant and included by the later author, but its secondary status is marked by this form, and it is not attributed.

Although the incident is narrated in full in the *Historia scholastica*, it is obvious from a comparison of the wording of the three versions that the Vulgate is the direct source of the main narrative:[41]

Exodus 2

11 in diebus illis postquam creverat Moyses
egressus ad fratres suos vidit adflictionem eorum
et virum aegyptium percutientem quendam de Hebraeis fratribus suis

1360HB: Exodus 2

Die text der bibelen

In dien daghen, na dien dat Moyses ghewassen was, soe ghinc hi uut te sinen bruederen ende sach haer vernoey. Ende hi sach dat een man van Egipten sloech enen hebreuschen man van sinen

Historia scholastica

Cap. VII. *De fuga Moysi, et affinitate Jethro.*

In diebus illis egressus Moyses ad fratres suos in terram Gessen, vidit afflictionem eorum, et praefectum operis Aegyptium percutientem quemdam de Hebraeis,

[40] In the manuscripts (and de Bruin's edition) these glosses are presented in inset blocks set into the text columns; here they are added in parentheses after the passage to which they correspond.

[41] De Bruin, *Oude Testament*, I, p. 77.

12cumque circumspexisset huc atque illuc et nullum adesse vidisset percussum Aegyptium abscondit in sabulo	brueders. Ende doe hi al om ghesien hadde herwaert ende ghinswaert ende hi sach datter niemant bi en was, soe sloech hi den man van Egipten ende barchene inden zavel. [Dese man van Egipten was een vande meesters die Pharao boven den kinderen van Israhel gheset had.]	et secrete percussum Aegyptium abscondit in sabulo. (col. 1145)

Comestor's version contains several omissions and additions. He omits the reference to Moses' adulthood and summarizes 'cumque circumspexisset huc atque illuc et nullum adesse vidisset' with 'secrete'; he adds that Moses went to his brothers 'in terram Gessen'. None of these changes are echoed by the Dutch text, which gives an entire and accurate translation of the Vulgate.

From the above analysis it is clear that in this chapter the author of the *Historiebijbel van 1360* carries out his intention to distinguish between scriptural and non-scriptural material consistently. The secondary status of the *Historia scholastica* is also apparent in the author's technique: where the Vulgate is the direct source he generally gives a very accurate translation, with changes only on the level of syntax, whereas passages from Comestor are paraphrased more freely, with omissions and additions of information.

However, the importance of the *Historia scholastica* should not be underestimated. In the section examined above almost all the extra information offered by Comestor is included by the Dutch author in some form, either in the longer passages introduced as 'Scolastica hystoria' or in the short glosses inserted into the columns of the main text.[42] This pattern continues throughout the work, with an increasing tendency to omit all material from the *Historia scholastica* which duplicates that in the Vulgate.[43]

42 The only details omitted altogether are: the composition of Moses' basket (which is substantially the same as in the Vulgate); Moses' beauty as part of the divine plan; the exact way in which the ibis attacks its prey; and the derivation of the name of Madian.

43 Ebbinge Wubben (*Middelnederlandsche vertalingen*, p. 114) points out that the amount of material from the *Historia scholastica* diminishes as *1360HB* progresses. This is confirmed by a qualitative analysis of the number of lines devoted to the translation of the *Historia scholastica* in the manuscript (London, B.L. MS Add. 15310): one can calculate that the 'Scolastica hystoria' sections make up 46% of the total of the book of Genesis (and for the first half of the book this figure is as high as 62%), but only 16% of the book of Judges. However, such analysis overlooks the fact that much of the *Historia scholastica* consists of narrative which overlaps with the Vulgate; of the commentary material provided by Comestor

5.3 Conclusion: The *Historia scholastica* as Source in the *Historiebijbel van 1360*

As has been discussed above, the *Historiebijbel van 1360* shows a level of awareness of the distinction between scriptural and non-scriptural biblical material which is not present in the other works included in this study. This entails a certain difference in the author's approach to the *Historia scholastica*; where the earlier authors drew mainly on the narrative component of Comestor's work, seeming to favour it over the Vulgate because of its concision and extra anecdotal detail (see sections 2.3.6, 3.3.3, 4.4 etc.), here it is mainly the commentary which is extracted by the author from its narrative context and included in separate sections. The relationship between the Vulgate and the *Historia scholastica* is now a different one: whereas in the *Schwarzwälder Predigten* and the *Weltchronik* of Rudolf von Ems the *Historia scholastica* is sometimes favoured over the Vulgate, here it is clearly in a subservient position.

Many of the functions of the *Historia scholastica* do overlap with those observed in the earlier works, however. Here too it furnishes extra narrative material from Josephus or the Midrash, though the non-scriptural status of this material is now acknowledged explicitly. It continues to provide a framework for relating biblical and secular history, as in the *Weltchronik* of Rudolf von Ems and the *Scolastica* of Jacob van Maerlant, and is perhaps all the more important in this capacity since, unlike these two, who treat these subjects in their other works, the author of *1360HB* seems not to be very familiar with this non-biblical material. The *Historia scholastica* influences the sub-structure of *1360HB*, as the author inserts *incidentia* and passages of commentary from Comestor even where this entails breaking up the unity of a chapter in the Bible.

The *Historia scholastica* serves as a link between the medieval lay reader of a text in the vernacular and the earlier learned exegetical tradition and provides references to authorities such as Josephus. However, the author of the *Historiebijbel van 1360* does not include Comestor's discussions of the variants from the Greek and Hebrew versions of the Bible, or etymological or

---

in his 'Historia Libri Judicum', 59% is included in *1360HB*. For detailed analysis of the adaptation of the *Historia scholastica* in the book of Judges in the *Historiebijbel van 1360*, see Sherwood-Smith, 'Reception', pp. 304–364.

onomastic material relating specifically to these languages, which would not be relevant to the readers of a vernacular Bible. Though Comestor himself is not mentioned by name, his work is cited repeatedly, so that here the *Historia scholastica* has a higher profile than in the other works. It is an important element in this early vernacular translation of the Bible, as it provides an orthodox interpretation of the text.

6 CONCLUSION: THE *HISTORIA SCHOLASTICA* AS SOURCE

The above studies each focus on the reception of the *Historia scholastica* in a particular work. Close textual analysis of selected sections of each work in parallel with the corresponding passages in the *Historia scholastica* explores the relationship between text and source. The following section will review the observations of the previous chapters, focusing on the function of Comestor's work for the vernacular authors who used it, their approach and attitude to it, and what this reveals about its status for them. It will highlight the common trends in the use of the *Historia scholastica* by the vernacular authors studied as well as their individual accentuation and differences.[1]

To explain the similarities, and divergences, in the selection of material from Comestor, and the fact that the non-scriptural status of the material is not normally noted, Andersson-Schmitt posits the existence of Bibles containing the full text of the Vulgate glossed with the *Historia scholastica*; the confusion between sources and the divergences in the selection of material are attributed to scribal laxity in distinguishing text from gloss in the manuscripts.[2] However, the familiarity of medieval scribes with the format of the glossed Bible, and their competence in distinguishing the various components of this genre, is attested by the strong textual tradition of the *Glossa Ordinaria*, so that this degree of inconsistency is unlikely.[3] Also, though abbreviations of, or collections of extracts from Comestor's work are not uncommon, particularly in the fourteenth and fifteenth centuries, no such hybrid between glossed Bible and *Historia scholastica* is known to survive.[4]

It would seem that the possible explanations for the conformity in the selection of Comestor material by later authors must be sought elsewhere.

[1] The observations in this section correspond closely with those in my article 'Die "Historia scholastica" als Quelle biblischer Stoffe im Mittelalter', in: *Die Vermittlung geistlicher Inhalte im Mittelalter*, ed. by Timothy R. Jackson, Nigel F. Palmer and Almut Suerbaum (Tübingen, 1996), pp. 153–165.

[2] Andersson-Schmitt, 'Die Verwendung', p. 19; see discussion above, section 1.4.

[3] Margaret Gibson, 'The Twelfth-century Glossed Bible', *Studia Patristica* 23 (1990), pp. 232–244.

[4] See discussion in section 1.4.

This forms part of the question at the heart of the present study, which investigates the way in which the *Historia scholastica* is used by a series of vernacular authors. The question is approached from the angle of the nature of the *Historia scholastica* itself, its sources, intended readership and transmission. This in turn is viewed within the context of the individual works of the German and Dutch authors selected, the other sources at their disposal and their attitude to these sources in the light of their own aims and intended readership (insofar as these can be determined). This can shed some light on other factors which play a role in the selection of material from a given source. Perhaps the conformity can be explained better in terms of the nature of Comestor's work, its function for the later authors, and their attitude to it, rather than through positing a nebulous intermediary tradition to account for both similarities and divergences.

Morey suggests that one of the reasons for the popularity of the *Historia scholastica* is that it is 'a book of *stories*'.[5] This is borne out by this series of studies; all five of the vernacular works discussed here use the *Historia scholastica* as a source of apocryphal stories derived from the Jewish legends of the Midrash, such as the non-scriptural accounts of the childhood and youth of Moses. These stories generally fill in the perceived gaps in the Bible, supplying more information about the motivation for the actions of biblical characters, missing links in the chain of biblical history. What differs here among the authors of the various works is the status of such non-scriptural anecdotes. Whereas the anonymous authors of the *Schwarzwälder Predigten*, Rudolf von Ems, and Jacob van Maerlant feel no need to display an awareness of the non-scriptural status of such stories, the authors of the 'Historiebijbels' are careful to distinguish them from the Bible sections of their works. A further gradation can be seen between the 'Historiebijbels' themselves; in the *Noordnederlandse Historiebijbel* non-scriptural details from the *Historia scholastica* are occasionally incorporated into the main, 'Bible' sections, but this does not occur in the *Historiebijbel van 1360*.

Another function which the *Historia scholastica* fulfils, in differing degrees, for all the authors studied, is that of providing historical and geographical information which adds definition to the narration of biblical events. This type of material from Comestor is included only once in the *Schwarzwälder Predigten* (the discussion about the availability of donkeys in Jerusalem in the sermon for Palm Sunday, T24), but is an important aspect of the use of the *Historia scholastica* by Rudolf von Ems and the authors of the 'Historie-

[5] Morey, 'Peter Comestor', p. 7.

bijbels'. Jacob van Maerlant, like Rudolf von Ems, relishes historical detail and is concerned to anchor his narrative firmly in time and place; he seldom omits this category of commentary. Etymological and onomastic material is also provided by the *Historia scholastica.* This material is not used by the authors of the sermons and seldom by Rudolf von Ems or the author of the *Historiebijbel van 1360*; Jacob van Maerlant, on the other hand, tends to retain Comestor's information about the derivation of place-names, and transposes the etymological discussions to suit Middle Dutch.[6]

Comestor furnishes straightforward literal interpretations of difficult passages in the Bible and reconciles apparent contradictions. The authors of the *Schwarzwälder Predigten* draw on the *Historia scholastica* in this capacity several times. The discussion of donkeys, mentioned above, attempts to reconcile the varying accounts in the Gospels; other examples are the interpretation, in the same sermon, of God's contradictory instructions to Balaam, and, in the sermon for Lent (T18/4), of His apparently gratuitous command to slaughter the herds of the Amalechites. This use of the *Historia scholastica* is also common in the *Historiebijbel van 1360*, but occurs infrequently in the *Weltchronik* of Rudolf von Ems, the *Scolastica* of Jacob van Maerlant, and the *Noordnederlandse Historiebijbel.* The latter generally translates such passages from the Vulgate without comment, whereas Rudolf and Maerlant tend rather to avoid the controversy from the outset by incorporating Comestor's interpretation or presenting a simplified version of events.[7]

[6] E.g. the derivation of the place-name 'Madian', *Sa*, ll. 3610–3614, discussed in section 4.3 above; the transposition of etymological material can be seen in the explanation of the word 'firmament' (*PL* 198, col. 1058): 'Dit firmament hevet hi ghenoemt, / spreket die boec, "hemel" bi namen, / omme dat beaect al te samen, / ende verhemelt die weerelt al', *Sa*, ll. 184–187; see Goudriaan, 'Maerlants bronnen', pp. 39–40.

[7] This can be seen by comparing the equivalent passages to those mentioned in connection with the *Schwarzwälder Predigten*, the instructions to Balaam (*PL* 198, col. 1237) and the destruction of the Amalechites (*PL* 198, col. 1309). Comestor's commentary is included in full by the author of the *1360HB* (London, British Library, MS Add. 15310, fols 120^{r} and 183^{v} respectively); *NNHB* translates the Vulgate without comment in each case (Numeri, 22 capittel and 'dat eerste boec der coninghen', 15 capittel). *Wchr* (ll. 14560–14616) and *Sa* (ll. 6030–6054) avoid controversy with relation to Balaam by focusing more on his belief in demons and false intentions than on God's command, thus absorbing part of Comestor's interpretation into the narrative; in the case of the Amalechites they include the animals in the command for wholesale destruction without comment (*Wchr*, ll. 23564–23622 and *Sa*, ll. 8985–8994). Jacob van Maerlant does retain Comestor's solution to the discrepancies in the accounts of the four Evangelists with regard to Christ's entry into Jerusalem: 'Ende ic wane hi teersten sat / Vp ionc ende vp die moeder na dat' (*Sa*, ll. 25024–25; *PL* 198, col. 1599).

The *Historia scholastica* provides an abridged version of the biblical narrative, giving the salient points in a concise form. Comestor digests the material, reducing the detail of the Pentateuch's account of Jewish laws and rituals, avoiding confusing repetition in the books of Joshua and Judges, collating the parallel accounts of the books of Kings and Chronicles or the four Gospels, omitting or explaining contentious issues. This is an important aspect of the use of the *Historia scholastica* by the vernacular authors studied, but for different reasons. When the authors of the *Schwarzwälder Predigten* take material for their 'urkünden' from Comestor they appear to be attracted mainly by the concision of the account, and this may also be a factor for Rudolf von Ems, whose prologue states his intention to tell the history of the world 'mit warheit, doh kúrzeklike' (l. 177). Brevity is also important for Jacob van Maerlant, but for him, and particularly for the author of the *Historiebijbel van 1360*, the issue would appear to be more one of how difficult the material is to understand and how suitable it is for lay people.[8]

Besides providing an abridging paraphrase of the narrative, Comestor draws on a large number of diverse sources of commentary material relating to the Bible and interweaves elements from these different sources into his account. This synthesis is in turn passed on to the authors who consult the *Historia scholastica*, and as such it forms a bridge between the lay recipient of the vernacular work and the learned exegetical tradition which informs Comestor's work. It provides the later authors with references to earlier writers such as Josephus, Methodius and Philo, whose names lend authority to the account. This function of the *Historia scholastica* is not important for the authors of the *Schwarzwälder Predigten*, but can be observed frequently in the *Weltchronik* of Rudolf von Ems and, though to a lesser extent, in the *Scolastica* of Jacob van Maerlant and the *Historiebijbel van 1360*. In this respect one is struck by the paradoxical fact that the *Historia scholastica*, whilst obviously a source of considerable authority, is not cited as such by Rudolf von Ems, for example, or by the authors of the *Schwarzwälder Predigten*, who instead take over Comestor's own source-references. There is nothing in the works studied here which corresponds to the situation observed by Morey in Middle English texts, which leads him to suggest that '[...] the citation of Comestor as an authority may have been an offhand convention'.[9]

In his preface, Comestor refers to his work as tracing the path of the 'rivulum historicum' which flows from the Creation of the cosmos to the

[8] See sections 4.2 and 5.1.

[9] Morey, 'Peter Comestor', p. 27, n. 96.

Ascension of Christ; as such the *Historia scholastica* provides a framework for the study of the Bible and of Universal History. It promotes an awareness of the Old Testament and of the (historical books of the) Bible as a consecutive whole. This is a possible explanation for the emphasis on Old Testament examples in the sermon collection, which far exceeds the typological interest of the material. An extension of this can be seen in the works by Rudolf von Ems and Jacob van Maerlant, where the *Historia scholastica* provides a framework for relating past and present within a single historical process. Both these authors elaborate on Comestor's information about the invention and transmission of various skills and customs.[10] Another facet of this, shared by the *Schwarzwälder Predigten*, the *Weltchronik* of Rudolf von Ems and the *Historiebijbel van 1360*, is the relation of Old Testament events and Jewish rituals to the contemporary ritual of the liturgy.[11] Comestor's *incidentia* provide a similar framework for relating sacred and secular history in the *Historiebijbel van 1360*, the *Weltchronik*, and the *Scolastica*, though the latter two both expand on the material in the *Historia scholastica*.

The above discussion reviews the various functions of the *Historia scholastica* as a source for the vernacular authors studied and the differing degrees of importance attached to each function in each work. There are also similarities in the approach of the authors and their attitude to the *Historia scholastica*. In all five works studied, Comestor is consulted in conjunction with the Vulgate, which, except in the *Scolastica* of Jacob van Maerlant, remains the main source. The main difference among the authors in this regard is the extent to which they distinguish between these two sources: in their use of the terms 'alte ê' and 'ewangelium', the authors of the *Schwarzwälder Predigten* do not make any distinction between the *Historia scholastica* and the Vulgate as sources of narrative examples; Rudolf von Ems uses the phrase 'dú schrift' indiscriminately to refer to either source. Jacob van Maerlant states in his prologue that his intention is to make the *Scolastica* available in Dutch (without

[10] E.g. the invention of various skills such as music, metal-work and weaving before the flood: *PL* 198, col. 1079, *Wchr*, ll. 520–544, *Sa*, ll. 973–995, *1360HB*, MS as n. 9, ff. 13^{v}–14^{r}; the transfer of skills from Egypt to Greece at the time of the plagues: *PL* 198, col. 1153, *Wchr*, ll. 10436–10499, *Sa*, ll. 4027–4035, *1360HB*, MS as n. 9, f. 64^{r}.

[11] E.g. the parallels drawn between Moses' holding up his arms in prayer to ensure the victory of the Israelites over the Amalechites and the gestures of the priest in the mass: *PL* 198, col. 1161, *SP*, Grieshaber I, p. 122, *Wchr*, ll. 11337–11347, *1360HB*, MS as n. 9, f. 69^{v}. Jacob van Maerlant consistently omits such references to the liturgy; see Goudriaan, 'Maerlants bronnen', p. 41.

ever explaining what is meant by this term except that it entails the history of the world from its creation until the ascension of Christ); thereafter, however, he introduces each book of the Bible without drawing attention to any difference between his direct source and the original.[12] As has been remarked above, whereas in the 'Historiebijbels' the main sources remain the same, the clear and explicit policy to differentiate between the Bible and the *Historia scholastica* sets them apart from the other works investigated.

If one considers what this reveals about the status of the *Historia scholastica* as source, it is striking that in some ways this is in inverse relation to its profile: in those works where it remains anonymous, the *Schwarzwälder Predigten* and the *Weltchronik*, it appears to be interchangeable with the Bible itself and is indeed often favoured over the Vulgate for its concision and extra detail; where it is named most frequently, in the *Historiebijbel van 1360*, its subservient status as a tool for understanding the 'Text der Bibelen' is stressed. From the relative chronology of the works studied, it would appear that there is an increasing awareness of the provenance of biblical material and a strengthening concern about the integrity of the Bible text. This supposition will have to be tested on a wider sample of works, but is corroborated by observations about changing attitude towards Comestor and the development of the translation of the Bible into the vernaculars throughout Europe.[13]

What is constant in the attitude to the *Historia scholastica* of the authors of the four works investigated, is the emphasis on Truth. The concern of the authors of the *Schwarzwälder Predigten* is reflected in their use of the term

[12] E.g. 'Hier na so comt exodus', l. 3371; 'Hier gaet an leuiticus / Dats moyses derde boec', ll. 5212–5213; 'Der coninghe boec die gaet hier an / Die jeremias die heleghe man / Versamede ende selue screef', ll. 8415–8417; 'Hier gaet vd doude testament / Dat nieuve dat si v bekent / Dat in dewangelie es bescreuen / Salic in dietsch nv vord gheuen', ll. 20926–20929. A possible exception is the book of Numbers, which is introduced as: 'Numeri na dat ict bekende / Beginnet hier verstaet dit wale / Dat ment den boec van ghetale./ Want de gesten ons bedieden / Dat tghetal van al den lieden [...]', ll. 5436–5440; 'de gesten' (and 'dese ystorie' in the prologue, l. 37) can be taken here to refer to the *Historia scholastica*, but both these terms are used so frequently in Maerlant's *Scolastica* in the more general sense of 'the narrative' (e.g., signalling the end of a section of *incidentia*, 'Nv willic an die geste keren', l. 8577), that this cannot be understood as a specific designation of the source.

[13] De Bruin, *Oude Testament*, I, pp. XIV–XV, points out that the first printed Bible in the Low Countries, printed in Delft in 1477, contains the Bible translation from the *Historiebijbel van 1360* without the sections which were based on the *Historia scholastica*; a similar principle would appear to have led to the expurgation of the Comestor passages in the Portuguese work *Historias d'abbreviado Testamento velho*, Vollmer, Materialien II,1, pp. XX–XXI.

'urkůnde': the biblical examples in their sermons, whether drawn from the Vulgate or the *Historia scholastica*, are adduced as documentary evidence for each individual point.[14] Rudolf von Ems stresses the truth of his account throughout in the use of such phrases as 'als dú warheit giht' (l. 11212, 11242 etc.), 'fúr war' (l. 11232), 'mit warheit' (l. 11370). In his prologue he connects this issue with the choice of source material: he will narrate the true history of the world 'als úns mit rehte warheit / dú buoch der warheit hant geseit, / dú mit der heiligen schrift / sint des geloubin rehtú stift' (ll. 181–184). That the *Historia scholastica* is perceived as a purveyor of Truth is demonstrated by the fact that material from this source is introduced as 'dú warheit' eight times in the course of the *Weltchronik*. A very similar attitude can be observed in the *Scolastica* of Jacob van Maerlant. He too stresses the importance of truth in his prologue: 'hier ne vint men no fauele no borde / No ghene truffe no faloerde, / Maer vraie rime ende ware woerd / [...] ware leeringhe' (ll. 27–29, 35), contrasting it with unspecified works of his earlier production which contained 'lueghelike[...] saken' (l. 71), and continuously draws attention to the truth of his account with phrases such as 'dans ghene saghe' (l. 1232), 'ghelouet das' (1434), 'weet vor waer' (l. 1492, 2554 etc.), 'sonder waen' (l. 2504).[15] For the author of the *Historiebijbel van 1360* also the *Historia scholastica* is an important ingredient for ensuring the truth and accuracy of his account. In his prologue to Genesis, he assures his readers that where he is not satisfied that his translation of a particular word adequately conveys its full meaning, he will elucidate it in a gloss based on what he finds in 'gheauctoriseerden boeken'. The *Historia scholastica* is the source for the vast majority of such marginal glosses.[16]

Truth and the *Historia scholastica* go hand in hand from the very conception of the work; the desire for truth, the request of his colleagues for a document 'ad quod pro veritate historiae consequenda recurrerent', is presented in Comestor's preface as the motivating factor behind the composition of the work.[17] It is in this capacity that it continues to be used by the vernacular authors for whom it is a source; the overriding function of the *Historia scholastica* for the authors studied is that of a supplier and guarantor of Truth.

[14] See the discussion of the term 'urkůnde' in section 2.3.3 above.

[15] See also Van Oostrom, 'Slotbeschouwing', p. 132.

[16] De Bruin, *Oude Testament*, I, p. 3; Guyart Desmoulins, whose *Bible Historiale* serves as a model for the *Historiebijbel van 1360*, is even more explicit in referring to the *Historia scholastica* as a source of 'pure verité', see Morey, 'Peter Comestor', p. 23.

[17] *PL* 198, cols 1053–1054; Morey, 'Peter Comestor', p. 23.

BIBLIOGRAPHY

Abbreviations

BÄDL	Beiträge zur Älteren Deutschen Literatur
CCCM	Corpus Christianorum. Continuatio Mediaevalis
CCSL	Corpus Christianorum. Series Latina
CMNT	Corpus van Middelnederlandse teksten
CSEL	Corpus Scriptorum Ecclesiasticorum Latinorum
CSSN	Corpus Sacrae Scripturae Neerlandicae Medii Aevi
DSAM	*Dictionnaire de spiritualité, ascétique et mystique*
DThC	*Dictionnaire de théologie catholique*
DTM	Deutsche Texte des Mittelalters
HThR	*Harvard Theological Review*
LexMA	*Lexikon des Mittelalters*
LThK	*Lexikon für Theologie und Kirche,* 2nd edn
GAG	Göppinger Arbeiten zur Germanistik
Materialien	Materialien zur Bibelgeschichte und religiösen Volkskunde des Mittelalters
MGH	Monumenta Germaniae Historica
MNW	*Middelnederlandsche Woordenboek*
NdJb	*Niederdeutsches Jahrbuch*
Nd Stud	Niederdeutsche Studien
PBB (H/T)	*Beiträge zur Geschichte der deutschen Sprache und Literatur* (Halle, Tübingen)
PG	*Patrologia Graeca*
PL	*Patrologia Latina*
RGG	*Die Religion in Geschichte und Gegenwart*
RTAM	*Recherches de théologie ancienne et médiévale*
TNTL	*Tijdschrift voor Nederlandse taal- en letterkunde*
TRE	*Theologische Realenzyklopädie*
TT	*Theologisch Tijdschrift*
VL[2]	*Die deutsche Literatur des Mittelalters. Verfasserlexikon,* 2nd edn
ZfdA	*Zeitschrift für deutsches Altertum und deutsche Literatur*
ZfdPh	*Zeitschrift für deutsche Philologie*

Manuscript Sources

Brussels, Koninklijke Bibliotheek, MSS 720–722; 19545; 15001
Freiburg i. Breisgau, Universitätsbibliothek, Hs. 460 (microfilm)
Hamburg, Staats- und Universitätsbibliothek, Hs. Petri 5
Leiden, Bibliotheek der Rijksuniversiteit, MS Letterk. 231
London, British Library, MSS Add. 10043, 15310/15311, 15410, 16951
Oxford, Bodleian Library, MS Add. B26 (Marshall 90); MSS Bodl. 164, 173, 208, 397, 711, 723, 748; MS Auct. D.1.16; MS Hatton 72; MS Lat. misc. b.15; MSS Lat. th. c.10, c.23; MS Laud Lat. 109; MSS Laud Misc. 74, 151, 270, 408, 446, 472, 518; MSS Lyell 8, 35, 70; MSS Rawl. 571, A 363, C 31, C 46, C 283, C 889, D 893
Utrecht, Bibliotheek der Rijksuniversiteit, MSS 2 B 13, 4 E 3, 5 E 6
Vienna, Österreichische Nationalbibliothek, MSS 2771/2772 (microfilm in Deutsches Bibelarchiv, Universität Hamburg)

Printed Sources

Primary Literature

Andrew of St. Victor, *Andreae de Sancto Victore Opera I. Expositio super Heptateuchum*, ed. Charles Lohr, CCCM 53 (Turnhout, 1986)
——, *Andreae de Sancto Victore Opera II. Expositio hystorica in librum Regum*, ed. Frans v. Lieve, CCCM 53a (Turnhout, 1996)
Augustine of Hippo, *Locutiones in Heptateuchum*, ed. I. Fraipont, CCSL 33 (Turnhout, 1958), pp. 379–465
——, *Quaestiones in Heptateuchum*, ed. I. Fraipont, CCSL 33 (Turnhout, 1958), pp. 1–377
Biblia sacra iuxta vulgatam versionem, 2 vols, ed. Robert Weber OSB (Stuttgart, 1969)
Biblia Sacra latinam iuxta vulgatam versionem, ed. Aidan Gasquet et al. (Rome, 1926–1978)
Blatt, Franz (ed.), *The Latin Josephus. I. Introduction and Text. The Antiquities: Books I–V* (Copenhagen, 1958)
Conrad (Holtnicker) of Saxony, *Sermones de tempore*, in: Bonaventura, *Opera Omnia*, III (Mainz, 1609), pp. 1–214
Eusebius/Jerome, *Sancti Hieronymi interpretatio chronicae Eusebii Pamphili*, *PL* 27, cols 11–676
——, *Eusebius' Werke*, 7 vols, ed. Rudolf Helm, 2nd edn (Berlin, 1956)
Frutolf von Michelsberg, *Chronicon Universale*, ed. Georg Waitz, MGH, SS 4 (Hannover, 1844, repr. Leipzig, 1925 and Stuttgart, 1980)
Giovanni de Balbi, *Catholicon* (Venice, 1495)
Glossa Ordinaria – Biblia latina cum Glossa ordinaria, facsimile reprint of the editio princeps Adolph Rusch of Strasburg, 1480/81 (Turnhout, 1992)
——, *Biblia sacra cum Glossa interlinearia, Ordinaria, et Nicolai Lyrani Postilla*, 5 vols (Venice, 1588)
Godfrey of Viterbo, *Pantheon*, in: J. Pistorius, B.G. Struve, *Scriptores rerum Germanicarum*, II (Regensburg, 1726)
Grieshaber, Franz Karl, *Deutsche Predigten des XIII. Jahrhunderts*, 2 vols (Stuttgart, 1844–46; repr. Hildesheim / New York, 1978)

Historiebijbel van 1360, see Bruin (ed.), *Het Oude Testament* below
Hugh of Amiens, *Tractatus in Hexameron*, *PL* 192, cols 1247–1256
Hugh of St. Cher, *Postilla – Textum Bibliae cum Postilla Domini Hugonis Cardinalis*, 6 vols (Paris, 1533–1539)
Hugh of St. Victor, *Adnotatiunculae elucidatoriae in Exodum*, *PL* 175, cols 61–74
Isidore of Seville, *Etymologiarum sive originvm libri XX*, ed. W.M. Lindsey (Oxford, 1911)
Jacob van Maerlant, *Scolastica – Rijmbijbel*, ed. Maurits Gysseling, 2 vols, CMNT II,3–4 (Leiden, 1983)
——, *Rijmbijbel*, ed. Jean David, 4 vols (Brussels, 1858–1859)
Jansen Enikel, *Jansen Enikels Weltchronik*, ed. Philipp Strauch, MGH, Dt. Chron. 3 (Hannover / Leipzig, 1891; repr. Dublin / Zürich, 1972)
Jerome, *De situ et nominibus locorum hebraicorum*, *PL* 23, cols 859–928
——, *Hebraicae quaestiones in libro Geneseos*, ed. P. de Lagarde, CCSL 72, pp. 1–56 (Turnhout, 1986)
——, *Liber interpretationis hebraicorum nominorum*, ed. P. de Lagarde, CCSL 72, pp. 57–161 (Turnhout, 1959)
Pseudo-Jerome, *Quaestiones hebraicae in libros Regum et Paralipomenon*, *PL* 23, cols 1391–1470
Josephus, Flavius, *Antiquitates Judaicae*, see Blatt
——, Josephus, *Ant – Josephi antiquitatis iudaice* (Augsburg: J. Schüssler, 1470)
——, *The Jewish Antiquities*, trans. by H. St. J. Thackeray and Ralph Marcus, in: *Josephus*, 9 vols (Cambridge, MA, 1934), IV–VIII
——, *Des Flavius Josephus Jüdischen Altertümer*, trans. by Heinrich Clementz, 2 vols (Berlin / Vienna, 1923)
Midrash Rabbah Translated into English with Notes, Glossary, and Indices, ed. H. Freedman and Maurice Simon, 3rd edn, 10 vols (London, 1983)
Nicholas of Lyre, *Postilla – Biblia sacra cum Glossa interlinearia, ordinaria, et Nicolai Lyrani Postilla* (Venice, 1588)
Noordnederlandse Historiebijbel, see Berg below
Otto von Freising, *Chronica sive historia de duabus civitatibus*, ed. Walther Lammers (Darmstadt, 1980)
Ovid, *Metamorphoses – P. Ovidii Nasonis metamorphoses*, ed. William S. Anderson (Leipzig, 1985)
Peter Comestor, *Historia Scholastica*, *PL* 198, cols 1045–1722; for early printed editions, see Table 3, p. 24
Peter Riga, *Aurora – Aurora Petri Rigae. Biblia versificata. A Verse Commentary on the Bible*, ed. Paul E. Beichner, (Notre Dame IA, 1965)
Pliny the Elder, *Naturalis historia – C. Plini Secundi Naturalis historiae libri XXXVII*, ed. Ludwig Ian and Carl Mayhoff, 6 vols (Stuttgart, 1967–70)
Rudolf von Ems, *Weltchronik. Aus der Wernigeroder Handschrift*, ed. Gustav Ehrismann, DTM 20 (Berlin, 1915)
Schwarzwälder Predigten, see Grieshaber

Secondary literature

Andersson-Schmitt, Margarete, 'Zwei niederdeutsche Bibelfragmente und die Überlieferungsgeschichte der "sogenannten ersten" niederländischen Historienbibel', *Niederdeutsches Wort. Beiträge zur niederdeutschen Philologie* 23 (1983), 1–37

——, 'Die Verwendung der "Historia Scholastica" in einigen volkssprachigen Bibelwerken des Mittelalters', *Årsbok Kungliga Humanistika Vetenskaps-Samenfundet i Uppsala / Annales Societatis Litterarum Humaniorum Regiae Uppsaliensis*, 1985 (1986), pp. 5–31

Balfour, Mark, 'Moses and the Princess: Josephus' *Antiquitates Judaicae* and the *Chansons de Geste*', *Medium Aevum* 64 (1995), 1–16

Baron, Salo, 'Rashi and the Community of Troyes', in: *Rashi Anniversary Volume*, ed. H.L. Ginsberg (New York, 1961)

Benson, Robert L. & G. Constable (eds), *Renaissance and Renewal in the Twelfth Century* (Cambridge MA, 1982)

Berendrecht, Petra, 'Maerlants "Scolastica" (c.q. "Rijmbijbel") in relatie tot zijn directe bron. Een verkenning', *TNTL* 108 (1992), 2–31

——, *Proeven van bekwaamheid. Jacob van Maerlant en de omgang met zijn Latijnse bronnen* (Amsterdam, 1996)

Berg, Marianus K.A. van den, 'Tekstgeleding in de "Noordnederlandse Historiebijbel"', in: *Boeken voor de Eeuwigheid*, ed. Thom Mertens (Amsterdam, 1993), pp. 266–81

——, (ed.), *De Noordnederlandse Historiebijbel: een kritische editie met inleiding en aantekeningen van Hs. Ltk 231 uit de Leidse Universiteitsbibliotheek* (Hilversum, 1998)

Berger, Samuel, *La Bible française au Moyen Âge. Étude sur les plus anciennes versions de la Bible écrites en prose de langue d'Oïl* (Paris, 1884)

Bode, Georgius Henricus, *Scriptores Rerum Mythicarum Latini* (Celle, 1834)

Brackert, Helmut, *Rudolf von Ems. Dichtung und Geschichte* (Heidelberg, 1968)

Brady, Ignatius, 'Peter Manducator and the Oral Teachings of Peter Lombard', *Antonianum* 41 (1966), 454–90

Bruin, Cebus Cornelis, de *Middelnederlandse vertalingen van het Nieuwe Testament* (Groningen, 1935)

——, 'Bespiegelingen over de "bijbelvertaler van 1360". Zijn milieu, werk en persoon' *Nederlands Archief voor Kerkgeschiedenis* 48 (1967–1968), 39–53; 49 (1968–1969), 135–53; 50 (1969–1970), 11–27; 51 (1970–1971), 16–41

——, (ed.) *Het Oude Testament*, CSSN, Series Maior, 3 vols (Leiden, 1977–1978)

——, 'De Prologen van de Eerste Historiebijbel geplaatst in het raam van hun tijd', in: *The Bible and Medieval Culture*, ed. Willem Lourdaux and D. Verhelst (Louvain, 1979), pp. 190–219

Cohen, Jonathan, *The Origins and Evolution of the Moses Nativity Story* (Leiden, 1993)

Coun, Theo, *De oudste Middelnederlandse vertaling van de Regula S. Benedicti* (Hildesheim, 1980)

Daly, Saralyn R., 'Peter Comestor: Master of Histories', *Speculum* 32 (1959), 62–73

D'Avray, David L., *The Preaching of the Friars. Sermons diffused from Paris before 1300* (Oxford, 1985)

De Hamel, Christopher F., *Glossed Books of the Bible and the Origins of the Paris Booktrade* (Woodbridge, 1984)

Deschamps, Jan, *Middelnederlandse handschriften uit Europese en Amerikaanse bibliotheken*, Handelingen van der Koninklijke Zuidnederlandse maatschappij voor taal- en letterkunde en geschiedenis 24 (Brussels, 1970)

Doberentz, Otto, 'Die Erd- und Völkerkunde in der Weltchronik des Rudolf von Hohen-Ems', *ZfdPh* 12 (1881), 257–301, 387–454; *ZfdPh* 13 (1882), 29–57, 165–223

Druten, H. van, *Geschiedenis der Nederlandsche Bijbelvertaling*, 3 vols (Leiden / Rotterdam, 1895–1906)

Duft, Jonannes, 'Die "Weltchronik" des Rudolf von Ems. Ihre Bedeutung und Überlieferung im Mittelalter', *Montfort* 36 (1984), 144–48

Ebbinge Wubben, Claudius Henricus, *Over Middelnederlandse vertalingen van het Oude Testament* (The Hague, 1903)

——, 'De zoogenaamde eerste Nederlandse historiebijbel', *Nederlandse Archief voor Kerkgeschiedenis*, n.s. 3 (1905), 323–50

Ebenbauer, Alfred, 'Das Dilemma mit der Wahrheit. Gedanken zum "historisierenden Roman" des 13. Jahrhunderts', in: *Geschichtsbewußtsein in der deutschen Literatur des Mittelalters*, ed. Christoph Gerhardt, Nigel F. Palmer and Burghart Wachinger (Tübingen, 1985), pp. 52–71

Ehrismann, Gustav, *Studien über Rudolf von Ems. Beiträge zur Geschichte der Rhetorik und Ethik im Mittelalter*, Sitzungsberichte der Heidelberger Akademie der Wissenschaften, Philologisch-historische Klasse (Heidelberg, 1919)

Englisch, Ernst, 'Deutsche Predigten als Vermittler zwischen Gelehrtenkultur und Volkskultur', in: *Volkskultur des europäischen Spätmittelalters*, ed. Peter Dinzelbacher and Hans-Dieter Mück, Böblinger Forum 1 (Stuttgart, 1987), pp. 147–48

Ertzdorff, Xenja von, *Rudolf von Ems. Untersuchungen zum höfischen Roman im 13. Jahrhundert* (Munich, 1967)

Feldman, Louis H., *Josephus and Modern Scholarship: (1937–1986)* (Berlin, 1984)

——, (ed.) *Josephus, Judaism and Christianity* (Detroit, 1987)

——, (ed.) *Josephus, the Bible, and history* (Detroit, 1989)

——, 'The Jewish Sources of Peter Comestor's Commentary on Genesis in his Historia Scholastica', in: *Begegnungen zwischen Christentum und Judentum in Antike und Mittelalter. Festschrift für Heinz Schreckenberg*, ed. Dietrich-Alex Koch and Hermann Lichtenberger (Göttingen, 1993)

Fischer, Bonifatius, 'Zur Überlieferung altlateinischer Bibeltexte im Mittelalter', in: Bonifatius Fischer, *Lateinische Bibelhandschriften im frühen Mittelalter*, Vetus Latina. Aus der Geschichte der lateinischen Bibel 11 (Freiburg, 1985)

Franz, Adolf, *Drei deutsche Minoritenprediger aus dem 13. und 14. Jahrhundert* (Freiburg i. Br., 1907)

Gärtner, Kurt, 'Überlieferungstypen mittelhochdeutscher Weltchroniken', in: *Geschichtsbewußtsein in der deutschen Literatur des Mittelalters*, ed. Christoph Gerhardt, Nigel F. Palmer and Burghart Wachinger (Tübingen, 1985), pp. 110–18

Gerhardt, Christoph, 'Historienbibeln', in: *VL*², IV (1983), cols 67–75

Gibson, Margaret, 'The Twelfth-century Glossed Bible', *Studia Patristica* 23 (1990), 232–44

Ginzberg, Louis, *The Legends of the Jews*, 8 vols (Philadelphia, 1909–1946)

Goudriaan, Koen, 'Maerlants bronnen in de *Scolastica*: Comestor en de anderen', in: *Scolastica willic ontbinden. Over de Rijmbijbel van Jacob van Maerlant.* ed. J. van Moolenbroek and M. Mulder (Hilversum, 1991), pp. 35–51

Grabois, Aryeh, 'The *Hebraica Veritas* and Jewish–Christian Intellectual Relations in the Twelfth Century', *Speculum* 50 (1975), 613–34

Hailperin, Herman, 'The Hebrew Heritage of Medieval Christian Biblical Scholarship', *Historia Judaica* 5 (1943), 133–54

——, *Rashi and the Christian Scholars* (Pittsburgh, 1963)

Hagenlocher, Albrecht, 'Quellenberufungen als Mittel der Legitimation in deutschen Weltchroniken des 13. Jahrhunderts', *NdJb* 102, 1979 (1980), 15–71

Haug Walter (ed.), *Traditionswandel und Traditionsverhalten* (Tübingen, 1991)

Henkel, Nikolaus, *Deutsche Übersetzungen lateinischer Schultexte. Ihre Verbreitung und Funktion im Mittelalter und in der frühen Neuzeit* (Munich, 1988)

Henkel, Nikolaus and Nigel F. Palmer (eds), *Latein und Volkssprache im deutschen Mittelalter 1100 – 1500* (Tübingen, 1992)

Herkommer, Hubert, *Der St. Galler Kodex als literarhistorisches Monument. Die 'Weltchronik' Rudolfs von Ems* (Lucerne, 1987)

Hindmann, Sarah, 'Fifteenth-century Dutch Bible Illustration and the *Historia Scholastica*', *Journal of the Warburg and Courtauld Institutes* 38 (1974), 131–43

——, *Text and Image in Fifteenth-century Illustrated Dutch Bibles*, CSSN Misc. I (Leiden, 1977)

Karp, Sandra R., 'The *Histories* of Peter Comestor: A Study of Literal Scriptural Exegesis' (unpublished doctoral thesis, Tulane University, 1978. UMI)

Kartschoke, Dieter, 'Biblia versificata. Bibeldichtung als Übersetzungsliteratur betrachtet', in: *Was Dolmetschen fur Kunst und Erbeit sey. Beiträge zur Geschichte der deutschen Bibelübersetzung*, ed. Heimo Reinitzer, Vestigia Bibliae 4 (1982), pp. 23–41

Kornrumpf, Gisela, 'Das "Buch der Könige". Eine Exempelsammlung als Historienbibel', in: *Festschrift Walter Haug und Burghart Wachinger*, ed. Johannes Janota et al., 2 vols (Tübingen, 1992), I, pp. 505–27

Lachs, Samuel Tobias, 'The Source of the Hebrew Traditions in Peter Comestor's *Historia Scholastica*', *HThR* 66 (1973), 385–86

Landgraff, Arthur, 'Recherches sur les écrits de Pierre le Mangeur', *RTAM* 3 (1931), pp. 292–306, 341–72

Löser Freimut and Christine Stöllinger-Löser, 'Verteidigung der Laienbibel. Zwei programmatische Vorreden des österreichischen Bibelübersetzers der ersten Hälfte des 14. Jahrhunderts', in: *Überlieferungsgeschichtliche Editionen und Studien zur deutschen Literatur des Mittelalters: Kurt Ruh zum 75. Geburtstag*, ed. Konrad Kunze, Johannes G. Mayer and Bernhard Schnell (Tübingen, 1989), pp. 245–313

Loewe, Raphael, 'The Medieval History of the Latin Vulgate', in: *The Cambridge History of the Bible*, ed. G.W.H. Lampe (Cambridge, 1969), II, pp. 102–55

Long, Isaac le, *Boek-zaal der Nederduytsche bybels* (Amsterdam, 1732)

Longère, Jean, *La Prédication médiévale* (Paris, 1983)

Lourdaux, Willem & D. Verhelst (eds), *The Bible and Medieval Culture* (Louvain, 1979)

Lubac, H. de, *Exégèse médiévale. Les quatre sens de l'Ecriture* (Paris, 1959–64)

Luscombe, David, 'Peter Comestor', in: *The Bible in the Medieval World. Essays in Memory of Beryl Smalley*, ed. Katherine Walsh and Diana Woods, Studies in Church History 4 (Oxford, 1985)

Manitius, Max, *Geschichte der lateinischen Literatur des Mittelalters*, III (Munich, 1931)

Martin, R.M., 'Notes sur l'oeuvre littéraire de Pierre le Mangeur', *RTAM* 3 (1931), 54–66

Merhavyah, C., *The Church versus Talmudic and Midrashic Literature* (Jerusalem, 1970)

Mertens, Volker, 'Der "implizierte Sünder". Prediger, Hörer und Leser in Predigten des 14. Jahrhunderts', in: *Zur deutschen Literatur und Sprache des 14. Jahrhunderts*, ed. Walther Haug, Dubliner Colloquium 1981, Reihe Siegen 45 (Heidelberg, 1983), pp. 76–114

Merzdorf, Theodor, *Die deutschen Historienbibeln des Mittelalters* (Stuttgart, 1870; repr. Hildesheim, 1963)

Minnis A.J. and A.B. Scott (eds), *Medieval Literary Theory and Criticism c. 1100–1375*, 2nd edn (Oxford, 1991)

Moolenbroek, Jaap van, 'Maerlants *Scolastica*: een Waagstuk?', in: *Scolastica willic ontbinden. Over de Rijmbijbel van Jacob van Maerlant*, ed. J. van Moolenbroek and M. Mulder (Hilversum, 1991), pp. 13–34

——, & Maaike Mulder (eds), *Scolastica willic ontbinden. Over de Rijmbijbel van Jacob van Maerlant* (Hilversum, 1991)

Morey, James H., 'Peter Comestor, Biblical Paraphrase, and the Medieval Popular Bible', *Speculum* 68 (1993), pp. 6–35

O'Carroll, Maura, 'The Lectionary for the Proper of the Year in the Dominican and Franciscan Rites', *Archivum Fratrum Praedicatorum* 49 (1979), 79–103

Oostrom, Frits P. van, 'Jacob van Maerlant: een herwaardering', *Literatuur* 2 (1985), 190–98

——, 'Slotbeschouwing: de *Rijmbijbel*, balans en perspectief', in: *Scolastica willic ontbinden. Over de Rijmbijbel van Jacob van Maerlant*, ed. J. van Moolenbroek and M. Mulder (Hilversum, 1991), pp. 127–43

——, *Aanvaard dit werk: over Middelnederlandse auteurs en hun publiek* (Amsterdam, 1992)

——, *Maerlants Wereld* (Amsterdam, 1996)

Palau y Dulcet, Antonio, *Manual del librero hispanoamericano*, 2nd edn, (Madrid / Oxford, 1950)

Patze H. (ed.), *Geschichtsschreibung und Geschichtsbewußtsein im späten Mittelalter* (Sigmaringen, 1987)

Postma, Ada, 'Voor wie schreef Jacob van Maerlant zijn *Rijmbijbel*?', in: *Scolastica willic ontbinden. Over de Rijmbijbel van Jacob van Maerlant*, ed. J. van Moolenbroek and M. Mulder (Hilversum, 1991), pp. 53–70

Potts McGerr, Rosemarie, 'Guyart Desmoulins, the Vernacular Master of Histories, and his Bible Historiale', *Viator* 14 (1983), 211–44

Prims, Floris, *Geschiedenis van Antwerpen*, 10 vols (Antwerp, 1927–49)

Proost, K.F., *De Bijbel in de Nederlandsche Letterkunde als spiegel der cultuur*, I: Middeleeuwen (Assen, 1932)

Reuss, Eduard, *Die deutsche Historienbibel vor der Erfindung des Bücherdrucks* (Jena, 1855; repr. 1966)

Rost, H., *Die Bibel im Mittelalter* (Augsburg, 1939)

Ruh, Kurt, 'Deutsche Predigtbücher des Mittelalters', in: *Beiträge zur Geschichte der Predigt*, ed. Heimo Reinitzer, Vestigia Bibliae 3 (1981), pp. 11–30

Sanders, Willy, 'Die unheile Welt. Zu einer christlichen Etymologie des Mittelalters', in: *Verbum et Signum. Beiträge zur mediävistischen Bedeutungsforschung. Festschrift für Friedrich Ohly*, ed. Hans Fromm, Wolfgang Harms and Uwe Ruberg (Munich, 1975), pp. 331–40

Schiewer, Hans-Jochen, *'Die Schwarzwälder Predigten'. Entstehungs-und Überlieferungsgeschichte der Sonntags- und Heiligenpredigten*, (Tübingen, 1996)

——, '*Et non sit tibi cura quis dicat sed quid dicatur.* Entstehung und Rezeption der Predigtcorpora des sog. Schwarzwälder Predigers', in: *Die deutsche Predigt im Mittelalter*, ed. Volker Mertens and H.-J. Schiewer (Tübingen, 1992), pp. 31–54

——, 'Schwarzwälder Predigten' in: *VL*², VIII (1992), cols 919–24

Schmidtke, Dietrich, Review of Gerhard Stamm, *Studien zum 'Schwarzwälder Prediger'*, *PBB* (T) 92 (1970), pp. 285–90

Schneyer, Johannes B., *Repertorium der lateinischen Sermones des Mittelalters für die Zeit von 1150 – 1350*, 10 vols, Beiträge zur Geschichte der Philosophie und Theologie des Mittelalters 43/1–10 (Münster, 1969–89)

Schönbach, Anton E., *Studien zur Geschichte der altdeutschen Predigt*, 3 vols (Vienna, 1886–1907; repr. Hildesheim, 1968)

Scholz, Manfred G., *Hören und Lesen. Studien zur primären Rezeption der Literatur im 12. und 13. Jahrhundert* (Wiesbaden, 1980)

Schreckenberg, Heinz, *Die Flavius-Josephus-Tradition in Antike und Mittelalter* (Leiden, 1972)

——, *Rezeptionsgeschichtliche und textkritische Untersuchungen zu Flavius Josephus* (Leiden, 1978)

Schwarz, Werner, *Schriften zur Bibelübersetzung und mittelalterlichen Übersetzungstheorie*, Vestigia Bibliae 7 (Hamburg, 1985)

Seybolt, Robert Francis, 'The Legenda Aurea, Bible and Historia Scholastica', *Speculum* 21 (1946), pp. 339–42

Shereshevsky, Esra, 'Hebrew Traditions in Peter Comestor's *Historia Scholastica*', *Jewish Quarterly Review*, NS 59 (1968/1969), pp. 268–89

Sherwood-Smith, Maria, 'Studies in the Reception of the *Historia Scholastica* of Peter Comestor in Medieval German and Dutch Literature' (unpublished doctoral thesis, University of Oxford, 1996)

——, 'Die "Historia Scholastica" als Quelle biblischer Stoffe im Mittelalter', in: *Die Vermittlung geistlicher Inhalte im Mittelalter*, ed. Timothy R. Jackson, Nigel F. Palmer and Almut Suerbaum (Tübingen, 1996), pp. 153–65

Smalley, Beryl, 'The School of Andrew of St. Victor', *RTAM* 11 (1939), pp. 145–67

——, *The Study of the Bible in the Middle Ages*, 3rd edn (Oxford, 1983)

——, 'Peter Comestor on the Gospels and his Sources', *RTAM* 46 (1979), pp. 84–129

——, *The Gospels in the schools, c. 1100–1280* (London, 1985)

——, *Medieval Exegesis of Wisdom Literature: essays by Beryl Smalley*, ed. Roland E. Murphy (Atlanta GA, 1986)

Smeets, J.R., 'Riga en Van Maerlants *Rijmbijbel*', in: *Handelingen 28ste Nederlands Filologencongres* (Groningen, 1964), pp. 124–27

Sneddon, Clive R., 'The "Bible du XIIIe siècle": its medieval public in the light of its manuscript tradition', in: *The Bible and Medieval Culture*, ed. W. Lourdaux, D. Verhelst (Louvain, 1979), pp. 127–40

Spicq, Bernard, *Esquisse d'une histoire de l'exégèse latine au moyen âge* (Paris, 1944)

Stamm, Gerhard, *Studien zum 'Schwarzwälder Prediger'*, Medium Aevum 18 (Munich, 1969)

Stedje, Astrid, *Die Nürnberger 'Historienbibel'* (Hamburg, 1968)

Stegmüller, Friedrich, *Repertorium biblicum medii aevi*, 11 vols, (Madrid 1950–1980), IV (1954) pp. 280–300

Tippelskirch, Ingrid von, *Die Weltchronik des Rudolf von Ems. Studien zur Geschichtsauffassung und politischen Intention*, GAG 267 (Göppingen, 1979)

Vercellone, Carolus, *Variae lectiones Vulgatae Latinae Bibliorum editionis* (Rome, 1860)

Vilmar, A.F.C., *Die zwei Recensionen und die Handschriftenfamilien der Weltchronik Rudolfs von Ems* (Marburg, 1839)

Vollmer, Hans, *Bibel und deutsche Kultur. Veröffentlichungen des deutschen Bibelarchivs in Hamburg*, Materialien 1,1–2 (Berlin, 1921)

——, *Eine deutsche Schulbibel des 15. Jahrhunderts. Historia Scholastica des Petrus Comestor in deutschem Auszug mit lateinischem Paralleltext, Materialien* 2, 1–2 (Berlin, 1925–27)

——, *Ein deutscher glossierter Auszug aus den alttestamentlichen Propheten*, Materialien 3 (Berlin, 1927)

——, *Die Neue Ee. Eine neutestamentliche Historienbibel, Materialien* 4 (Berlin, 1929)

Wenzel, Horst, *Höfische Geschichte. Literarische Tradition und Gegenwartsdeutung in den volkssprachigen Chroniken*, BÄDL 5 (Bern / Frankfurt a. M. / Las Vegas, 1980)

Williams-Krapp, Werner, 'Das Gesamtwerk des sogenannten "Schwarzwälder Predigers"', *ZfdA* 107 (1978), 50–80

Zielemann, Gerrit C., *Middelnederlandse epistel- en evangeliepreken*, Kerkhistorische bijdragen 8 (Leiden, 1978)

——, 'Das Studium der deutschen und niederländischen Predigten des Mittelalters', in *'Sô predigent etelîche.' Beiträge zur deutschen und niederländischen Predigt im Mittelalter*, GAG 378 (Göppingen, 1982)

Zimmermann, Erich, *Die deutsche Bibel im religiösen Leben des Spätmittelalters*, Neue Beiträge zur Geschichte der deutschen Bibel im Mittelalter 8 (Hamburg, 1938)

www.ingramcontent.com/pod-product-compliance
Ingram Content Group UK Ltd.
Pitfield, Milton Keynes, MK11 3LW, UK
UKHW042007190726
13854UKWH00005B/2206